Transforming Law's Family

Law and Society Series
W. Wesley Pue, General Editor

The Law and Society Series explores law as a socially embedded phenomenon. It is premised on the understanding that the conventional division of law from society creates false dichotomies in thinking, scholarship, educational practice, and social life. Books in the series treat law and society as mutually constitutive and seek to bridge scholarship emerging from interdisciplinary engagement of law with disciplines such as politics, social theory, history, political economy, and gender studies.

A list of titles in the series appears at the end of this book.

Transforming Law's Family

The Legal Recognition of Planned Lesbian Motherhood

FIONA J. KELLY

UBCPress · Vancouver · Toronto

20 19 18 17 16 15 14 13 12 11   5 4 3 2 1

Printed in Canada on FSC-certified ancient-forest-free paper
(100% post-consumer recycled) that is processed chlorine- and acid-free.

Library and Archives Canada Cataloguing in Publication

Kelly, Fiona J., 1975-
    Transforming law's family : the legal recognition of planned lesbian motherhood / Fiona J. Kelly.

(Law & society, ISSN 1496-4953)
Includes bibliographical references and index.
ISBN 978-0-7748-1963-3 (bound)
ISBN 978-0-7748-1964-0 (pbk.)

    1. Lesbian mothers – Legal status, laws, etc. – Canada. 2. Gay parents – Legal status, laws, etc. – Canada. 3. Parent and child (Law) – Canada. I. Title. II. Series: Law and society series (Vancouver, B.C.)

KE600.K44 2011   346.7101'7   C2010-908006-8
KF547.K44 2011

---

e-book ISBNs: 978-0-7748-1965-7 (pdf); 978-0-7748-1966-4 (epub)

Canadä

UBC Press gratefully acknowledges the financial support for our publishing program of the Government of Canada (through the Canada Book Fund), the Canada Council for the Arts, and the British Columbia Arts Council.

This book has been published with the help of a grant from the Canadian Federation for the Humanities and Social Sciences, through the Aid to Scholarly Publications Program, using funds provided by the Social Sciences and Humanities Research Council of Canada, and with the help of the K.D. Srivastava Fund.

Printed and bound in Canada by Friesens
Set in Myriad and Sabon by Artegraphica Design Co. Ltd.
Copy editor: Joyce Hildebrand
Proofreader: Andrea Kwan
Indexer: Christine Jacobs

UBC Press
The University of British Columbia
2029 West Mall
Vancouver, BC V6T 1Z2
www.ubcpress.ca

For Finlay, who deserved better,

and Maia,

who reminds me that it is important

to keep fighting

Contents

Acknowledgments

A project of this magnitude is never the work of just one individual. While many people have helped me along the way, several stand out for the enormity of their contributions.

First and foremost, I would like to thank Professor Susan Boyd, the PhD supervisor every graduate student wishes she had. I am enormously grateful for Susan's endless support, encouragement, and editing. I would also like to thank Professors Catherine Dauvergne, Becki Ross, and Margot Young, each of whom provided invaluable guidance and support.

Thanks must also go to Jodie Gauthier for her indispensable research assistance, the anonymous referees who provided thoughtful and provocative feedback, and the staff at UBC Press for their assistance in bringing this book to fruition. I would also like to thank the Trudeau Foundation for its financial support.

Finally, I would like to thank the forty-nine women who entrusted me with their stories. It was an honour to be welcomed into their lives. While the interviews covered set topics, few of the women simply told me the pertinent information. Instead, they disclosed stories of coming out, falling in love, wishing for a child, searching for a donor, and the instantaneous love that their children produced within them. Many also spoke of the heartbreak of infertility, miscarriage, premature birth, postpartum depression, and parental separation. More often than not, the women spoke honestly about their fears, the lack of role models available to them and their children, and the societal, legal, and familial pressure to identify the "real" mother. Some expressed anger and outrage, and many cried. It was an enormous honour and privilege to be invited into their homes and to be offered a glimpse of what it meant to be a lesbian mother living in Canada in 2005. It is my hope that in this book, I have gone beyond the academic to capture some of the poignancy of their stories.

This manuscript was edited and finalized during the first year of my daughter's life. Much of the work was done while Maia slept in her carrier against my chest. Her presence while I worked served as a constant reminder of exactly why we need to change the law. Maia, I hope that when you are grown, the issues raised in this book will no longer be worthy of discussion.

Transforming Law's Family

Introduction

Just weeks before Canada became the fifth country in the world to legalize same-sex marriage, I interviewed Yael, a lesbian mother of two children conceived via donor insemination. As her story unfolded, it became apparent that Yael had been one of the pioneers of the planned lesbian family, defined here as families in which a single lesbian mother or a lesbian couple decide to have a child using some form of alternative conception method, typically donor insemination. With children aged 28 and 21, Yael had become a mother almost two decades before most of the other women I interviewed in 2005 for my study on planned lesbian families. In fact, Yael and her partner became lesbian mothers well before social scientists identified a "lesbian baby boom" and before same-sex couples had even the most basic legal protection. She had parented in a legal vacuum, and she suggested several times in her interview that recent legal victories meant that lesbian mothers today "had it easy."

Yael and her partner, Judy, began their journey towards parenthood in 1974. Drawing on the services of a women's health collective, they found a doctor who was willing to perform an insemination using anonymous-donor sperm. However, they were warned that they could never present themselves as a couple at the doctor's surgery or give any indication to the receptionist that they were there for insemination services. This initial experience was re-lived over and over for the next twenty years. Yael recounted numerous stories of exclusion, isolation, denial, and discrimination. She described watching her daughter scream-ing in pain in a hospital waiting room as the nurse informed her that they had to wait for the child's "mother" to give her consent to medical treatment. She recounted the refusal of her daughter's school to refer to her as anything but a "babysitter" and the years of fear she endured after she and Judy separated and she found herself with no legal access rights to her non-biological daughter. When Judy refused to financially support their son, Yael had no way to enforce the obligation. While Yael tried desperately to invoke the law, she also feared it, not "wanting to get too close ... 'cause you don't know if it will bite you." Even today she remains angry, primarily at the legal system that, in spite of her social and financial commitment to her children, "gave [her] no recognition at all."

When I suggested to Yael that she was a "pioneer" of planned lesbian motherhood, she agreed. Forced to "invent everything from the ground up," Yael feels quite strongly that she "broke *new* ground." She referred to herself and her family as a "fragile little island," often invisible while at other times a very public object of attack. However, she believes that by being open about her identity and the nature of her family, she has contributed to the process of change. In fact, she has a hard time recon-ciling the current treatment of lesbian mothers with her own experience. When I told her that several Canadian provinces allow two women to appear on a child's birth certificate from birth, she rolled her eyes and laughed, unable to believe how much had changed. To her, life seems easier for many lesbian mothers today, and she flippantly suggested that the "revolution" might be over.

In some ways, Yael is right. Many lesbian mothers parenting today do have it easy, or at least easier. Most have legal options available to them that Yael could barely have imagined when she was raising her children. They also enjoy a level of societal acceptance that Yael was routinely denied. But the more I thought about it, the more complicated it seemed. Without in any way diminishing the harrowing experiences Yael had endured, I wondered whether the path of "progress" was as straightforward as she and I had presumed. I reflected on whether the inclusion of lesbian mothers within law might sometimes come at a price: Do strategies matter? Should we be careful about what we ask for? I thought about the long-term effects of the existing approach to reform, which tends to rely on the assertion that lesbian mothers are indistinguishable from their heterosexual counterparts. I wondered which lesbian mothers this might ultimately exclude. At the same time, I could see how much easier Yael's life would have been had she had access to exactly the same legal rights as non-biological fathers whose partners conceived through donor insemination. Identical treatment would have actually served Yael very well. Yet for other lesbian mothers, it would do little to meet their needs. In thinking about these issues, it seemed that the question to be asked was not *whether* planned lesbian families should be legally recognized – Yael's story highlighted exactly why they should – but rather *on what terms* recognition should be granted. Absent an attentiveness to both the inclusionary *and* exclusionary implications of different modes of recognition, there was a very real chance that law reform would reinforce existing norms and thus exclude lesbian families who parented outside of them.

The Visible Lesbian Family

Yael's story indicates that lesbian motherhood is by no means a new phenomenon. However, planned lesbian families are greater in number and more visible today than ever before, prompting a number of social scientists to declare that we are witnessing a lesbian "baby boom."[1] While the number of lesbian mothers in Canada is difficult to determine, the 2006 census found that of the 20,610 female same-sex couples who were willing to have their relationships recorded, 3,359 (or 16.3 percent) were raising children.[2] These numbers represent a 47 percent increase in the number of children being raised by lesbian couples since the 2001 census.[3] Arguably, the census underestimates the number of lesbians raising children because not all lesbians would have chosen to respond candidly to the census question. Nor do the census figures include those lesbian mothers who are single or separated from their child's other parent, or who are non-custodial parents.

Another indicator of the rise in lesbian motherhood in Canadian society is the increasing presence of lesbian women among the clientele of Canadian fertility clinics. In 2001, the Genesis Fertility Centre in Vancouver, British Columbia, noted that 15 to 20 percent of their clients were lesbian couples.[4] In some clinics in the United States, lesbians make up over 60 percent of the clientele.[5] Thus, while it is difficult to determine exactly how many lesbian mothers there are in Canada, a variety of social indicators suggest that the phenomenon is increasing, and at a fairly rapid rate.

While lesbian motherhood may not be an altogether new concept, lesbian families in the twenty-first century often look very different than they did in the past. Historically, most lesbian mothers conceived within the context of a heterosexual relationship.[6] After separating from their children's father, many of these women repartnered with another woman and raised the children together.[7] Some of these children considered themselves to have two mothers, while others viewed their mother's new partner as something other than a parent. However, with the increasing societal acceptance of lesbian relationships, as well as the younger age at which lesbians now "come out,"[8] the number of children born to lesbian women within the context of heterosexual relationships has steadily declined.[9] Not surprisingly, the number of children being born into lesbian relationships or to lesbian single mothers has simultaneously risen. This new type of lesbian family – a *planned* lesbian family – presents some unique and complex challenges for both the law and wider society.

Despite the significant increase in planned lesbian families in Canada, lesbian mothers, particularly non-biological mothers, remain legal outsiders. Excluded in almost all provinces from both legislative presumptions of parentage and statutory provisions addressing parentage within the context of assisted reproduction, non-biological lesbian mothers have little access to Canada's legal parentage laws. As a result, planned lesbian families, and particularly non-biological mothers, must contend with a great deal of legal uncertainty. In situations where conception has been achieved using the sperm of a known donor, the uncertainty is exacerbated by the absence in all but one Canadian province of any legislation addressing the legal status of donors. In the face of legislative exclusion, lesbian mothers have turned to the courts. While this has been a relatively successful strategy in terms of individual outcomes, litigation has created an uneven patchwork of promising but incomplete provisions across the provinces, none of which fully meet the needs of lesbian families. Most notably, none of the litigation to date has fully resolved the legal status of either non-biological mothers or known donors, whether they donate to a lesbian couple or a single lesbian mother.

The considerable number of parentage cases initiated by lesbian mothers would suggest that the desire for law reform is high, but the process of reform is complicated by the lack of knowledge about planned lesbian families. Few studies have addressed how lesbian mothers living in Canada understand or define their various family relationships,[10] and no empirical research has specifically explored the *legal* aspects of lesbian parenting in Canada. As a result, we have little sense, beyond what has been argued in individual cases, of how lesbian mothers define their family relationships or what they need from the law. This substantial gap in our knowledge poses a significant limitation on the law reform process.

The need for empirical research attentive to the specific legal needs of planned lesbian families is made all the more urgent by the tendency within the existing case law to equate lesbian families with other forms of "alternative" family – such as stepfamilies and heterosexual families created via assisted reproduction – without any inquiry into whether the comparison is helpful or accurate. While an equivalency approach, typically grounded in formal equality, may be adopted because of the strategic advantage it presents in the courtroom, the risk is that it will underplay the differences between lesbian and heterosexual parenting relationships and thus limit reform to that which can be understood within the existing normative framework. For example, while lesbian families created through the use of anonymous-donor sperm may benefit from the extension of the parentage laws that apply to heterosexual couples who conceive via the same method, for the many planned lesbian families created using the sperm of a known donor, a practice almost unheard of in the heterosexual community, the existing legal framework is inadequate. Known-donor families must grapple with the legal effect (if any) of inseminating outside a medical environment,[11] the legal status of the known donor, and the related legal status of the non-biological mother. These issues would remain unaddressed by a law reform strategy that simply maps the existing heterosexual framework onto the lesbian family. The legal challenges of having a known donor are exacerbated for single lesbian mothers who are unable to provide a second parent: these mothers cannot take advantage of reforms based on equal treatment where the comparator is a heterosexual, two-parent family.

Equating lesbian families with heterosexual stepfamilies is similarly unhelpful. Unlike most heterosexual step-parents, non-biological lesbian mothers typically take part in the planning of the child, are present at conception, and raise the child from birth. In other words, most non-biological mothers are not step-parents: they are equal co-parents from the outset. Accordingly, existing laws designed to recognize the role of step-parents in children's lives, such as step-parent adoption, fail to fully capture the role played by non-biological lesbian mothers. The inability of existing legal parentage laws to respond adequately to lesbian families suggests that a new legal framework is needed. Empirical research attentive to the specific legal needs of planned lesbian families is essential to the development of such a framework.

The research findings presented in this book, which derive from an interview-based qualitative study of planned lesbian families living in British Columbia and Alberta, are designed to redress the existing empirical gap. The purpose of the study was twofold. First, speculating that the differences between planned lesbian families and other forms of family might lead lesbian mothers to define their familial relationships along non-normative lines, the study sought to investigate how lesbian mothers define and understand key familial concepts such as "family" and "parent." Without law or biological assumptions to fall back on, lesbian mothers must define for themselves what makes someone a parent and where the boundaries of family might lie. Exploring these definitions would be essential to developing a responsive law reform proposal.

The second purpose of the study was to explore the possibility of law reform. At present, Quebec is the only province to have addressed the assignment of legal parentage within lesbian families by way of legislation.[12] It is also the only province to have expressly addressed the legal status of known donors. Limited parental recognition has been achieved in some provinces through the courts, but it remains both uneven and inadequate. No province has addressed the legal issues raised by single mothers-by-choice, some of whom conceive with known donors and many of whom are lesbians. While lesbian single mothers may have more in common with heterosexual single mothers-by-choice (who also conceive via donor insemination) than with lesbian couples, I consider them to be part of the planned lesbian family spectrum and thus relevant to a discussion of law reform.

Recognizing the severe limitations of the existing legal framework, the second purpose of the study was to develop, in conjunction with lesbian mothers, a legislative reform model that addresses the assignment of legal parentage within planned lesbian families.[13] Key to this undertaking was the issue of the terms upon which law reform should be pursued. As noted above, most of the legal successes to date have relied on a formal equality model in which lesbian families are equated with heterosexual families created via anonymous-donor insemination. While such an approach has produced numerous legal victories, it has failed to address the needs of planned lesbian families that deviate from existing norms, such as those that include a known donor or are created by a single lesbian woman. Because the existing reform strategies might be creating new exclusions, the study sought to explore the mothers' responses to a variety of law reform models, each of which captured a different strategic approach to recognition. To address these two research questions, a qualitative study of planned lesbian families was devised.

Researching Lesbian Mothers: Design, Method, and Participants

The difficulties inherent in obtaining representative samples of marginalized groups such as lesbian women have been well documented.[14] The stigmatization and relative secrecy that continue to characterize lesbian existence makes it very difficult to select participants through any kind of random modelling. Because of the difficulties associated with identifying participants, most research with lesbian women relies on "convenience sampling" whereby participants are found through advertising in written materials directed at lesbian readers, in physical locations frequented by lesbian women, or on email listservs to which lesbian women subscribe. Convenience sampling was employed in this study, with email listservs for lesbian and gay parents living in British Columbia and Alberta producing the bulk of the study's participants.

While convenience sampling is often the only method by which to build a sizeable group of participants from within a marginalized community, it can produce highly self-selected samples of friends or networks within the particular community in question.[15] To overcome some of these deficiencies, study participants were gathered from as diverse a variety of backgrounds as possible. Foremost, I sought to maximize the range of family configurations represented within the study. This diversity was important for a number of reasons. First, I was concerned that the vast majority of research related to planned lesbian parenthood has deliberately focused on lesbian nuclear families, usually for the purposes of comparison with heterosexual families.[16] Such a starting point inevitably prioritizes the nuclear family and may imply that families that take some other form are somehow inadequate or illegitimate.[17] By actively recruiting lesbian mothers who parented outside of the nuclear model, I sought to displace the nuclear family as the reference point from which all discussion flows. Similarly, I made efforts to include mothers who parented within diverse family configurations because of their remarkable absence from the mainstream legal debate over parental and family recognition. I was concerned that the singular focus on the lesbian nuclear family in recent Canadian litigation has overlooked alternative approaches to parenthood emergent within the lesbian community or has deliberately omitted them because they did not fit easily into a formal equality framework. Finally, I hoped that by including participants who parented within a diverse array of family configurations, I might draw attention to new and innovative approaches to parenthood that are easily overlooked or even elided in narrower studies. Revealing these alternative approaches might help highlight the constructed nature of existing legal and social norms.

To achieve the greatest diversity possible, I created a list of the various family configurations that might exist among planned lesbian families. The final list comprised the following: two-mother families with anonymous donors, two-mother families with known donors, multiple-parent families, single-mother families by choice, separated lesbian families, reconstituted families (both nuclear and non-nuclear), couples in which only one parent identified as a mother, non-conjugal same-sex co-parents, and non-conjugal opposite-sex co-parents (where the mother identified as a lesbian). Saturation point was reached only after concerted effort had been made to attract participants from across the full spectrum of configurations. Some configurations were better represented than others, though I suspect the frequency with which they appear might be an accurate reflection of their actual numbers within society.

As the list of possible family configurations suggests, a significant limitation was placed on the sample: only women who had conceived at least one of their children via either donor insemination or in vitro fertilization were included. In other words, the focus was on planned lesbian families that were created through some form of alternative conception method and that therefore included at least one biological parent. While this approach ran the risk of reproducing the discourse of biologism, the decision to focus on women who became parents in this particular context – and not on those who became parents through adoption, fostering, or a heterosexual relationship – was based on a number of reasons. First, there is at least anecdotal evidence that lesbian families created through alternative conception methods represent the fastest growing group of lesbian parents in Canada, yet no Canadian empirical research addresses their legal needs.[18] Second, while most provinces offer some method by which to acquire legal recognition for planned lesbian families, such recognition is both incomplete and inconsistent. Significant issues, such as the legal status of known donors, remain unclear. In addition, unlike lesbian women who adopt, foster, or conceive in the context of a heterosexual relationship, there is no established legal framework to fall back on. Legal recognition has thus become a matter of urgency for this particular group of lesbian mothers. Finally, because planned lesbian families challenge so many of the traditional signifiers of legal parenthood, perhaps more than any other family form, they provide an unprecedented opportunity to unpack the various assumptions upon which the current law is based. Such a discussion is likely to make a significant contribution to the more general debate about how legal parenthood should be defined in the twenty-first century.

Despite my original intention to include gay fathers and donors (due to their role as significant stakeholders in the debate about the legal recognition of lesbian parents), they are also omitted from the sample. Because many lesbians conceive using anonymous-donor sperm, I had not expected to locate as many gay donors and fathers as lesbian mothers. Despite these low expectations, the failure to recruit sufficient numbers to constitute a sample was disappointing. In recruiting the men, I used all of the same techniques I had used with the mothers. I also contacted two support groups for gay fathers, but both informed me that their members were men who had become parents in the context of a hetero-sexual relationship. From all of my advertising, I received only three responses.

It is difficult to know exactly why the response rate from fathers and donors was so low. They are certainly not a large population, but that alone cannot explain the numbers. Perhaps because some donors do not see themselves as parents, they were poorly represented on the various *parenting* listservs used to recruit participants, yet the study was advertised within the gay community more generally. It is also possible that donors may not have been sufficiently invested in parenting to feel that the study was relevant to them. As my own data suggests, most donors are "occasional parents" at best, and they may not feel that their stories are particularly important to a study such as this. Finally, most gay donors and fathers may feel satisfied with their existing parenting arrangements and therefore have no concerns about reforming the current legal framework.

While locating mothers who parented within a diverse range of family configurations was the central focus of my sampling strategy, participants were also sought from a variety of racial, cultural, and economic backgrounds. I felt that it was possible that the different social, racial, and cultural positions women occupy might inform their experiences of and attitudes towards both parenting and the law. In an effort to locate participants from different backgrounds, the email advertisement was sent to a number of social groups directed towards racialized lesbians, as well lesbians who are members of religious minority groups. Also contacted were several lesbian and gay social and community groups that were located within, and presumably drew their members from, lower-income areas of the regions in which the interviews were conducted.

The final decision with regard to sampling was to determine from which geographical regions participants would be drawn. Ultimately, interviews were conducted with women who lived within a two hundred-kilometre radius of Vancouver, Calgary, or Edmonton. Vancouver, a city of approximately 2 million people with a thriving and visible lesbian and gay community, seemed a logical choice. Calgary and Edmonton were chosen partly because they varied in size both from each other and from Vancouver. Their lesbian and gay communities were thus much smaller and far less visible than Vancouver's. In addition, the location of Calgary and Edmonton within Alberta, a socially conservative province often perceived as being hostile to lesbians and gay men, was expected to increase the range of configurations and understandings of family represented within the study. However, few distinct trends emerged between the provinces.

The Interviews

Thirty-six interviews were conducted between February and October 2005. Twenty-four occurred in the Vancouver area, seven in the Calgary area, and five in the Edmonton area. Thirty-six families and forty-nine mothers are represented within the sample. Twenty-two of the interviews were conducted with one mother alone, though most were members of a couple, and the remaining fourteen included both mothers together.

The interview schedule took a semi-structured form and was designed to address four key research questions. The first question focused on how mothers defined "family": mothers were asked to describe their own families and who they included within them. During these discussions, concepts such as chosen family, social family, and biological family were explored. The mothers were also invited to articulate where they would ideally draw the boundaries around the concept of family and why. Discussions centred on whether the mothers endorsed the law's existing preference for the nuclear family or whether they preferred a more expansive concept of family, perhaps capable of including three or more parents and/or other chosen family members.

The second research question involved an exploration of how parenthood is understood and defined within the lesbian family. Mothers were asked to provide their own definitions of parenthood and to describe how these understandings were enacted within their own families. Did they draw any distinction between biological and non-biological motherhood and, if not, how did they work to displace the significant social meaning attached to biological relationships?

The third question addressed the role of sperm donors within the lesbian family. The mothers, whether they had conceived using the sperm of anonymous or known donors, were asked how they understood the role of donors in lesbian families and in what circumstances (if any) they might understand a donor to be a parent. They were specifically asked about the meaning (if any) they attached to the biological connection between donor and child. The mothers who had conceived using the sperm of a known donor were asked to describe the role (if any) their donor actually played in their family and the language they used to define his identity.

The final research question focused explicitly on law reform: If the mothers were able to create their own model for parental recognition, what would they propose? The mothers were first invited to explore their attitudes towards law and legal engagement. They were then asked to describe what *kind* of law reform they would ideally pursue. To initiate the law reform conversation, the mothers were asked to respond to three loosely defined recognition models gathered from the international literature on same-sex parenting: What were the pros and cons of each model? Which model did they prefer? And, if necessary, what limitations or additions would they add to their preferred model so that it adequately met their needs?

While the interview schedule was relatively well defined, it was used more as an *aide-mémoire* in an effort to achieve what feminist researchers have described as a "dialogical" mode of interaction.[19] Dialogical interviews are designed to look less like question/answer sessions and more like fluid "conversations with a purpose." Such a model can assist in overcoming the hierarchical nature of subject/object interactions that are inherent in interview practice. In this study, the fluid nature of the interview was established with the first question: "Can you tell me the story of how you came to be a mother?" The answers to this question often extended to twenty to thirty minutes of narration as mothers pieced together the various elements of their family history. Answers often went well beyond the basic details to include very personal and often emotionally charged stories about failed relationships, unsuccessful negotiations with donors, fertility problems, miscarriages, infant death, and postpartum depression. I was often surprised by the ease with which mothers talked to me, as well as by their willingness to share stories outside of the study's parameters. Ultimately, I attributed their openness to the dialogical model, my commitment to active listening and a non-judgmental approach, and my own identity as a lesbian.

The Participants: A Summary

Recent research on planned lesbian families has revealed that they are far from a homogenous group.[20] The thirty-six families and forty-nine women who participated in the study were no different. Together, the women were the parents of forty-six children – twenty-six girls and twenty boys. The children ranged in age from four months to twenty-eight years, though the vast majority were under the age of seven. Eighteen of the mothers interviewed were biological mothers and five were non-biological mothers; in fourteen instances, both mothers were interviewed together.[21] While most of the families lived in one of the three cities, approximately 15 percent were located in suburban areas and small towns.

In accordance with the study's sampling goals, I recruited mothers who parented in a number of different family configurations. The complexity of these configurations makes it difficult to categorize them, and in several cases, the categories overlap. Short summaries of the characteristics of each family can be found in the appendix. The most common family configuration, with eighteen of the thirty-six families falling within it, was the two-parent nuclear model with an anonymous donor. The prevalence of this model within the sample, despite my best efforts to de-centre the nuclear family, suggests that it may be the most common parenting model within the lesbian community.

In addition to the anonymous-donor nuclear family, however, the sample included a variety of other family constellations. Twelve known-donor families were represented, each demonstrating a slightly different approach to the known-donor relationship. Seven of the thirty-six families had experienced parental separation, and in three of these families, the mother interviewed remained single. In an additional three families, the biological mother had planned at least one of her children as a single parent, raising legal issues that pertain to both lesbian mothers and single mothers by choice. Finally, in one of the thirty-six families, the biological mother parented with a non-conjugal, non-cohabiting female co-parent, an arrangement that had been agreed upon prior to conception.

As suggested above, a variety of donor relationships were identified within the sample. Two of the families who used anonymous donors had conceived at a time when lesbian access to fertility clinics was prohibited. These women, whose children were considerably older than the average, had accessed sperm through a third-party intermediary, in both cases a friend who self-identified as a feminist. The remaining twenty-two anonymous-donor families had purchased sperm from a sperm bank. The twelve families with known donors tended to define their donor's role in one of three ways.[22] In seven of the families, the donor was understood as a significant male figure in the child's life who exercised regular contact but was not considered a parent. In some instances, the children (where old enough) and their mothers used the word "father" to refer to these men, while in other families the man's first name was used to identify him. In two of the twelve families, donors played the role of "symbolic father."[23] These men were not involved in the child's life but were known to the child and could be pointed to in the event that the child needed to identify someone as "dad." Finally, in two of the known-donor families, the donors (and their male partners) were active, practicing parents with all of the rights and responsibilities implied by that status, though without legal custody. In these families, the mothers considered their children to have four parents. In all but one of the families with a known donor, the donor identified as gay.

Despite my attempts to recruit mothers from a diverse array of racial, ethnic, and social backgrounds, the sample remained largely middle class, urban, able-bodied, and Anglo-Canadian. Forty-two of the forty-nine women were of Anglo-European descent. Of those who were not, three identified as French Canadian, two claimed a Jewish ethnic heritage (one of these women was Israeli), one hailed from South Africa, and one was Aboriginal. The vast majority of the women were also well educated, most had professional qualifications, and several worked in senior positions. However, because they were clustered in the "caring industries" – teaching, nursing, and social work – few were high earners.

A high representation of white, middle-class, well-educated mothers is a general feature of most studies of planned lesbian parenthood.[24] There is no doubt that at least part of the explanation for this lack of diversity lies in the use of convenience sampling. Some researchers have argued, however, that the over-representation of race- and class-privileged mothers in studies about lesbian motherhood may reflect the actual racial and economic composition of planned lesbian families.[25] For example, Stacey and Biblarz have suggested that there may be more white and middle-class lesbian mothers because socially privileged lesbians are more likely than the less privileged to possess the required sense of entitlement to have children in the face of considerable moral judgment and disapproval of their actions.[26]

Beyond the question of entitlement, there are a number of other possible explanations for why white, middle-class families are so well represented within the sample. The most obvious relates to the costs associated with becoming a lesbian mother, particularly if the services of a fertility clinic are utilized.[27] The cost of buying and storing sperm, as well as insemination and other consulting services, means that lesbian women who conceive using anonymous-donor sperm face pre-conception costs of between $1,500 and $20,000, depending on the number of attempts necessary to become pregnant and the difficulties experienced along the way. Even the easiest conceptions are expensive. For example, a single insemination attempt (including the purchase of sperm) at any of the five clinics used by my study participants cost between $500 and $800. A single in vitro fertilization cycle, including the required medications, could cost up to $10,000.[28] It is thus possible that lower-income women are less likely to conceive using donor insemination. Conception using known-donor sperm obviously reduces the cost, and some researchers have suggested that lower-income lesbians might be more likely to choose this option.[29] In my own study, however, I found no discernible connection between income level and donor choices.

The prevalence of middle-class participants in the study may also be explained by the fact that the sample was drawn from three of the wealthiest areas of Canada. The average median incomes in Vancouver, Calgary, and Edmonton are above both the Canadian average and the average for other regions within the two provinces.[30] It is therefore not entirely surprising that many of the participants were comfortably middle class. It is also possible that the study's focus on law may not have been particularly appealing to working-class lesbians. While the middle class often perceive law to be a tool of social justice and progressive change, the working class are more likely to experience law as a tool of oppression. For example, working-class women may have experienced some form of state surveillance, perhaps in the context of social assistance law or child protection law, and are thus less likely to perceive legal mechanisms as positive or capable of assisting them in any way. The generally privileged nature of the study participants may mean that their approach to law reform is not representative of lesbian mothers from more marginalized backgrounds. This concern will be revisited in the law reform chapters.

Overview of the Book

The book is divided into three sections. The first section comprises the Introduction and Chapters 1 and 2, and addresses the contextual, methodological, and theoretical aspects of the study. The second section comprises Chapters 3, 4, and 5, and is based on analysis of the interviews. Chapter 3 addresses definitional issues, while Chapters 4 and 5 focus on law reform. In the third section, a concluding chapter draws together the main legal, theoretical, and policy implications of the study and makes recommendations for further research. Each chapter is discussed in more detail below.

Chapter 1 situates the study in its broader legal, social, and political context. First, it outlines the existing legal framework available to lesbian mothers, including its strengths and limitations. Second, it identifies some of the wider trends in Canadian family law, such as the influence of the fathers' rights movement and the rise of neo-conservatism, that form additional barriers to the legal inclusion of planned lesbian families.

Chapter 2 addresses the theoretical and policy dimensions of the study. It situates the issue of lesbian and gay parental recognition within the wider debate about the terms upon which lesbians and gay men have sought entry into legal "family." Focusing initially on relationship recognition, the chapter questions the continued reliance by lesbians and gay men on formal equality or "sameness" strategies, and suggests that these strategies may have the effect of reinforcing existing hierarchies and erasing lesbian and gay difference. The chapter then considers whether the critique of a formal equality strategy in the relationship recognition context resonates in the context of parenting. It posits that while the use of formal equality to achieve parental status raises numerous concerns, there may also be fundamental differences between parental and adult relationship recognition that make the critique less convincing in the parental context.

Chapter 3 presents the first stage of the data analysis. Drawing on the mothers' voices, it explores how the mothers understand and define key familial concepts, including "family" and "parent." The mothers' definitions are discussed in the context of wider debates about the meaning of kinship in contemporary Western society. Particular attention is given to what the mothers understand to be the key signifiers of parental status, analyzed first in the context of their own parent/child relationships and then with regard to donor relationships. Chapter 3 also considers the extent to which the mothers embrace or reject some of the key features of the traditional family. For example, it explores their attitudes towards parenting outside of a nuclear model, as well as the relationship between parenting and legal marriage.

Building on the mothers' definitions and understandings of key familial concepts, Chapter 4 considers how they might approach law reform directed towards recognizing their parental relationships. Acknowledging that legal engagement may be hazardous for marginalized groups, the chapter begins by considering the mothers' attitudes towards engaging with law. Given the tentative willingness on the part of most of the mothers to pursue a law reform agenda, particularly a legislative one, the second half of the chapter explores both existing and proposed law reform.

Continuing the discussion of law reform, Chapter 5 considers how the mothers' parental definitions might translate into a reform context and what kind of a legislative model would be required. Ultimately, it argues that the most appropriate reform proposal would combine the automatic extension of legal parentage to non-biological lesbian mothers with additional, more expansive provisions that capture the desire among the mothers for a more flexible definition of family.

The concluding chapter addresses the question of how progressive social change might be achieved. In particular, it considers how lesbian mothers might encourage government to pursue legislative change and what additional work still needs to be done.

The Legal and Social Context   **1**

As planned lesbian families have emerged as a significant component of Canada's demographic makeup, the assignment of legal parentage within them has become a contentious issue for Canadian family law. Traditionally, legal parentage has been granted to the "natural" or biological parents of a child and limited to two individuals of the opposite sex. The traditional parameters of legal parentage obviously exclude many lesbian parents. In an attempt to counter the existing exclusions, lesbian mothers have sought relief through the courts; after a decade of relatively successful litigation, they have access to some of the most inclusive laws in the world. However, significant gaps remain: the legal framework is uneven across the country, non-biological mothers continue to be treated as second-class parents or even legal strangers to their children, and the legal status of known donors remains unresolved.

This chapter discusses the existing provincial laws, as well as the broader legal and social context within which planned lesbian families must assert their parentage claims. I argue that while planned lesbian families have been reasonably successful through the courts in securing a number of methods by which non-biological mothers can proactively seek legal recognition following the birth of their child, the legal benefits they have gained fall well short of what is needed. Planned lesbian families may be able to erect a variety of legal structures around themselves in the months following their child's birth, but legal parentage laws – for example, laws that would treat non-biological lesbian mothers (and not known donors) as *presumptive* legal parents from the time of their child's birth – remain elusive. Influenced by the fathers' rights movement and broader neo-conservative rhetoric, neither the courts nor legislatures have been willing to create a legal framework that treats a two-mother family as complete.

The Existing Legal Framework: A Limited Model

In Canada, legal parentage is addressed primarily, though rarely explicitly, at the provincial level in family law, vital statistics, and adoption legislation.[1] In almost all instances, legal parentage is conferred on the child's "natural" or biological parents, the assumption being that these individuals are easily identified. Though legal parentage can be transferred in a number of strictly defined circumstances to someone other than a biological parent, such as in an adoption scenario, the undisturbed assumption is that the biological parents are the child's legal parents at the time of birth.

The focus on biological parenthood has been historically straightforward in the context of assigning legal maternity. Though rarely defined in legislation, it is presumed that the woman who gives birth to a child is the child's (biological) "mother."[2] As Roxanne Mykitiuk explains, "Because birth can be witnessed, the biological and social/legal aspects of maternity have been construed as inextricably linked."[3] Thus, while BC law does not define "mother" or legal maternity in any of its statutes, the provincial *Vital Statistics Act* does refer to the child's "mother" in the context of its definition of "birth."[4] Section 1 defines "birth" as "the complete expulsion or extraction from its *mother*, irrespective of the duration of the pregnancy, of a product of conception" (emphasis added).[5] The act therefore assumes that the woman who gives birth is the child's legal mother. Until fairly recently, such an assumption was likely to be biologically accurate; however, with the advent of surrogacy and egg donation, which will be discussed below, a new dimension of complexity has been added.

In contrast to maternity, paternity has always been a complicated designation because of the impossibility, until fairly recently, of proving biological fatherhood. The category of legal paternity has thus always been more of a social construction than an accurate statement of biological fact.[6] In the absence of clarity, a series of legislative "presumptions of paternity" have developed, and though it was historically impossible to know whether the presumptions accurately identified the biological father, underlying them was a belief that they did.[7] The original presumption of paternity derived from the Latin maxim *pate rest quem nuptia demonstrat* (by marriage the father is demonstrated) and typically stated that if a man is (or was at the estimated time of conception) married to – or, more recently, in an opposite-sex common-law relationship with – the mother, he is presumed to be the legal father. No additional proof of parentage was required. Underlying this presumption is the belief that the only man with sexual access to a woman is her husband or, more recently, her husband or male common-law partner.

In conjunction with the traditional marriage presumption, additional paternity presumptions are included in most provincial family law statutes, though their focus is primarily on parentage for the purpose of paying child support. A survey of provincial family law legislation indicates that a man may be presumed to be the father of a child for at least some legal purposes if (a) he was married to the mother of the child and the marriage was terminated within three hundred days of the birth; (b) he married the mother of the child after the birth and acknowledged that he was the father of the child; (c) he was cohabiting with the mother in a relationship of some permanence at the time of the birth of the child, or the child was born within three hundred days after the person and the mother ceased to cohabit; (d) he has acknowledged paternity of the child and is so registered under the *Vital Statistics Act* or similar legislation; or (e) he has been found by a court of competent jurisdiction in Canada to be the father of the child.[8] Now that paternity testing is widely available, a presumptive father's status can be challenged on the basis of genetic information to the contrary. Otherwise, the presumptions simply apply.

One might expect that the law would choose to be more exact with its assertions now that biological paternity can be proven absolutely.[9] However, the paternity by presumption regime remains active today, enabling a significant number of non-biological fathers to secure legal parentage.[10] While this could be understood as an important step towards the recognition of social fatherhood, Maguire Schulz suggests that the continued reliance on the presumption regime is more about preserving normative claims about the nature of marriage and family:

> What purports to be an inference about biological fact may actually grow out of a normative aspiration and may readily be transformed into a prescriptive command about marriage and family, often without acknowledgement that such a transformation has taken place. The important issue becomes not who is, but who *should* be having sex with the mother: her husband. Thus, the social construct, in fact normative and mutable, draws substantial but disguised legitimacy from the representation that it simply expresses "givens" of nature.[11]

In this statement, Maguire Schulz captures the ways in which the existing paternity regime permits the selective deployment of either biological or social paternity to fulfill its particular ideological ends. As will be seen later in this chapter, the ideology typically underlying the deployment of paternity presumptions is the preservation of the patriarchal nuclear family. In fact, the ease with which men can achieve legal parentage, particularly in contrast to the rather limited means by which women can claim the same identity, makes it very difficult for lesbian mothers to assert the completeness of a fatherless family.

While DNA testing has made traditional paternity presumptions increasingly difficult to sustain, perhaps the most significant challenge to existing parentage laws comes from the rapid growth in the use of assisted reproductive technologies. The conception of children via sperm and egg donation, or as a result of surrogacy agreements, has challenged the law to rethink the traditional bases upon which parentage is assigned. Presumptions built around a child's biological or "natural" parents are simply no longer sustainable. In a situation of sperm donation, the mother's male partner is clearly not the child's biological father, and in the case of surrogacy or egg donation, the woman giving birth may be neither the genetic nor intentional mother of the child. In other words, biological relationships may not be parental ones, and parental relationships may have no connection to either biology or genetics. In response to the legal and social conundrums presented by reproductive technologies, a number of provinces have introduced new parentage presumptions that apply specifically to situations of assisted conception. Replacing traditional parentage presumptions, which tend to rely on (assumed) biological relationships, the new presumptions derive from a mix of intention, relationship status, and genetics. For example, section 13 of Alberta's *Family Law Act*, which is replicated in a number of other provinces, addresses the assignment of parentage in the context of donor insemination. The section declares that a man is the legal father of a child conceived via assisted conception (with his consent) in circumstances where he is married to, or in a relationship of interdependence of some permanence with, the child's mother. The man's parental status thus derives from the conjugal relationship he shares with the child's biological mother and his consent to the assisted conception. Section 12 of the act addresses surrogacy. It permits the genetic mother of a child carried by a gestational surrogate to be named the sole legal mother, providing the surrogate consents. In the surrogacy case, the genetic (though not biological) link between the mother and the child is sufficient to displace the gestational mother's legal status, providing the gestational mother agrees.

What appears to underlie both provisions, though it is not explicit, is a desire to manipulate legal parentage laws in the assisted conception context so that they reflect the parties' pre-birth intentions. The non-biological father who consents to his female partner's assisted conception *intends* to play the role of father: section 13 gives legal force to that intention through the extension of legal paternity to such a man. Similarly, in the context of a surrogacy agreement, both the "commissioning" or intentional mother and the surrogate mother intend that the commissioning mother be the legal parent: section 12 gives that intention legal force. Though not available in all provinces, provisions such as those found in Alberta's *Family Law Act* suggest that the law is willing, where the child will be raised by two parents of the opposite sex, to sever the traditional link between biological and legal parenthood (whether actual or created via legal presumptions), replacing it with a form of social parenthood derived from pre-birth intentions and/or relationship status. The limiting of the applicability of section 13 of the *Family Law Act* to heterosexual couples was successfully challenged in 2005 by a married lesbian couple, who argued that it violated section 15 of the *Canadian Charter of Rights and Freedoms*.[12] The court allowed their application on the basis that section 13 created legislative consequences for same-sex couples that it did not create for heterosexual couples and was thus in violation of the *Charter*. The solution provided by the court was to read a provision into the act that did not limit the deeming provision to only a male spouse or partner. The act itself has not been amended.

Despite the Alberta example, most provinces explicitly exclude lesbian mothers from traditional presumptions of parentage as well as from the new laws pertaining to assisted conception. Recent attempts by non-biological lesbian mothers to utilize statutory paternity presumptions on the analogous basis that they frequently enable social fathers to secure legal parentage have been rejected because the assumption under-lying the legislation – that the mother's male partner *could* be the bio-logical parent of the child – could never be factually accurate in a lesbian context.[13] That the presumption is not always factually accurate in the heterosexual context was considered irrelevant. Similarly, legislation assigning legal parentage in cases of assisted conception is, in all provinces but Quebec, available only to heterosexual couples, thus excluding lesbian mothers from its benefits. As a result of these exclusions, non-biological lesbian mothers living in common law Canada have no statutory authority to assert legal parentage at the time of their child's birth.[14] For families that include known donors, there is a very real pos-sibility that the *donor* is in fact the child's second legal parent.

In the absence of legislative authority, lesbian mothers have turned to litigation to secure their parenting relationships. Perhaps surprisingly, given the lack of legislative interest in the issue, Canadian courts have exhibited a tentative willingness to extend a number of existing legal mechanisms by which non-biological lesbian mothers can secure legal rights with respect to their children, particularly in the absence of con-flict.[15] However, access to these mechanisms is limited, depends on the consent of the biological mother and donor (if known), and cannot always be utilized at the time of birth.

The most common way by which non-biological mothers secure legal parentage in relation to their children is through a second-parent adoption. Similar to a step-parent adoption, though available to parents of the same sex and typically completed as soon after the child's birth as legally possible, a second-parent adoption allows a non-biological mother to adopt the biological child of her partner without the biological mother losing her legal status. In such circumstances, the non-biological mother becomes a legal parent, and the parental rights of the donor, if he is known, are severed. The introduction of second-parent adoption was a significant breakthrough for lesbian mothers because, unlike traditional step-parent adoption, which requires that the adoptive parent replace the biological parent of the same sex, second-parent adoption allows two parents of the same sex to enjoy legal parentage simultaneously.

First secured via litigation in Ontario in 1995 and now available in all but two Canadian provinces/territories, second-parent adoptions are currently the only way by which non-biological mothers can secure all of the rights and responsibilities of parenthood.[16] However, they come with significant limitations. Second-parent adoptions require the consent of the biological mother (and the biological father in the case of a known donor), typically involve a waiting period of several months after the birth of the child, necessitate hiring a lawyer, and cost several thousand dollars to complete. The waiting period and the ease with which biological mothers and donors can withhold or withdraw consent leave non-biological mothers extremely vulnerable. For example, in the BC case of *K.G.T. v. P.D.*, the biological mother refused to consent to the non-biological mother's adoption of her daughter, instead consenting to her new partner adopting the child. The non-biological mother challenged the adoption, arguing that she was entitled to adopt the child on the basis that the two women had intended to co-parent and had done so for over five years. While the court ultimately barred the new partner from adopting, it also refused to dispense with the biological mother's consent to the non-biological mother's adoption, stating that any anticipated benefits for the child of having a second legal parent were "nebulous." In effect, the decision enabled the biological mother to bar her child's second mother from securing legal parentage. The court also rejected the non-biological mother's application for joint custody, preferring to award guardianship and access. The effect was that while the non-biological mother had some rights and responsibilities in relation to her daughter, she was denied actual legal parentage.

Another significant limitation of second-parent adoptions is that they cannot be utilized to secure legal parentage at the time of birth. Rather, they require the non-biological mother to take some positive action after the birth of the child. In some provinces, an application for adoption cannot be filed until the child is three or six months old. This waiting period leaves non-biological mothers vulnerable to a change of heart on the part of either the biological mother or the donor. As the facts in *K.G.T.* illustrate, the effects of not securing a second-parent adoption can be dire. While most lesbian mothers take advantage of second-parent adoption laws, it is difficult to secure an adoption without the assistance of a lawyer. Thus, mothers must not only be aware of the availability of second-parent adoptions; they must also be able to afford the services of a lawyer. Further complicating the situation is the fact that very few lawyers have any familiarity with second-parent adoptions. Even in Vancouver, a city with a large lesbian population, only two lawyers regularly complete second-parent adoptions.

In addition to second-parent adoption, and as a result of litigation, a number of provinces allow two mothers to appear on the child's birth certificate from birth.[17] The "gender-neutral birth certificate" was considered to be a significant breakthrough for lesbian mothers because, unlike second-parent adoption, it can be utilized at birth. It is therefore possible to assert the legal status of the non-biological mother as a "co-parent" from the moment of the child's birth. However, unlike an adoption, the gender-neutral birth certificate does not actually secure legal parentage. Similar to the traditional presumptions of paternity, it is presumptive proof of parentage only and is thus rebuttable by either the biological mother or a known donor. Furthermore, in Ontario and British Columbia, the new birth certificate can only be used if the child was conceived using the sperm of an anonymous donor, implying that if the donor is known, *he* is the child's second parent. The gender-neutral birth certificate therefore does nothing to address the vulnerability of lesbian families vis-à-vis known donors.

The final area in which lesbian mothers have made limited legal inroads through litigation is in relation to the recognition of multiple-parent families. While my study shows that most lesbian mothers *and their donors* wish to exclude donors from the status of legal parent, a small number of participants have chosen to co-parent their children within a three- or four-parent unit. Unfortunately for these families, the law has traditionally limited parentage to two individuals. However, in a recent case initiated by two mothers and their donor, *A.A. v. B.B.*, the Ontario Court of Appeal held that a child could have three legal parents – his two mothers and his donor father.[18] While *A.A. v. B.B.* is the only decision of its kind and is not applicable outside of Ontario, or perhaps even beyond the individual facts of the case, it suggests that in families in which three adults agree that they are all parents, the courts *may* be willing to give legal recognition to the arrangement.

As is the case with second-parent adoptions, the decision in *A.A.* does not address legal parentage at birth. Rather, it requires parents to initiate a legal process after the child is born. *A.A.* also seems to continue to prioritize the biological parents over the non-biological mother. In *A.A.*, it was the non-biological mother, not the donor, who sought to be added as the child's third parent, the donor having been listed on the child's birth certificate. While the parties' decision to name the two biological progenitors as the child's "parents" may have been strategic – the child's biological parents can be named on the birth certificate without challenge – the effect of the strategy was that the donor's biological relationship was prioritized and the burden of applying for third-parent status fell on the already vulnerable non-biological parent. The irony of this situation would be less if the three parties were sharing responsibility for the child, but the reality was that the child was being raised primarily by his two mothers, with the donor having much more limited contact and not taking part in any of the day-to-day decision making.

Given the significant, though limited, legal changes achieved via litigation, it is surprising that so few provinces have been willing to consider a legislative response to planned lesbian families. As noted above, while several provinces have legislated with regard to parentage in cases of assisted conception within heterosexual families,[19] the only province to do the same for lesbian families is Quebec. Introduced in 2002 as part of a review of provincial filiation laws, Quebec's *Civil Code* includes a series of parental presumptions applicable at the time of the child's birth to all individuals or couples who conceive using third-party gametes.[20] Article 538.3 of the code states that "if a child is born of a parental project involving assisted procreation between married or civil union spouses during the marriage or the civil union or within three hundred days after its dissolution or annulment, the spouse of the woman who gave birth to the child is presumed to be the child's other parent."[21] This article extends traditional paternity presumptions to couples who enter into a medically assisted "parental project." The term "parental project" is defined in article 538: "A parental project involving assisted procreation exists from the moment a person alone decides or spouses by mutual consent decide, in order to have a child, to resort to the genetic material of a person who is not party to the parental project." Thus, a parental project can be entered into by a couple or by a single person, and the gender-neutral terminology indicates that the provision applies to both same-sex and opposite-sex couples. Finally, article 538.2 states, "The contribution of genetic material for the purposes of a third-party parental project does not create any bond of filiation between the contributor and the child born of the parental project." Article 538.2 appears to exclude sperm donors from being awarded parental status if they are not parties to the parental project. Thus, in cases of assisted insemination involving a parental project, a same-sex couple or single lesbian woman is treated in the same manner as a heterosexual couple or single woman who conceives using the same method. However, Quebec remains the only province in which the assignment of legal parentage is addressed in this way.

Changing Families, Changing Attitudes

While the existing legal framework is limited in its capacity to meet the needs of planned lesbian families, the challenges that lesbian families encounter in asserting their legitimacy do not end with inadequate provincial law. Lesbian mothers must also contend with broader legal and social trends that work to exclude them, such as the recent resurgent interest within both family law and wider society in biological family, and biological fathers in particular.[22] While the impact of these trends is at least somewhat offset by the concurrent, and seemingly contradictory, willingness on the part of some courts to extend limited forms of legal recognition to non-normative families, they nonetheless make it very difficult for lesbian couples to assert the legitimacy of their families.

In 1996, Judith Stacey described planned lesbian families as the "pioneer outpost of the post-modern family" – perhaps the most complex example of the improvisation, ambiguity, and diversity that characterize twenty-first-century families.[23] However, Stacey was careful to note that lesbian families are by no means the only family form confronting traditional norms. They are part of a much broader shift in Canadian family demographics: in Canada, just over a third of children are being raised in homes that do not resemble the married, nuclear, heterosexual norm.[24] In fact, the sharp rise in divorce, single motherhood, stepfamilies, common-law relationships, and the use of assisted reproductive technologies have made it increasingly difficult to assert that the heterosexual biological nuclear family is any longer the norm. Lesbian mothers obviously benefit from this demographic and ideological shift, as it enables them to position themselves as just one more type of a growing number of alternative families. In fact, it comes as no surprise that the increased willingness on the part of the courts to recognize planned lesbian families as "functional families" has occurred in tandem with the recognition and growing acceptance of alternative family forms more generally.[25]

While non-normative family arrangements have reached new levels of legal and social acceptance in recent decades, the path of progress is by no means straightforward. At the same time that non-normative "functional" families, including lesbian and gay families, have received unprecedented legal support, a backlash against non-normative family practices, particularly those that exclude or marginalize biological fathers, has simultaneously emerged. Bolstered by an increasingly powerful fathers' rights movement, the emergence of a neo-conservative political agenda, and an unprecedented adherence to gender-neutral formal equality in family law, fathers have emerged as critical to both the preservation of "the family" and children's best interests. The resurgent interest in fathers, and biological fathers in particular, has made the legal terrain a complicated one for lesbian mothers who wish to assert the completeness of their two-mother family unit.

Fathers' Rights and Father Presence

A key impetus behind the increased focus on fathers in both Canadian family law and broader state policy has been the emergence over the past two decades of a vocal fathers' rights movement.[26] Frustrated by what they believe to be the favouring of mothers within the family law system, fathers' rights groups have become active participants in Canadian family law reform. While their legal interventions have not always been successful, fathers' rights discourse exerts considerable influence in Canadian family law. In fact, the "best interests of the child" test, which governs both custody and access law in Canada, has been so influenced by the fathers' rights agenda that there now appears to be a de facto presumption that father access is in a child's best interests.

It is difficult to pinpoint exactly why the fathers' rights movement has been so successful in influencing family law and policy in Canada. The explanation may lie with the fact that much of what the movement promotes resonates with the neo-conservative and neo-liberal agendas that currently dominate the Canadian political landscape.[27] Neo-conservatives respond positively to the movement's desire to preserve the traditional patriarchal family, while neo-liberals presume that maintaining father/child relationships following parental separation will reduce the economic burden on the state.

The key site of critique for the fathers' rights movement is the family law system, which the movement accuses of favouring mothers and marginalizing fathers. Along with complaints about child support, the movement's primary focus has been on custody and access law and, in particular, the importance of maintaining father/child access in separated and divorced families. Arguing before numerous government committees on custody and access law that it is in the best interests of children to have regular access with their fathers, fathers' rights groups have lobbied for both enhanced access rights as well as a legislative presumption in favour of joint custody.[28] The right to access and/or joint custody is presented by fathers' rights groups as deriving from two sources: (1) the father's biological tie to the child, which is understood to entitle him to access, independent of the nature or quality of the relationship he may (or may not) share with the child; and (2) the notion that parents should be treated as formal equals, with no reference to previous or existing caregiving patterns. It is therefore assumed by fathers' rights advocates that access or joint custody should prevail even in circumstances where the father has exercised little or no caregiving responsibility or where the father may have previously harmed the child or the child's mother.[29]

While fathers' rights groups have not succeeded in securing a legislative presumption in favour of joint custody, they have had significant influence on Canadian custody and access decision making in both the courtroom and non-judicial settings. Many judges, lawyers, social workers, and psychologists who participate in children's disputes appear to have unquestioningly accepted the view that contact between fathers and their children is in children's best interests. For example, in her review of reported Canadian custody and access decisions from 1990 to 1993, Dawn Bourque found that "paternal access is viewed by judges as paramount in the 'best interests of the child' test, eclipsing virtually all other factors. A child's supposed 'need' for or 'right' to a father, irrespective of the quality or quantity of his parenting, has superseded virtually all other considerations."[30]

The conviction that paternal access is in a child's best interests, no matter the nature or quality of the relationship between father and child, has been sustained in part by section 16(10) of the *Divorce Act* – known as the "maximum contact" rule – which states that "the court shall give effect to the principle that a child of the marriage should have as much contact with each spouse as is consistent with the best interests of the child." While section 16(10) clearly limits contact to what is "in the best interests of the child," Bourque's research suggests that in the current pro-father climate, it is presumed by many judges that maximum contact is always in the child's best interests. A similar approach appears to have

emerged in the context of custody law. In her research on custody decision making, Boyd found that although Canada has never adopted a
presumption in favour of joint custody, the philosophy behind it – that
children should be shared equally between their parents – "nevertheless
influences the broader trends in redefining custody and access."[31] In the
absence of a legislative presumption, a de facto presumption appears to
prevail.

Research also suggests that the presence of factors that diminish the
benefits of access between biological fathers and their children, such as
spousal abuse, has little effect on the pro-access/joint custody position.[32]
For example, in her study on spousal abuse, children, and the legal system
in Canada, Neilson found that many family lawyers, who obviously have
a significant influence on post-separation negotiations between spouses,
consider abuse of partners to be of little importance in access decision
making.[33] Many of them felt that "bad spouses" do not necessarily make
"bad parents" and endorsed the need for children to have regular access
with both biological parents: "However incapable an abusive spouse
may be at appreciating the needs and respecting the rights of his former
spouse, he is still a parent; a child separated from a parent needs to see,
feel and appreciate *this half of who he or she is*" (emphasis added).[34]

Neilson also found that partner abuse seemed to have little effect on
judges' decisions about access.[35] In fact, her analysis of reported cases
and court files indicates that fathers who abuse their partners are awarded
access to their children most of the time by Canadian courts.[36] In justify-
ing their position, both judges and lawyers made a distinction between
spousal abuse and child abuse, taking the view that only in cases of direct
child abuse should there be any limitations on access.[37] Such an approach
appears contrary to social science research in the area, which shows that
in families where there is spousal violence, children have a significant
probability of suffering direct physical abuse (40 to 50 percent) or sexual
abuse (30 percent).[38] This approach also underestimates the impact on
children of witnessing violence between their parents, which often
continues into the post-separation period if access or joint custody is
ordered.[39] Despite the social science evidence on the issue, and no doubt
influenced by assertions that father involvement is *always* in a child's

best interests, judges remain reluctant to bar biological fathers from having access to their children, even in circumstances of abuse.

The trend towards equating biological fatherhood with an automatic right of access is epitomized by cases such as *Johnson-Steeves v. Lee*, where the Alberta Court of Appeal awarded access to a biological "father" largely on the basis that fathers are simply "good news."[40] *Johnson-Steeves v. Lee* was an access dispute between the child's two biological parents; however, the unusual facts of the case demanded that the court make a specific pronouncement about the significance of the biological tie between father and child. Caroline Johnson-Steeves, who lived in Calgary, asked King Tak Lee, an old university friend who lived in Toronto, whether he would act as a sperm donor. Johnson-Steeves chose a donor arrangement because she wanted to protect any future children from the conflict that her two existing children had experienced as a result of their parents' separation. The parties made an oral agreement that Lee would either donate sperm or father the child via intercourse and provide some financial support. However, he agreed not to interfere with decision making around the health and welfare of the child. Access was discussed briefly by the parties, with Johnson-Steeves indicating that Lee could see the child whenever he passed through town. The child, Nigel, was conceived via intercourse. Lee was not listed on the birth certificate but was acknowledged as Nigel's father for the purpose of providing maintenance.

Lee visited with Nigel several times over the first ten months of his life. Following a series of disagreements, however, Johnson-Steeves prevented Lee from exercising access. The case arose when she applied for an order of sole custody, an order that Lee be denied access to Nigel, and an order for child support. In support of her application for denial of access, Johnson-Steeves argued that the court "must distinguish between a biological father who is not entitled to access as of right and a social father who would have rights of access."[41] She submitted that Lee was only a biological father and, given the circumstances surrounding the conception and birth of Nigel, was not entitled to access. To grant access would be to "impose on her a family relationship she specifically did not want, hence the agreement."[42] Lee responded by arguing that it was always his intention to be a parent, that Nigel had a right to know his biological father, and that it was in the child's best interests that access be granted.

From the outset, the court rejected Johnson-Steeves's argument that Lee was a "sperm donor" and thus "just a biological father."[43] Focusing on Lee's financial contributions, the Court of Appeal stated that "the suggestion that the respondent agreed to provide financial support for the child without having any opportunity to develop a relationship with the child is incomprehensible to us."[44] Drawing a nexus between the payment of maintenance and a right of access, the court refused to believe that a man would provide financial support without getting something in return. Turning to the issue of access, the court relied on both a generic and essentialized view of fatherhood to reject Johnson-Steeves's suggestion that Lee needed something more than mere biology to assert his right to access. Drawing heavily on the evidence of a child psychologist, Dr. Kneier, who had met neither of the parties nor Nigel, the court concluded that it was in Nigel's best interests to have access to his biological father. The court stated:

> It is in children's best interests to have the influence of a "good or adequate" father than to not have that relationship at all. Although a child can develop normally in a one parent household, they do better with the influence of both parents. Dr Kneier says fathers are important to young boys, they yearn for a father and a child may wonder why he has no father when other people do. A child would be happy, curious, and interested to know the man who was their dad. As he said, "it's good news to have a dad."[45]

The court also relied on Dr. Kneier's suggestion that boys in particular need to develop relationships with their fathers, citing with approval the psychologist's assertion that a boy's relationship with his father helps "develop intelligence and drive, improve academic achievement and helps develop independence, empathy and social adequacy with peers."[46]

The decision in *Johnson-Steeves* illustrates the renewed emphasis on biological fatherhood as an essentialized identity giving rise to certain defined rights. Rather than considering the specific relationship between

Nigel and his father or a particularized best interests analysis, the court relied on generic statements about fatherhood from an expert who had met neither the parents nor the child. In fact, it seems that in the context of Canada's pro-access family law system, biological fathers are simply "good news," and a best interests analysis is no longer required. A consideration of Nigel's best interests may have produced the same result, but rather than applying the test, the court allowed biology to serve as a proxy. The court also seemed to accept the argument made by many fathers' rights advocates that fathers are the "antidote" to social problems, particularly those experienced by boys. (Essentialized) fathers are alleged to give their children, particularly their sons, drive, ambition, and intelligence and to help them develop independence and social adequacy. In the context of the court's construction of biological fatherhood, there is no room for the kind of chosen family Caroline Johnson-Steeves imagined.

Rights based solely on biological paternity have also been successfully asserted beyond the custody and access arena. For example, the Supreme Court of Canada's decision in *Trociuk v. British Columbia*, a dispute quickly embraced by the fathers' rights movement, dealt with whether a biological father had the right to have his children share his surname.[47] Like *Johnson-Steeves*, the case highlights the willingness of courts to guarantee rights to biological fathers even in circumstances where those fathers have taken little responsibility for the child. *Trociuk* arose after the children's mother, Rene Ernst, recorded their father as "unacknowledged" on their birth certificates and gave them her surname only. While Ernst later expressed a willingness to hyphenate the children's names, she otherwise refused to alter the birth registration.[48] As she explained at trial:

> I felt there was no reason why the children should bear the last name of somebody that I was not married to and had no plans to set up a life with. I saw no important connection between Darrell's ability to be a good father, if that is what he wanted, and the children bearing his last name. My view was that the children were carried by me, raised by me, and that they should bear my last name. I am their primary caregiver, and, despite the Petitioner's protestations to the

contrary, he has made very little effort outside of the litigation arena to be part of their lives.[49]

Ernst's assertion was well supported by the sporadic nature of her relationship with Trociuk and his apparent lack of interest in the children. Ernst and Trociuk had never lived together for long enough to qualify as "spouses" under British Columbia's *Family Relations Act*,[50] and, though he was awarded six hours of access per week, Trociuk had exercised access only twice in the six months following the order. Without marriage, cohabitation, or a social relationship with the children, Ernst could see no reason why Trociuk should be able to influence the naming process. For her, a biological relationship was not enough. Trociuk, however, brought the matter to court, arguing that section 3(1) of the BC *Vital Statistics Act,* which permitted Ernst to unilaterally choose her children's surname, offends section 15 of the *Canadian Charter of Rights and Freedoms* on the basis that the provision draws an explicit distinction on the basis of sex.

Finding in favour of Trociuk, the Supreme Court held that certain rights attach to the status of biological fatherhood and that those rights are operational even in the absence of a relationship between father and child. In other words, fathers' rights prevail even in the absence of any responsibilities.[51] Noting that affirmation of the biological tie through processes such as birth registration and naming is "a significant means by which some parents participate in a child's life,"[52] the court appears to have equated participation through naming with other forms of participation, such as the actual work of raising a child. In fact, by stating that having one's name on a child's birth certificate is a significant means of participating in a child's life, the court completely diminished the years of caregiving work that Ernst had undertaken alone. Ultimately, the court held that allowing a mother to unilaterally exclude a biological father from a child's birth certificate "cannot be presumed to be in the best interests of the child."[53] By linking children's best interests to the protection of fathers' rights, the court makes it almost impossible to assert an alternative position.[54]

Decisions such as *Trociuk* and *Johnson-Steeves* are emblematic of a much larger trend in Canadian family law towards prioritizing the rights of biological fathers. Father rights and children's best interests are increasingly equated, even in circumstances where the relationship between father and child is limited at best. The effect of this trend is not only an increase in fathers' rights, but also a simultaneous diminishing of the significance of mothers' actual responsibilities for the work of caregiving. When biology alone is sufficient to warrant extensive legal rights, the significance of parental responsibilities is quickly diminished, or worse, taken for granted when performed by women.

Lesbian Mothers in the Era of Fathers' Rights

For planned lesbian families, the increased emphasis on biological fatherhood is troubling. Planned lesbian families rarely include a traditional father within their family configuration, either because anonymous-donor sperm has been used or because it has been agreed in advance between the mother(s) and the donor that his role, if any, is something other than parental. Arrangements with known donors are often put in writing, but such agreements have no legal effect. Where conflict arises with known donors, attempts by lesbian mothers to assert that a donor is not a father have largely failed. In fact, while courts have expressed a tentative willingness to extend limited forms of legal recognition to planned lesbian families who conceive using the sperm of an anonymous donor, they remain resolutely resistant to excluding a known donor from a lesbian family if it means the child will not have a "father."

As yet, very few Canadian decisions have addressed the legal status of known donors to lesbian women (though decisions such as *Johnson-Steeves* are obviously relevant). Three of the cases that address this issue are from Quebec, the sole Canadian province in which the relationship between assisted reproduction and legal parentage is directly addressed by legislation that includes same-sex couples within its parameters.[55] The decisions are thus not necessarily representative of how the issue would be resolved in common law Canada where no such legislation exists. The first of the cases, *S.G. v. L.C.*, dealt with the status of a known sperm donor to a lesbian couple in an interim access application filed by the donor and determined by applying Quebec's unique filiation laws.[56] The child in *S.G.* was conceived via donor insemination and raised by her lesbian mothers. The two women, L.C. and K.S., who had undergone a civil union ceremony a month before the child was born, were listed on the child's birth certificate as her parents. While the mothers initially allowed some contact between the donor (S.G.) and the child, when they began to limit contact, S.G. sought an order of filiation. He argued that a parental project, as defined by article 538 of the Quebec *Civil Code,* existed between himself and the biological mother. He also argued that it had always been his and the biological mother's intention that the two of them raise the child as mother and father. S.G. supported his claim with an affidavit in which he asserted that the non-biological mother had opposed the biological mother's decision to have a child and had suggested that she might end the relationship if the biological mother went ahead with the plan.[57] Though the non-biological mother did not end the relationship, and in fact went on to co-parent the child and enter into a civil union with the biological mother, the court relied on S.G.'s assertions to suggest that the non-biological mother was not a party to the parental project. The two mothers opposed the application, arguing that S.G. was not a parent and had no legal standing to ask for access. They submitted that because the child's birth was medically assisted and the parenting plan was between themselves, S.G. had no more rights to the child than would a complete stranger.

As noted above, Quebec has the most inclusive laws in Canada when it comes to recognizing lesbian parents.[58] Under the recently reformed filiation provisions, if a child is born of a parental project involving assisted conception, it is presumed that the spouse of the woman who gave birth to the child is the child's other parent.[59] The sex of the spouse is irrelevant. Furthermore, where a child is conceived via assisted conception, the contribution of genetic material does not create any automatic bond of filiation between the contributor and the child.[60] A sperm donor is only a legal parent if he is also a party to the parental project.

In making her decision in *S.G.,* Courteau J. relied heavily on the donor's affidavit, which was unopposed at the interim hearing, and concluded that the parental project in this case was between S.G. and L.C., not between L.C. and her civil union spouse.[61] Article 538.2 was therefore not applicable because S.G. was not considered a third-party contributor of genetic material. Rather, he was a party to the parental project. That S.G. could have been constructed as such is baffling. The child was planned by a lesbian couple and born into a lesbian relationship that was later solemnized via a civil union. The two mothers had parented the child from birth within their nuclear family. Yet Courteau J. was unwilling to recognize the social bond between non-biological mother and child, or the autonomy of the lesbian nuclear family, prioritizing instead the biological link between donor and child.

Citing the donor's affidavit with approval, Courteau J. held that the mothers' attitude to access was "totally destructive" and that they were denying the child her "rights to her father."[62] These comments highlight Courteau J.'s refusal to accept that lesbian families, like their heterosexual counterparts, are entitled to a degree of family autonomy. Viewing the lesbian family as inherently incomplete, Courteau J. treated the inclusion of the donor as *positive* rather than destructive. In fact, the donor was understood to add something to the family that was lacking: a father. In a final affront, Courteau J. accused the non-biological mother of having created her parental relationship with the child "artificially," particularly with regard to her appearing on the child's birth certificate.[63] This assertion is revealing of the ways in which biology, particularly biological fatherhood, trumps social relationships, even in the face of legislation designed specifically to protect social parenting by permitting non-biological parents to appear on a child's birth certificate. In the judge's mind, however, the absence of a biological link makes the (statutorily protected) relationship between the non-biological mother and her child "artificial," while a biological tie between the donor and child, even absent a social relationship, warrants the court's protection.

The second Canadian case addressing paternity via sperm donation, *L.O. v. S.J.*,[64] also arose in Quebec but produced a different result. Given the clarity of the factual evidence in *L.O.*, the court had little choice but to follow the clear instruction of the filiation provisions in the *Civil Code*. The parties had a donor agreement that specified that the donor agreed to relinquish all rights he may have as a legal parent. The court relied on the agreement as written confirmation of the intention of the parties with regard to the "parental project." In addition, the court relied on the fact that the women already had two children conceived using the sperm of a different donor to support the assertion that the donor was not intended to be part of the family. Based on these facts, the court held that the parties to the parental project were the two women and that the donor was a third-party gamete provider. The donor was thus excluded from the status of father. By way of counter-argument, the donor asserted that the parental project involved three individuals – himself and the two mothers – but the court rejected the claim on the basis that Quebec law did not permit three legal parents.

The decision in *L.O.* suggests that sperm donors will not always be successful in asserting paternity. However, the clarity of both the facts and Quebec's legislation left the court with little choice but to make the decision it did. By contrast, the lack of factual clarity in *S.G.* meant that the judge had the discretion to make a decision influenced by her desire for a normative family arrangement. In fact, the decision in *S.G.* suggests that in situations where donors show an interest in being involved in a child's life, the courts may use this "positive" desire on the part of the donor to support a decision in favour of access. Such an approach is even more likely in common law Canada, where no legislation exists to protect planned lesbian families.

The final decision from Quebec is *A v. B, C and X*.[65] In this case, the court again characterized a biological lesbian mother as being party to a parental project with a known sperm donor to the exclusion of her former partner, the non-biological, social lesbian mother. According to the court, despite having had virtually no contact with the child and openly acknowledging his role as a donor and not a father, the donor was designated a "father" because the child had been conceived via intercourse.[66] The lesbian co-mother, despite having actively parented the child since birth, was not granted parental rights.

A final case addressing the legal status of known donors in Canada, *M.A.C. v. M.K.*, arose in Ontario where there is no legislative regime addressing parentage in such situations.[67] The case differs from the Quebec decisions due to the presence of a three-way co-parenting agreement entered into prior to the child's conception. During the early years of the child's life, the donor played an active role, both in terms of caregiving and decision making. However, when the parties had a falling out, the mothers asserted that their nuclear family should be protected against the now-unwanted intrusion of their known donor. They applied for a second-parent adoption and requested that the court dispense with the donor's consent.[68] Their application was rejected on the basis that the parties had agreed that the donor play a role from the outset and that he had in fact played such a role. Given his active role in the child's life, the court was unwilling to dispense with the donor's consent. The effect of the decision was the denial of the non-biological mother's parental status in favour of that of the known donor.

While there is little Canadian jurisprudence addressing the legal status of known donors, there are a considerable number of cases from other comparable jurisdictions, such as the United States, Australia, the United Kingdom, and New Zealand. Because none of the these jurisdictions had, until very recently, legislation addressing the assignment of legal parentage within same-sex couples, they may be more helpful in predicting how common law Canada might approach the issue than the decisions arising out of Quebec. In her recent analysis of lesbian/donor access litigation across a number of common law jurisdictions, Jenni Millbank found that despite efforts on the part of lesbian mothers to assert the legitimacy of their functional two-mother families, the trend has been to prioritize the biological tie of the donor over all else: not a single donor has lost his application for access.[69] In fact, reminiscent of the Supreme Court's reasoning in *Trociuk,* Millbank found that even in situations where donors have no contact with their children whatsoever, they are uniformly treated by the courts as "enduring and significant figures in their children's lives."[70] By contrast, non-biological mothers engaged in the daily work of caregiving often find their parental status denied or diminished because of the absence of a biological link.

Millbank also found that courts uniformly refuse to accept that a distinction can be made between a (known) biological progenitor and a parent. Even in cases where written contracts specify that the two mothers are intended to be the sole legal parents of the child and that the donor is to play an "avuncular" role only, courts reject this construction as "distorting" the child's "family relationships," where "family" is defined solely according to biology.[71] Preferring to treat all donors as fathers in "the traditional sense of the word," courts routinely interfere with written agreements in order to "find fathers" for the children of lesbian mothers. Millbank also found that courts regularly reject the assertion made by lesbian mothers, such as the mothers in *S.G. v. L.C.*, that the insertion of a donor into their functional family would be destructive. Rather, courts treat the inclusion of donors as "adding" to lesbian families. As Millbank explains:

> Functional family is invisible in [lesbian/donor access cases]; because it is same-gendered parenting, the addition of a male parent is not seen to *take away anything* from the family (for example, by intruding on their autonomy or invalidating their family form), it only *adds* to it. The mothers are viewed as inexplicably trying to deny their child something good, something special and something that their family lacks: a daddy. The mothers' behaviour in resisting a third parent in their family is therefore selfish, non-child centred and weird; while the donor/father's behaviour in trying to join or control that family is *natural*, understandable and loving.[72]

While courts are more than willing to insert donors into lesbian families, Millbank notes that heterosexual families rarely fall victim to such intervention.[73] Heterosexual families created via donor insemination are treated as complete because of the presence of a male parent, whereas lesbian families created in the same circumstances are viewed as deficient. For example, in the New Zealand decision of *P v. K & M*, the court went to great lengths to explain why lesbian and heterosexual families created via donor insemination *should* be treated differently.[74] At the heart of the distinction is the court's belief that lesbian families lack the qualities that might entitle them to family autonomy. The court states that the exclusion of donors from heterosexual families can be justified for "plausible policy reasons": the need to "[protect] the security of the traditional nuclear family."[75] Lesbian families, by contrast, lack traditional nuclear family status and are therefore subject to intervention, there being nothing "valuable" to protect. The approach in *P v. K & M* highlights the extent to which courts can view lesbian families as incomplete and thus appropriate candidates for legal intervention.

Conclusion

While planned lesbian families have come a long way in recent decades in asserting their right to call themselves "family," serious barriers to inclusion remain. Some barriers are easy to address, such as the exclusion of lesbian mothers from legal presumptions of parentage, while others, such as the recent valorization of biological fatherhood, require more sophisticated responses. While the legal and social context in which lesbian mothers assert their right to parenthood is complex, at no other time in Canadian history has the prospect of reform seemed so likely. In fact, given the increased visibility of lesbian mothers, the growing acceptance of lesbian and gay relationships more generally, and the variety of legal victories lesbian mothers have already achieved through the courts, the time is ripe for a comprehensive revisiting of the law's response to planned lesbian families. However, as noted above, the *terms* upon which reform is pursued remains a critical issue. The challenge for lesbian mothers is to secure legal recognition in a manner that does not exclude those lesbian families that parent outside of traditional norms.

The terms upon which lesbians and gay men have engaged with law have, until recently, been largely unquestioned. Challenging explicit inequalities and relying primarily on strategies grounded in formal equality, lesbians and gay men have based their entitlement to legal inclusion on their "sameness." For example, the successful same-sex marriage litigation was built entirely on the premise of formal equality, with the entitlement to marry being presented as deriving from the similarities between same-sex couples and opposite-sex couples. The second-parent adoption and gender-neutral birth certificate litigation took a similar approach. Though the application of formal equality can often succeed in dismantling the most blatant forms of discrimination and has produced numerous legal victories for lesbians and gay men in Canada, it remains a problematic strategy for a population that is as much characterized by diversity and difference as it is by sameness. Reform based exclusively on a formal-equality strategy will inevitably leave people out. Pursuit of formal equality also makes it very difficult to question the existing law and the assumptions that underlie it. It is thus important, before any reform process begins, to explore the terms upon which reform is to be pursued. In the next chapter, I address this debate, situating lesbian parenting claims within the much broader discussion about the terms upon which lesbians and gay men have sought entry into legal "family."

On Whose Terms? On What Terms? **2**
Lesbian and Gay Family Recognition

Over the past two decades, lesbians and gay men in Canada have enjoyed considerable courtroom success challenging the various legislative provisions that excluded them from the domain of legal "family." Relying primarily on formal equality – typically a straightforward "sameness" argument that assumes that equality requires no more than equal treatment – lesbians and gay men have successfully challenged everything from the definition of "spouse" in the pension provisions of the federal *Income Tax Act*[1] to the differential treatment of same-sex "spouses" under provincial adoption legislation.[2] There is no doubt that within the lesbian and gay community, or at least among its most vocal and publicly recognizable members, the dominant perception of the lesbian and gay trajectory towards "family" is a positive one. Legal victories have been understood almost exclusively through the lens of progress. In fact, throughout the recent same-sex marriage campaign, both litigants and their organizational advocates, such as EGALE,[3] went so far as to assert that it was only through access to marriage that lesbians and gay men could achieve "full citizenship" in Canadian society.[4]

With lesbian and gay access to the trappings of the traditional family tied to concepts as powerful as citizenship, it seems almost impossible to understand the recent spate of legal successes as anything but victories. To suggest otherwise might be understood as a rejection of lesbian and gay equality. There has, however, emerged what I have termed a "quiet critique" of the lesbian and gay equality-seeking movement, which has, often in opposition to the most vocal voices within the lesbian and gay mainstream, expressed reservation about the terms upon which family recognition has been argued for and won. Articulated predominantly by lesbian feminists,[5] as well as by lesbians and gay men who might align themselves with a more liberationist agenda, the critique suggests that by seeking inclusion within the family on the basis of formal equality or sameness, lesbians and gay men validate and perpetuate the hierarchies, inequalities, and oppressions that characterize traditional familial ideology. Because formal equality demands little more than identical treatment, reforms that evolve out of a formal-equality strategy tend to expand existing categories but rarely question the nature of the categories themselves.

Those who have offered the quiet critique do not suggest that equality seeking is, in itself, problematic. Rather, they challenge the trend among lesbian and gay advocacy groups to rely almost entirely on a formal-equality model that tends to emphasize the similarities between same- and opposite-sex families. In particular, they question why a more substantive version of equality has not been adopted. In contrast to formal equality, substantive equality takes into account social circumstances and differences, and is thus more likely than formal equality to respond to the lived realities of lesbian and gay families. For example, a substantive approach to equality for lesbians and gay men would not presume that equal treatment under Canadian family law would necessarily result in equal familial recognition. Lesbian and gay families are not necessarily structured in the same way as heterosexual families, yet equal treatment will provide familial recognition only to those that are. In contrast, a substantive-equality approach, because it favours a wider contextual analysis, is much more likely to produce laws that cater to families of difference, whether they include three parents, non-conjugal co-parents, or involved known donors. Perhaps because of the possibilities presented by a more nuanced version of equality, few proponents of the quiet critique suggest that lesbians and gay men should refuse to engage with the struggle to achieve legal recognition of their familial relationships altogether. Rather, they argue that engagement with the existing framework must be done critically, with a view to effecting progressive social change.

The significant reliance by lesbian and gay rights advocates on formal-equality strategies in the face of these criticisms can be explained in a number of ways. First, the tendency to emphasize similarities between opposite- and same-sex families may be the product of engaging with Canada's constitutional equality-rights guarantee. As part of any equality claim under section 15 of the *Canadian Charter of Rights and Freedoms*,[6] it is necessary that the claimant identify a "comparator group" against whom he or she wishes to be compared for the purpose of the discrimination inquiry.[7] For lesbian and gay litigants who seek legal recognition of their familial relationships, the most obvious and strategic comparator to choose is heterosexual relationships and the easiest way in which to frame the claim is to argue, "We, Y group, want the same rights that X group already possesses, because we are essentially the same as X group in terms of the quality and security of our intimate relationships."[8] This formal-equality analysis is both straightforward and strategically attractive to lesbian and gay litigants. A second explanation for the reliance by lesbian and gay rights advocates on formal-equality strategies may lie in the origins of Canada's most vocal lesbian and gay rights organization, EGALE. Formed in the wake of the 1985 House of Commons Standing Committee hearings on equality rights, EGALE has been committed from the outset to using "constitutional litigation" as a vehicle for change.[9] The limits that characterize equality claims under section 15 have inevitably shaped the claims brought forward by EGALE and its supporters. The final explanation for lesbian and gay reliance on formal equality is that while it might be an insufficient long-term strategy, it tends to alleviate the most extreme forms of discrimination, providing a "first step" towards more substantive change. As Shelley Gavigan puts it, formal equality can never fully resolve relations of inequality, but it can at least *inhibit* them.[10]

Although it is possible to explain why formal equality has been relied upon so heavily by lesbian and gay rights advocates, these explanations do not obviate concerns that formal equality is increasingly being understood as an end in itself. Opportunities to rally for more substantive changes once formal equality has been achieved are often lost when assimilation into the existing framework becomes the purpose of the movement. This has played out most recently in the context of same-sex marriage, where lesbian and gay entry into the institution has been celebrated as the *final* step, the ultimate equality-rights victory. That the institution of marriage itself might be problematic no longer enters the discourse.

While proponents of the quiet critique have now produced a significant body of literature questioning the terms upon which same-sex partnership recognition (including marriage) has been advocated for and achieved, little consideration has been given to whether the same arguments resonate in the context of parenting.[11] In other words, few people have investigated the terms upon which lesbian and gay parental recognition has been sought or, in the event that a formal-equality framework has been relied upon, whether it warrants the same critique as has been directed towards its use in the context of relationship recognition. The fact that the majority of legal efforts in the parenting arena have focused on recognizing the two-mother nuclear family suggests that the quiet critique has some relevance in the parenting debate. By arguing for parental recognition on the basis that lesbian parents mirror the heterosexual "norm," lesbian litigants necessarily exclude from "family" those who parent outside of the traditional model. Furthermore, because lesbian parents often rely in their equality claims on many of the same family signifiers as those who advocated for same-sex marriage – monogamy, financial interdependence, jointly held property, shared caregiving – they also perpetuate the idea that there is only one way to "do family."

At the same time, there may be fundamental differences between seeking parental recognition and seeking adult-relationship recognition that make the critique of a formal-equality strategy less convincing in the parental context. First, it could be argued that the stakes are simply higher in the parenting context and that a pragmatic approach might be more easily justified. For example, failure to legally recognize a non-biological mother could result in the complete severance of the relationship between mother and child. Such a scenario is likely to affect not only the non-biological mother, but also the child who has a significant interest, both emotionally and economically, in having her parental relationships recognized. Second, it could be argued that the alternative to the nuclear family – some kind of multiple-parent model – is extremely risky for lesbian mothers given the ongoing influence of the fathers' rights movement in Canada. In fact, by willingly expanding the family beyond a two-parent model, lesbians arguably run the risk of having "fathers" imposed upon them. Finally, it is possible to argue, as Nancy Polikoff has, that the legal validation of a two-mother family supports a woman's right to make reproductive decisions autonomously from men.[12] Thus, while the nuclear family is ultimately reinforced when applying a formal-equality model, the absence of a patriarch creates space for new meaning. None of this is to suggest that a formal-equality approach to parental recognition is not problematic or that it is the only way in which lesbian mothers can be legally protected. However, these arguments do make the complete rejection of a formal-equality strategy more difficult to sustain. Perhaps most importantly, they emphasize the need for critical engagement with law, and ultimately, a willingness to move beyond either/or solutions.

In this chapter, lesbian and gay parental recognition is situated within the wider debate about the terms upon which lesbians and gay men have sought entry into legal family. First, I outline the dominant approach taken by the lesbian and gay communities towards family recognition. Focusing in particular on the marriage campaign – which is, in many ways, emblematic of the wider discourse – I highlight the enormous reliance that key advocates have placed on formal equality. Second, I provide an overview of the critique of the formal-equality approach to family recognition, illustrating the many ways in which "sameness" strategies can reinforce existing hierarchies and render invisible non-normative lesbian and gay relationships and family configurations. Finally, I explore how these debates, which have unfolded largely in the context of adult-relationship recognition, might play out in the parenting context.

"We Are Family": Lesbian and Gay Claims to Family

The formal-equality framework that has come to dominate lesbian and gay claims to family tentatively emerged within lesbian and gay politics in the mid-1980s, no doubt the product of the constitutional entrenchment of the *Canadian Charter of Rights and Freedoms* and the coming into force in 1985 of section 15 (equality rights) in particular. Equality seeking through the courts was not an entirely new strategy for lesbian and gay activists. In fact, alongside political protest and civil rights action, equality seeking had played a significant role in the early liberation movement.[13] What had changed, however, was the "meaning frame" through which litigation was understood.[14] Prior to the *Charter*, litigation was often understood as a means to an end, a tool by which to draw attention to discrimination, politicize a community, and build a social movement.[15] In other words, what went on in court was only part of the battle: a legal loss could be understood as a victory if it contributed to community consciousness. In contrast, after the introduction of the *Charter*, litigation was increasingly (though not always) understood as an end in itself.[16] Struggles for legislative reform continued, but in the post-*Charter* era, litigation came to dominate the time and resources of the most prominent lesbian and gay rights organizations.[17] Thus, while not necessarily a new tactic, the courtroom-based equality-seeking strategy that characterizes modern-day lesbian and gay claims is guided by a new meaning frame, one that prioritizes legal change, formal equality, and "rights talk."[18]

The initial lesbian and gay claims to family were varied in subject matter, ranging from access to bereavement leave to challenges to the old age security scheme. Despite the diversity of their focus, almost all of the cases involved a challenge to the opposite-sex definition of "spouse." This usually took the form of an assertion by the lesbian or gay litigant that his or her same-sex relationship was the same as an opposite-sex spousal relationship. The first in this series of "spousal" cases was *Andrews v. Ontario*, an unsuccessful attempt by a lesbian woman, Karen Andrews, to obtain "family" provincial health insurance benefits for her same-sex partner and her partner's children.[19] Relying on both section 15 of the *Charter* and the Ontario *Human Rights Code*,[20] Andrews argued that the lives and relationships of same-sex couples closely resemble those of opposite-sex couples, and thus the exclusion of her partner from the definition of "spouse" for the purpose of family benefits was discriminatory. The court rejected the plaintiff's assertion that she and her partner were "the same as" a heterosexual couple, holding that their inability to procreate naturally was too significant a difference to overcome.[21] Brenda Cossman argues that despite the loss, *Andrews* effectively launched the lesbian and gay "We Are Family" strategy and the formal-equality approach that came to underlie it.[22]

The first successful challenge to a federal spousal exclusion came in 1998 with the Ontario Court of Appeal's decision in *Rosenberg v. Canada (Attorney-General)*. *Rosenberg* involved a constitutional challenge to the opposite-sex definition of "spouse" in section 252(4) of the *Income Tax Act*. The opposite-sex definition meant that a private pension plan could only be registered with Revenue Canada if the plan restricted survivor benefits to spouses of the opposite sex. Plans not registered with Revenue Canada could not receive the significant tax benefits available to registered plans. Applying a strict formal-equality analysis to find in favour of the applicants, the majority held that the opposite-sex definition of "spouse" violated section 15 of the *Charter* and could not be saved by section 1. As aging and retirement was not unique to heterosexuals, and there was nothing about being heterosexual that warranted the preferential attention to the possibility of economic insecurity, it could not be a pressing and substantial objective to single out for exclusive recognition the income protection of those older Canadians whose sexual preferences were heterosexual. The solution of the court was thus to read the words "or same-sex" into the act's definition of "spouse."[23] The effect of the decision was the extension of entitlement to survivor benefits under occupational pension plans to the partners of lesbians and gay men who died while covered by the plan. Choosing not to appeal the decision, the federal government subsequently amended the definition of "spouse" in section 254(2) of the *Income Tax Act* to include same-sex cohabitants as spouses for all tax purposes.[24]

The next significant decision, and the first success in a traditional family law dispute, came in 1999 when, in *M v. H*, the Supreme Court of Canada expanded the definition of "spouse" in Ontario's *Family Law Act* to include same-sex partners for the purpose of spousal support.[25] The case arose when, after a ten-year lesbian relationship ended, one of the women (M), whose earning capacity was significantly lower than her ex-partner's (H), sought a spousal support order. However, because Ontario's *Family Law Act* allowed only opposite-sex cohabitants and married spouses to make such a claim, it was necessary for M to bring a constitutional challenge to the act's definition of "spouse." She did so by arguing that the opposite-sex definition in the act discriminated against her on the basis of sexual orientation and therefore infringed her section 15 *Charter* equality rights. Once again, the claim was presented largely through the lens of formal equality. By highlighting the monogamous conjugal nature of the relationship, its significant length, the emotional and economic interdependency of the parties, and what might be considered a traditional gendered division of labour in which one partner focused primarily on domestic tasks while the other attended to business, M engaged (whether intentionally or not) in an explicit exercise in comparison. In other words, at least part of M's case rested on the perceived similarities between her intimate relationship and what might be described as the "model" heterosexual relationship. Interestingly, the Supreme Court noted in its decision that lesbian litigants need not portray their relationships as "just like" heterosexual ones.[26] However, as Boyd and Young note, *M v. H* highlights the degree to which "assimilation discourse that reinforces the heterosexual norm has been built into the legal process."[27] Ultimately, the court's decision rested on the fact that, like heterosexuals, same-sex partners form relationships of permanence that are characterized by financial interdependence. Discrimination against same-sex couples, particularly in circumstances where their relationships look so much like those of heterosexuals, could therefore not be sustained.

The positive decision in *M v. H* forced the federal government, as well as some provinces, to extend the rights and responsibilities enjoyed by opposite-sex cohabitants to same-sex cohabitants. In fact, the federal government response – the *Modernization of Benefits and Obligations Act* in 2000 – was the single most comprehensive attempt to date to remove legal distinctions between same-sex couples and opposite-sex couples in Canada.[28] The act amended sixty-eight pieces of federal legislation in order to extend a variety of rights and responsibilities to "common-law partners," which was defined to include same-sex couples. The legislation covered everything from income tax to conjugal visits with same-sex partners in prison. While the act was obviously a major breakthrough for lesbian and gay relationship-recognition advocates, it was generally understood to contain two significant limitations. First, the interpretation section of the act included language defending marriage as an opposite-sex relationship only. Second, a legal distinction was drawn between married "spouses" and "common-law partners," with the "spousal" category reserved for opposite-sex couples only. Thus, while the act extended to lesbian and gay couples rights and responsibilities that had previously been denied, it did so through what might be described as a "separate but equal" legislative framework.

While each of the mounting legal successes was celebrated by lesbians and gay men as a further step towards equal family status, the most celebrated victory of all was the legalization at a federal level in July 2005 of same-sex marriage.[29] Quickly renamed "equal marriage" by its proponents, same-sex marriage was understood by many to be the Holy Grail of equality claims. Kathleen Lahey, for example, argued that without access to marriage, lesbians and gay men did not have full legal personality.[30] Others saw it as the final goal at the end of a lengthy road to equality. For example, in their joint affidavit, the same-sex couples from Ontario ("the Ontario marriage litigants") who first challenged the opposite-sex definition of marriage argued that marriage was "the last bastion of discrimination against lesbians and gays and bisexuals in Canada's legal culture."[31] Thus, perhaps more than any other legal victory, "equal marriage" was understood by a significant portion of the lesbian and gay population to bring them, and the relationships they formed, within the domain of "family." Success was achieved, however, through an extremely narrow formal-equality paradigm. In fact, it might be argued that more than any other lesbian and gay rights campaign, "equal marriage" was about sameness.

Shelley Gavigan has insightfully argued that the campaign for equal marriage was organized on two fronts: first, at the formal level as an equality right to equal treatment and benefit of the law, and, second, at the equally important ideological level.[32] Arguably, one bled into the other. The positioning of the equality right as one of *formal* equality necessarily invoked a particular ideological framework: the existing one. Thus, marriage was understood, somewhat ironically, by both (lesbian and gay) supporters and (heterosexual) opponents of same-sex unions as "without dispute" one of the most basic elements of social organization and civic life. For example, the Ontario marriage applicants described the "freedom to marry" as "central to our definition of humanity,"[33] while opponents of same-sex marriage, such as the Interfaith Coalition on Marriage and the Family, similarly characterized marriage as one of Canada's "foundational social institutions."[34] With this kind of deference to the existing institution exhibited by *both* sides of the debate, it is not surprising that the lesbian and gay marriage litigants supported their claims by highlighting how same-sex relationships compared favourably to the heterosexual "norm."

In proving the sameness of their relationships, the marriage case litigants tended to focus on three relationship qualities: (1) monogamous conjugality, (2) the capacity to maintain long-term relationships, and (3) economic interdependency. Each of these qualities was understood to be fundamental to the (idealized) institution of marriage, and thus each of the litigants pointed to the ways in which their own relationships emulated the "norm." The following statement, typical of those made by other litigants, epitomizes this trend:

> During our thirty-two years together, Bob and I have shared our lives, plans and finances. We have always purchased things together and have never owned anything separately. We have always had joint bank accounts, we owned a home together and we have wills, leaving all of our possessions to each other.[35]

Similarly, a second litigant provided the following reasons for why she and her partner should be able to marry:

> I love Michelle. She is the only person I ever want to be with. I want to raise children with her, build a family, and buy a house, a car, and a deep freezer ... My parents just celebrated their 25th wedding anniversary. There is nothing I look forward to more than Michelle and our family celebrating ours.[36]

By pointing to their economic interdependence[37] and the long-term monogamous nature of their relationships, the marriage case couples asserted that they were virtually the same as heterosexual couples.[38] In fact, as Boyd and Young argue, the litigants seemed to imply that the only difference between themselves and heterosexual couples was their sexual orientation.[39] As noted above, the invocation of formal equality by the couples was not necessarily an active choice. Narrow judicial interpretation of section 15 has meant that equality arguments under the *Charter* typically require a comparative analysis and, in the context of "family," this often involves comparing oneself to a relatively conservative norm. However, it is important to note that none of the litigants attempted in any way to assert a more substantive model of equality, despite the availability of such an argument under section 15.[40] For example, none of the litigants argued that while their relationships might differ in some ways from the (idealized) norm, they should still be entitled to equal access to marriage.

Interestingly, many of the marriage case litigants pointed to the procreative nature of their relationships as further evidence of the similarities they shared with heterosexual couples. For example, the Ontario marriage case factum stated that "six of the seven Applicant couples are or plan to be parents. They, like many other same-sex couples, believe that marriage will benefit their children."[41] Adopting language that bears a startling resemblance to that used by conservatives to decry the increase in divorce and single-parent households, many of the couples argued that they should be allowed to marry because it would provide their children with a "better sense of legitimacy and belonging."[42] Applicants also relied on "expert" evidence to assert that allowing same-sex couples to marry would be good for their children because marriage "promotes emotional well-being, greater maturity, and better psychological adjustment."[43] One of the litigants went so far as to state that she wanted to marry her partner because she would "never bring a child into this world without the safety net that a legally recognized marriage creates."[44] As Gavigan notes, the couples never precisely identified the danger to which children of unmarried same-sex couples are exposed, but they argued that marriage provides some kind of "insurance" against it.[45] Thus, while the marriage case litigants stopped short of arguing that procreation was an essential element of marriage, they did use the fact that many of them were parents to further bolster their claim to "sameness."

The rhetoric of sameness during the marriage debate was by no means the sole domain of the litigants. Similar arguments were invoked by lesbian and gay advocates during the same-sex marriage hearings of the House of Commons Justice and Human Rights Committee that preceded the introduction of the civil marriage bill.[46] Assertions of sameness also dominated the more progressive elements of the mainstream press. Supportive media outlets, for example, profiled same-sex couples who excelled in their middle-class, white "ordinariness."[47] A *Globe and Mail* editorial suggested that lesbians and gay men should be commended for their desire to reinforce traditional marriage:

> By embracing marriage, homosexuals remind others that it is, or should be, the norm for committed couples. It is the best place to experience love, sex and companionship together. It is the best place to raise children. Marriage's "till death do us part" pledge of permanence gives people the security they need to give themselves fully to the other. It is one of the ironies of the same-sex marriage debate that conservatives who once condemned the hedonistic, selfish and licentious "gay lifestyle" would now deny homosexuals the right to opt in to the bourgeois comfort of marriage.[48]

The presumption behind this statement seems to be that lesbians and gay men have now "grown up" and that any negative attributes that might have once characterized their relationships have evaporated through the process of maturation. Having now shed the trappings of their "hedonistic" and "selfish" past, lesbians and gay men are proving to be no different than their heterosexual counterparts.

The rhetoric of formal equality also dominated the statements of groups such as EGALE and Canadians for Equal Marriage (CEM). For example, emphasizing the simplicity of the formal-equality argument, CEM produced "public service advertisements" comparing the treatment of same-sex couples in Canada to the treatment of African Americans under the "separate but equal" Jim Crow laws of the southern United States.[49] Depicting identical park benches and public telephones with signs on them saying "Gay" and "Straight," the advertisements presented the issue as one of straightforward equal access.

While there were no doubt opportunities over the years for lesbians and gay men to demand inclusion within the "family" without invoking its most traditional characteristics, few activists have taken such a position. From the early claims to state benefits through to the recent marriage litigation, lesbians and gay men have succeeded in the courts on the basis of formal equality. Throughout this process, there has been little suggestion, at least within the mainstream debate, that such an approach to equality has been anything but positive.

"We Are Not Family" (at Least as You Define It): The Quiet Critique

The dominance of the formal-equality framework and the attractiveness of its simple comparative logic makes it very difficult to assert an alternative meaning frame. In fact, as noted earlier, to do so might be understood as a challenge to lesbian and gay equality claims. Despite the risks associated with critiquing the formal-equality discourse, a small group of lesbian feminists and gay liberationists have questioned the terms upon which lesbian and gay inclusion within the family has been achieved. While advocates of this critique raise numerous concerns with regard to the use of formal equality, two issues dominate their position. First, they argue that by seeking entry into the family on the basis of formal equality, lesbians and gay men effectively reify traditional familial ideology and thus reinforce its internal inequalities and oppressions. Second, by seeking entry into the family on the basis of its existing terms, opportunities to problematize marriage as a raced, gendered, and classed institution are greatly diminished. While those who engage in the quiet critique recognize why the formal-equality framework has been so heavily relied upon and generally avoid attacking those who have chosen to do so, they worry that the effect of a may be further exclusions.

Reifying the (Unequal) Family

The most common argument made by those who critique the formal-equality approach is that by seeking entry into family on the basis of sameness, lesbians and gay men reinforce the inequalities that characterize traditional familial ideology and ultimately subject themselves to a process of assimilation. The effect of adhering to the existing framework is that lesbians and gay men become participants in the system of exclusions and oppressions that operates within it. Arguably, this not only maintains the status quo but also leads to new hierarchies within the lesbian and gay communities. Ruthann Robson refers to this process as one of "domestication," whereby lesbian and gay cultural categories and concepts are replaced by those of the heterosexual mainstream: "Domestication occurs when the views of the dominant culture become so internalized that they seem like common sense."[50] For example, lesbians and gay men who internalize heterosexual "norms" such as monogamy and financial interdependence in order to gain access to marriage become "domesticated."

The process of domestication has the potential to create new exclusions within the lesbian and gay communities, primarily between those who endorse traditional norms and those who are unable or unwilling to conform. "Good" gays and lesbians (or "clean sexual deviants," as Joan Nestle refers to them)[51] are those who embrace marriage and who organize their relationships in accordance with heterosexual norms. In contrast, "bad" gays and lesbians are those who resist the mainstreaming of their intimate relationships or who suggest that the institution of family itself is in need of reform. Thus, rather than alleviating exclusions, formal equality creates a new set of hierarchies and a new kind of surveillance in the lives of lesbian and gay men. The crucial difference is that the new hierarchies are now embedded within the lesbian and gay communities themselves, creating the possibility of an internalized policing of lesbian and gay behaviour. In addition, the people most capable of transforming the institution of family – arguably the "bad" gays and lesbians – remain largely excluded from the conversation.

A related issue raised by adopting a formal-equality framework is that the "norms" to which lesbians and gay men must necessarily subscribe arguably have little foundation in reality. They are not reflective of actual practice but rather represent what Judith Butler has referred to as a "fantasy of normativity." In other words, the existing framework "does not always seek to order what exists but to figure social life in certain imaginary ways."[52] This means that while lesbians and gay men can turn to formal equality as a means by which to render their families "family," formal equality commits them to a familial ideology that, while powerful, is little more than fiction. The effect of this need to position oneself as "straighter than straight" is illustrated quite clearly in the marriage case affidavits, as well as in the submissions of lesbians and gay men before the House of Commons Standing Committee on same-sex unions, where it was not uncommon to hear parties describe their relationships in language usually associated with the 1950s.[53]

Those who critique the formal-equality strategy have also argued that it has the potential to co-opt lesbians and gay men into the systems of oppression that characterize the traditional family and its accompanying legal structures.[54] The family is not an innocent institution. Rather, it is classed, raced, and gendered. In fact, as Boyd and Young argue, "the struggles over the last few decades [to secure lesbian and gay relationship recognition] have been about the acquisition of a limited set of legal rights that themselves rest on profoundly hierarchical social relations."[55] The effect of these embedded hierarchies is that inclusion within the family has a differential impact, particularly with regard to class, race, and gender.

It is commonly assumed that inclusion within the family will produce only positive outcomes for lesbians and gay men when, in fact, it may lead to economic disadvantages, particularly for lesbians and the poor. This is because built into the existing framework are a number of classed, raced, and gendered inequalities. For example, the recognition of a non-biological lesbian mother as both a "spouse" and a "parent" has the effect of reducing state assistance for the family. Because the child now has a second parent whose income is combined with that of the biological mother, the family is not only taxed at a higher rate, but also experiences a reduction in any income-tested benefits they may receive, such as the Child Tax Benefit. This obviously has the greatest impact on the poorest families, who are more likely to receive income-tested benefits in the first place. Gender and racial inequalities are also implicated. Because women (especially women of colour) earn, on average, less than men and because lesbians are more often parents than gay men, it is lesbians (especially lesbians of colour) who are likely to suffer the majority of the negative consequences of legal recognition. Thus, in seeking entry into family on the basis of its existing terms, lesbians and gay men arguably become party to economic, racial, and gender-based oppression, oppression felt even within their own ranks.

A second, but related, economic implication of the formal-equality approach is that it results in lesbian and gay support, whether intentional or not, for the privatization of economic and social responsibility within the family. By relying so heavily on their financial interdependence as evidence of their sameness, lesbians and gay men effectively accept that an individual's economic security is the responsibility of the private family. When this position is asserted in the context of widespread cuts to social welfare programs, lesbians and gay men arguably become participants in the wider "privatization project."[56] The effect of familial privatization is that spouses will be expected to absorb economic hardship within the private domain, whether by way of provision of home-based care, retirement planning, spousal support, or child support. An inability to absorb economic burdens within the family is likely to be understood as an instance of individual, rather than collective, failure. Furthermore, by situating responsibility for social welfare within the private family, cuts to welfare programs are more easily justified. As Boyd and Young argue, "Trends that bolster privatization of economic responsibility tend to diminish general public support for publicly funded programs."[57] Thus, by endorsing an essentially privatized model of family through their emphasis on financial interdependence, lesbians and gay men become participants in privatization. Furthermore, lesbian and gay willingness to endorse a privatized vision of family inevitably makes it harder for others to oppose it.

Formal Equality and the Limits of Change
The second critique of the formal-equality strategy to have emerged from among those engaged in the quiet critique is that formal equality necessarily forecloses the possibility of problematizing the institution of family itself. Because entry into the family is sought on the basis of sameness – the extent to which lesbians and gay men mirror the existing framework – it becomes very difficult to simultaneously suggest that the existing framework is in any way flawed. The challenge is further exacerbated by the fact that those who oppose lesbian and gay inclusion within the family prioritize its most traditional aspects. In order to meet

this most conservative of standards, lesbians and gay men must silence any doubts they have about the institution itself. By relinquishing the ability to critique the existing social, legal, and ideological framework, lesbians and gay men arguably diminish the possibility of achieving significant social change.

There is no doubt that the legal recognition of same-sex relationships has had a positive impact on the average Canadian's conception of family. In fact, the public's growing support for same-sex relationship recognition over the past two decades suggests that an increasing number of Canadians understand family as an evolving and diverse institution.[58] In critiquing a strategy of formal equality, the growing public support it has generated for lesbians and gay men should not be downplayed. However, the prospect of achieving more radical social change is severely curtailed if formal equality is the only strategy employed. Focussing the process of inclusion entirely on sameness leaves no forum in which to suggest that marriage, for example, is implicated in women's inequality or that spousal relationships should not be the primary site to which state benefits flow. In other words, the extent as well as the kind of social change available is limited by the framework within which change is sought. By limiting themselves to a comparative framework, the kind of social change lesbians and gay men can actually achieve is relatively narrow.

Some participants in the relationship-recognition debates did attempt to turn the conversation towards a more transformative agenda. In most instances, this was done by suggesting that discrimination might be best addressed through a more substantive model of equality. For example, in its submission to the House Committee on same-sex marriage, West Coast LEAF, a feminist organization focused primarily on seeking equality for women, attempted to introduce a gendered analysis of marriage. LEAF's submission noted that marriage plays a significant role in women's inequality and that equal access to marriage by previously excluded groups will not change the hierarchical nature of marriage itself.[59] Revealing the inability of the committee to see beyond a formal-equality framework, only one member responded to LEAF's critique, and then only to use it to suggest that lesbians and gay men should not have access to marriage.[60] LEAF's experience was by no means unique.

Gary Kinsman's submission, which argued that marriage should be abolished on the grounds that the state sanctioning of marriage is itself a practice in discrimination against other forms of social and sexual relationships, was similarly met with silence.[61] It was as if committee members could not understand a position that was neither for nor against same-sex marriage. The formal-equality framework within which the debate unfolded had rendered unintelligible any options beyond the existing norm.[62]

Parental Recognition and the "We Are Family" Debate

As the discussion above suggests, while a small but significant group of scholars and activists have questioned the terms upon which lesbian and gay claims to family have been made, their focus has been almost exclusively on adult-relationship recognition. Very little attention has been given to whether the same critique resonates in the parenting context. This is somewhat surprising, given that lesbian and gay claims to parental status have also relied on formal-equality arguments and that references to same-sex parenting have often been made to support claims for relationship recognition.[63] The absence of a critique may stem from a sense that parental recognition is somehow different from adult-relationship recognition.

Equal Families, Equal Parents: Recognizing Lesbian Motherhood

Given the success of a formal-equality approach in the relationship-recognition context, it is not surprising that lesbian and gay parental claims proceeded on a similar basis. Focusing on their sameness, lesbian parents have argued that their families function in the same way as heterosexual families with children and that the children lesbian mothers raise are identical to those raised by heterosexual parents. To support these claims, lesbian mothers have focused on the traditional nature of their intimate relationships, the nuclear structure of their families, and social science evidence that reveals the similarities between children raised by lesbian mothers and children raised by heterosexual parents.

Re K, the first Canadian decision to extend second-parent adoption rights to non-biological lesbian mothers, exemplifies the use of formal equality in the parental context. In fact, almost all parental recognition cases since *Re K* have adopted a similar analysis.[64] In *Re K*, the mothers made two assertions to support their section 15(1) *Charter* claim: (1) that their intimate relationships were no different than those of heterosexual "spouses" and (2) that their children were the same as children raised in heterosexual families. In order to prove the sameness of their intimate relationships, the mothers in *Re K*, not unlike the marriage case litigants, pointed to their economic interdependence, the length of their relationships, and the nuclear nature of their families. In fact, the picture of normality they created was so striking that Nevins J. noted that the mothers' intimate relationships had "all the characteristics of ... [relationships] formalized by marriage."[65] He explained:

> Each of the couples have cohabited together continuously and exclusively for lengthy periods, ranging from six to 13 years; their financial affairs are interconnected; they share household expenses, have joint bank accounts and in some cases, they own property together in joint tenancy; they share the housekeeping burdens to the extent that they are able in light of their respective careers and employments; the individual partners share a committed sexual relationship. Most importantly, they all share equally the joys and burdens of child rearing.[66]

In addition to evidence pertaining to the traditional nature of their relationships, the mothers also provided social science evidence illustrating the similarities between their children and the children of heterosexual parents. Central to this evidence were findings that the children of lesbian mothers are no more likely than children raised by heterosexual parents to develop gender roles or identities "inconsistent with their biological sex" or outside of the "normal range."[67] The court also relied upon research showing that the children of lesbian mothers are no more likely than the children of heterosexual parents to be lesbian or gay themselves.[68] Thus, central to the mothers' claim for recognition was the assertion that their children, when compared to the children of heterosexuals, were "normal." This assertion provided great comfort to Nevins J., who, no doubt influenced by the materials he had been provided by the parties, clearly understood difference as deficit. Interestingly, the mothers in *Re K* also attached their curricula vitae to their affidavits. Obviously impressed by what he read, Nevins J. referred to the mothers' credentials as "nothing short of staggering."[69] The reference suggests that the women bringing the claim – well-educated and economically privileged – were significantly assisted by their class position. A court may not have looked so favourably upon a group of women with less privilege. Thus, their sameness operated at multiple levels. The mothers were not the same as just any heterosexual parents: they were the same as middle-class, well-educated parents.

In the more recent two-mother birth certificate cases, a similar pattern of sameness analysis emerged. For example, in the 2006 decision of *M.D.R. v. Ontario*,[70] the lesbian litigants framed their case using an extremely narrow formal-equality lens. Relying again on section 15 of the *Charter* and choosing as their comparator group "heterosexual non-biological fathers who plan a pregnancy with a spouse using assisted reproductive technology," the mothers left little room for non-normative family practices. Their equality was based on looking like a heterosexual nuclear family with a fertility problem. The effect of this choice was that lesbian women who parented outside of the nuclear norm – for example, those who conceived using the sperm of a known donor and were thus the most vulnerable – were excluded from the benefits of the decision. In fact, on more than one occasion, the court distinguished the claim in *M.D.R.* from a concurrent claim being made by a three-parent queer family, who were considered to be justifiably excluded from recognition because they challenged the nuclear norm.[71]

The pervasiveness of nuclear family rhetoric – an inevitable by-product of adopting a formal-equality framework – is hard to ignore in the parental recognition cases. It is, after all, the lesbian *nuclear* family to which both second-parent adoption and the gender-neutral birth certificate extend protection. Neither option is capable of providing any form of recognition to a three- or four-parent family or any guidance as to the circumstances in which such a family might be recognized. The pervasiveness of nuclear family rhetoric can also be seen in a second lesbian parenting context that arguably involves quite different dimensions: that of access disputes between lesbian mothers and their sperm donors. Asserting their right to parent free from donor intervention, lesbian mothers who find themselves subject to unanticipated donor access claims often argue that donors should be denied access because they fall outside the parameters of the nuclear family. For example, in one of the first reported donor access decisions, the US case of *Thomas S. v. Robin Y.*, the child's two mothers sought to exclude the donor from the life of his biological child on the basis that their family was already "complete."[72] Comparing themselves to any other two-parent nuclear family, the mothers argued that their nuclear family unit was equally entitled to the protection of the law. At the same time, they argued that their donor was neither a parent nor family because he existed outside of the nuclear framework.[73] While the mothers eventually lost their case,[74] their assertion of the lesbian nuclear family as a functional equivalent of the heterosexual nuclear family continues to dominate these kinds of disputes.

As noted in Chapter 1, there are few Canadian decisions addressing the issue of donor access.[75] Most have been decided in Quebec, the only province in Canada where parenting presumptions apply equally to lesbian parents who conceive using donor sperm as to heterosexual parents who conceive through the same method.[76] Thus, the need to rely on nuclear family rhetoric is lessened by the fact that the legislative scheme itself is framed in the terms of a nuclear family. In the Quebec cases, however, the mothers relied on the "completeness" of their nuclear families as at least part of the justification for excluding their donors from access. In both situations, the mothers asserted that the donor was simply a third-party gamete provider to their lesbian nuclear family.[77] While the mothers provided significant evidence that this was in fact the case, their claims were nonetheless framed by a nuclear family discourse.

The only other case in Canada addressing donor access is *M.A.C. v. M.K.*[78] As noted above, the dispute involved a three-way co-parenting agreement entered into prior to the child's conception. When the mothers and donor experienced conflict, the mothers asserted that their nuclear family should be protected against the now-unwanted intrusion of their known donor. Their application was rejected. Unlike the two Quebec decisions, there was little evidence that the mothers in *M.A.C.*

had in fact parented as a nuclear family unit. The donor had played a significant role in the child's life and had been a party to both caregiving arrangements and decision making. Yet the mothers pursued a nuclear family discourse, arguing that the protection of their nuclear unit was essential to their family's survival.

The only instance in the Canadian context in which a formal-equality, and thus a nuclear family, analysis has not been relied upon in the parenting context is the 2007 case of *A.A. v. B.B.* As discussed in Chapter 1, the parties in *A.A. v. B.B.*, a lesbian couple and their gay sperm donor (who was listed on the child's birth certificate), jointly petitioned the court to recognize that their son had three legal parents. In order to achieve this outcome, the court was asked to extend legal recognition to the non-biological mother without simultaneously severing the parental status of the donor.[79] While the mothers were the child's primary caregivers and the donor played a secondary role, the parties felt that it was in the child's best interests to have all three of them legally recognized. Thus, rather than relying on a purely comparative analysis grounded in the (same-sex) nuclear family, the mothers and donor sought to assert an alternative version of family grounded much more in their common intention and the relationships between the child and relevant adults. Whether *A.A. v. B.B.* will elicit a legislative response remains unknown, but there is no doubt that the decision signals a possible deviation from the application of a straightforward formal-equality analysis.

Despite the decision in *A.A. v. B.B.*, it is fair to say that lesbian parental recognition has been achieved, by and large, through the application of a formal-equality framework. Lesbian mothers have asserted their right to legal recognition on the basis that their families and children closely resemble the heterosexual norm (even in instances where this is not in fact the case, such as in *M.A.C.*). The mothers' claims have been further bolstered by the work of social scientists who also tend to adopt a comparative analysis whereby the nuclear family unit is the standard against which other family types are measured. The question that then arises is whether relying on formal equality in the parenting context is as problematic as it is in the relationship-recognition context, or whether the nature of parenting relationships makes the critique more difficult to sustain.

Critiquing Formal Equality and the Parenthood Debate

Relying on a formal-equality framework to achieve parental recognition raises many of the same concerns as it does in the adult-relationship context. By asserting the sameness of their families, lesbian mothers necessarily reinforce the traditional nuclear family, and dyadic parenting in particular. The impact of this approach is twofold. First, it leaves little space for those lesbian mothers who understand difference from hetero-sexual norms in a positive light. Second, it excludes from recognition those women who parent outside of a dyadic framework or with indi-viduals who are not their conjugal partners. Thus, as Julie Shapiro argues, formal-equality strategies may ultimately "divide those [they were] in-tended to benefit."[80] Furthermore, by focusing exclusively on formal equality, and thus the nuclear family, the opportunity to challenge the nuclear family as the optimal or only framework within which to raise children is arguably lost. This latter point is extremely problematic, as it has the potential to limit the kind of change that is possible.

While the use of formal equality to achieve parental status raises numerous concerns, there are arguably fundamental differences between parental and adult-relationship recognition that make the critique less convincing in the parental context. In fact, this belief emerged among my study participants, many of whom supported the legal recognition of their parental relationships but remained ambivalent about or actively opposed to same-sex marriage. The most obvious distinction between the two scenarios is the presence of a vulnerable third party – a child – whose protection and security arguably rests on the law recognizing the adults (however many or few) who parent them. For example, a non-biological parent who has no legally recognized relationship with her child cannot consent to the child's medical treatment or enrol her in school. In the event of the death of a biological parent, a non-biological parent has no automatic legal rights in relation to the child and must seek leave of the court to even apply for custody.[81] These restrictions on a non-biological parent's ability to carry out the daily tasks of parenting put the children of lesbian mothers in an extremely vulnerable position and ultimately deny them the equal protection of the law. In some situations, it could, quite literally, render a child "parentless." My study participants, particularly those who had their children prior to the introduction of the second-parent adoption laws, alluded frequently to the daily burden of these inequalities. It can thus be argued that the stakes are higher in the parenting context and that a pragmatic approach, such as that provided by formal equality, might be more easily justified.

A second reason why formal equality might hold more appeal in the parenting context is that the alternatives to it, such as a more substantively based multiple-parent approach, are extremely risky for lesbian mothers in light of the dominance of fathers' rights rhetoric in Canadian family law. As several of my own study participants argued, by embracing a more expansive concept of family that extends beyond the nuclear model, lesbians run the risk of having "fathers" imposed upon them.[82] In fact, as discussed in Chapter 1, biological fatherhood has emerged as one of the most protected identities in Canadian family law.[83] Whether motivated by neo-conservative arguments about the importance of fathers to the healthy raising of children or neo-liberal arguments about the economic benefits to the state of maintaining father-child relationships,[84] courts are generally willing to extend parental rights (and at least financial responsibilities) to biological fathers in the absence of a social, or even healthy, relationship with the child.[85] In other words, father-child contact, independent of the actual relationship between them, is increasingly understood as being in a child's best interests.[86] The fact that the "father" is actually a sperm donor is of little consequence.

Conclusion: Moving beyond Either/Or

Moving beyond either/or is a complicated matter. The legal recognition provided by formal equality promises benefits that lesbian mothers and their children desperately need. At the same time, formal equality involves accepting harmful exclusions and restraints. Thus, it appears that one must be either for or against formal equality. To avoid the political impasse that will necessarily result from the framing of the issue as one of either/or, I turn to Julie Shapiro's critical analysis of second-parent adoption.[87] One of the few legal commentators to apply the relationship-recognition critique to the parenting context, Shapiro argues that the solution lies in a *critical* engagement with law. Critical theory does not conclude that lesbians should never engage with the existing legal framework, she explains, "but [it] teaches that *when* they do, it must be with a skeptical view and vigilant attention to the alluring perils that may await."[88]

Thus, the first step in responding to the either/or dilemma may well be to acknowledge the potentially damaging effects of a recognition strategy grounded solely in formal equality. In other words, some skepticism and vigilance needs to be injected into the current debate. Acknowledging that the existing solutions are imperfect is perhaps all the more important given the dearth of critical commentary around the issue of parental recognition. In fact, as Shapiro argues, there has been an almost uncritical acceptance of reforms such as second-parent adoption.[89] This is in sharp contrast to same-sex marriage, where critique has almost always accompanied the mainstream debate in Canada. While the lack of critique in the parenting context may stem from the additional complexity of the parental-recognition debate, this alone does not explain the absence of critical work. Thus, an important first step in moving forward is the encouragement of dialogue about the implications of adopting a formal-equality approach to parental recognition and an acknowledgement of its limitations as a strategy. At the same time, for those who have adopted a critical position with regard to relationship recognition, it will be important to acknowledge that the unique vulnerabilities of lesbian mothers make a complete abandonment of formal equality in the parenting context more difficult to justify.

Once the limitations of formal equality are acknowledged, the law reform process can be pursued with a more critical eye. Formal equality is unlikely to be abandoned altogether, but future reform efforts will hopefully involve an examination of its limitations and at least some attempt to counteract them. Oppositional strategies might include litigants refusing to invoke the most traditional aspects of familial ideology, or activists and academics proposing reform models that at least diminish the significance of the nuclear family. As Weeks, Heaphy, and Donovan have argued in the UK context, perhaps the goal for progressive reformers should be to "not necessarily ... make governments give [same-sex families] equal access to the same legislative and policy provisions heterosexuals enjoy, but [to consider] how approaches to legislative and policy provisions can be changed to include a plurality of relationships without a hierarchical ordering of them."[90] Such an approach presents a middle ground that acknowledges the importance of legal recognition for lesbian mothers but refuses to accept that recognition be at the expense of those who eschew traditional family forms. In many ways, it is this middle ground that my study participants chose to occupy. By ultimately choosing a reform proposal that includes both formal and substantive elements, the participants sought to overcome the dilemma posed by either/or solutions.

Finally, lesbians must continue working to change the social conditions that make recognition as a traditional family so important in the first place. While it might be necessary within the current political and legal climate to focus at least some attention on the extension of legal recognition to the lesbian nuclear family, it is equally important that lesbians work to strengthen the social and collective responsibility owed to those who are *not* regarded as family (or the "right kind" of family). For example, lesbians need to be part of the debate around the extension of family status to non-conjugal relationships. They must also reject the continuing emphasis on the middle-class nuclear family as the primary site to which state benefits flow. It is also important that they oppose welfare cuts that drive single mothers and their children further and further into poverty. All of these issues are lesbian issues for no other reason than that each of them involves the prioritizing of one form of family over others. Lesbian mothers should thus see themselves as political allies of those engaged in these debates, as women who have an interest in protecting *all* forms of family.

Because there has been so little acknowledgment of the potentially damaging effects of the current approach to parental recognition, there has also been little exploration of how law reform, particularly legislative reform, might be done differently. For this reason, one of the questions driving this research was which parental-recognition framework lesbian mothers themselves might choose if they were given the opportunity to draft such a framework. Would they support a formal-equality approach or would the existing strategy be abandoned in favour of a more substantive vision of equality? What kind of critique (if any) might they have of formal equality, and would it resonate with that expressed by those engaged in the quiet critique? If formal equality is not understood to be capable of meeting their needs, what alternatives would they suggest and would any of them provide a solution to the either/or dilemma? Finally, would they have any reservations about engaging with law at all? The next chapter explores each of these questions through consideration of the interview data.

Defining Queer Kinship   **3**
How Do Lesbian Mothers Understand
Their Familial Relationships?

To be a lesbian mother is to engage constantly in definitional acts. With little direct guidance (though substantial influence) from either law or society, the lesbian family must self-define. Rights and responsibilities, as well as nomenclature, must be distributed by the mothers among the various individuals through which connection – whether biological, social, or semiotic – is dispersed. This can often lead to creative reinterpretations of family that differ markedly from traditional norms. I agree, however, with Corinne Hayden that we should resist the temptation to argue that lesbian mothers are engaged in a process of developing *wholly novel* conceptualizations of kinship.[1] Rather, a more accurate understanding might be reached by showing how old ideas and symbols are being "pressed into new service" by lesbian mothers, often resulting in a destabilizing of traditional meanings and a creative (re)formulating of family.[2]

This chapter analyzes how the study participants understand and define key familial concepts. I will discuss their definitions in the context of wider debates about the meaning of kinship in contemporary Western society. The discussion begins by considering how the mothers defined "family." Given the rapid growth in the legal recognition of same-sex family relationships in recent years, I was particularly interested in whether the mothers would continue to employ Kath Weston's notion of "chosen family" or whether it would be replaced by more conventional definitions now that they were available to lesbian families.[3] Second, the chapter explores how the mothers defined their parenting relationships, both vis-à-vis each other and in relation to their donors. In the course of these discussions, two related issues are explored: (1) whether the law should be capable of recognizing more than two legal parents and (2) what role, if any, marriage should play in parental recognition.

Families of Choice? The Lesbian Family in the Twenty-First Century

"Family" is a powerful and pervasive word, embracing a variety of social, cultural, economic, and symbolic meanings. In more recent times, it has also become a hotly contested term, the subject of numerous polemics, anxiety, and political concern about the "crisis of the family."[4] As noted in Chapter 2, the family has always been a controversial topic for gays and lesbians. While the early gay liberationists and many lesbian feminists deliberately situated themselves outside the family, in more recent decades, lesbians and gay men have sought recognition of their families as a legitimate form of kinship. Perhaps the first tentative steps towards gay families came in the form of what Kath Weston labelled "families of choice."[5] "Families of choice" were understood by lesbians and gay men as a distinctive and alternative form of kinship that decentres legal and biological definitions in favour of a more practical model grounded in choice and love. Thus, lesbian and gay families of choice were defined not so much by analogy as by contrast, whereby gay kinship was seen as one *type* of multiple kinship possibilities.

In the 1980s, when the concept of families of choice first emerged in the academic literature, there was very little legal, institutional, or social recognition of the lesbian and gay family.[6] Attempting to exist within the traditional kinship framework was thus not really an option for such families. Lesbians and gay men were denied the legal mechanisms and social support that would have given recognition to their sexual and parental relationships, let alone their extended families of choice. Obviously, a great deal has changed since the 1980s. At the most basic level, lesbian and gay attitudes towards the family appear to have shifted, at least among a certain very vocal portion of the lesbian and gay community. Rather than rejecting family or asserting gay and lesbian families of choice as a distinctive form of family, many lesbian and gay activists now rely on the notion of formal equality to argue that gay and lesbian and heterosexual families are essentially the same. In addition to this ideological repositioning, an enormous shift in the legal treatment of lesbian and gay families has occurred, often as a result of litigation mounted on the basis of formal-equality arguments. For example, gays and lesbians in Canada can now legally marry, adopt their non-biological children, and access many of the government benefits traditionally reserved for heterosexual conjugal partners. Each of these changes has allowed gays and lesbians to position themselves closer to traditional nuclear models of kinship. In contrast, little attention has been given by the lesbian and gay community to seeking legal recognition of the extended networks of chosen family, such as the long-term non-conjugal relationships of care that were so frequently discussed by the narrators in Weston's study.[7] Given this enormous shift in recent years in the ideological and legal positioning of gays and lesbians, it was perfectly plausible that my study participants might have abandoned chosen family in favour of a more traditional definition. When a lesbian couple can legally marry and have both of their names on their child's birth certificate from birth, might a more "respectable" lesbian nuclear family be the new family of choice? This was, in many ways, the question I pondered when I started speaking with the mothers.

Given the dramatic changes that have occurred since Weston's study, I was somewhat surprised to find that the vast majority of the forty-nine mothers I spoke to continued to define family, sometimes quite self-consciously, through the concept of chosen family.[8] While many of them had also entered into certain legal arrangements that gave them the outward appearance of a more nuclear unit, they continued to include chosen family members in the daily lives of themselves and their children. For example, Yael, the biological mother of an adult son and the non-biological mother of an adult daughter, defined her family as the people she had "collected" over her lifetime, none of whom were blood relatives:

> It's interesting 'cause my family's so large. Most of it is family I've collected over time, like friends that I've had for forty years plus. So it's probably a core of about [counting] probably a core of about six, seven people. It's whoever you make your family. And that can, I guess, that can change through time, but I found that it doesn't really.

While Yael was one of the older narrators in my sample, and thus closer to the generation that first adopted the concept of chosen family, a number of younger narrators asserted a similar position. For example, Michaela, the biological mother of an infant son, noted that while chosen family might be a cliché in the lesbian and gay community, it remains the lens through which she understands family:

> I think family, being gay I mean it's the cliché, but it is true to a certain degree that you make your own family. Because, you know I have my aunts that are lovely, but I've lots of other family members that are not that lovely about [me] being gay. Like I've had no interest in seeing them and hanging out, so. [sigh] Um, what is the definition of family? It is, it's a combination of those that you're biologically related to and those that, [pause] you're not. Like I think you can meet people in your life and include them [in your] family. Or consider them to be family. And they're people that you rely on. The people that you have a deep connection with. That, um, [pause] you know, I mean I always like to think that they are there, are gonna be there during the tough times and the good times. Like really there, more than a friendship.

For Janet, the biological mother of two children aged seven and three, chosen family includes a combination of her nuclear household and other people she has "brought in." In Janet's family, these additional people serve as aunts to her two children:

> [Family is] your immediate household and then it's all of the people that you bring in as your family. Like, I have two friends that are the

kid's aunts that aren't related to me, but they have been friends for, you know, over twenty years. So they, they are our family.

As Janet's comments suggest, kinship ties were often created between the mothers' chosen family and their children, with many of the adults serving as godparents or aunts and uncles. These relationships often became very important to the children, who, like their mothers, incorporated these individuals into their understanding of family. For example, Paula's two-year-old daughter, who is very close to a male friend whom her mothers consider "part of the family," would list the important people in her life as "my Mamma, my Mommy, and my Daniel." Daniel was not the child's sperm donor, nor does he live with the family, but Paula considers him to be closer to her daughter than most of her extended family. This was not the only instance where biological family was treated as secondary to chosen family. In five of the families, chosen family, often the children's lesbian "aunts" or gay "uncles," are named in wills as the legal guardians of the children in the event of both mothers dying. This designation has created an enormous amount of conflict among the women's families of origin, who cannot understand how a "non-family member" could be chosen for this role. For example, the decision of Sally and her partner to name a gay male couple whom they considered to be family as the guardians of their son greatly angered Sally's parents because the mothers' decision involved going "outside the family."[9] Conflict was often exacerbated in these cases when the mothers explained to their families of origin that their decision was based on a belief that the guardians they had chosen would raise their child in a manner that respected the child's own sense of family. Thus, while few of the mothers excluded biological families from the category of family, biological family members were not, even in instances where relations were good, automatically awarded priority over chosen family. As Julia put it, "The emotional connection supersedes any biological connections."

Given that I was interviewing a group of mothers, one might expect that they would make links between having a child and being a family. After all, procreation has traditionally been linked to "becoming a family." What I discovered, however, was that most of the mothers resisted the idea that one needs to have children in order to be a family. In fact, all of the mothers saw themselves as a family prior to the birth of their children, though several feel that having children "solidified" their family. The views of Maureen and Gillian are representative of many of the mothers:

> *Maureen:* We considered ourselves a family before [our son] came. Which I know is unusual, you know, not always the case.
> *Interviewer:* Yeah, I actually tend to ask about that, you know, does the child make it a family or?
> *Maureen:* No.
> *Gillian:* We made it very clear that we were adding to our family, not making a family when we were trying to conceive.
> *Maureen:* Yes. I don't like the term "starting a family." You know. "We're gonna start a family." No, we've been a family for, for years.

That a group of parents would sever the link between being a family and having children is perhaps unusual. Procreation is often treated as the *purpose* of marriage and family life, and the inability of same-sex couples to procreate without assistance continues to be used to treat them as not only outside of, but dangerous to, the family.[10] Given that their exclusion from family rests in part on their inability to procreate, it is interesting that now that they are parents themselves, these mothers have not appropriated procreation as a signifier of family. Rather, most of the mothers understand their families in opposition to this norm, having viewed themselves as family long before their children were born. This ongoing commitment to a definition of family that eschews traditional norms, even in the face of biological procreation, is perhaps testament to the ongoing power of the concept of chosen family within the lesbian and gay community.

In only two interviews did mothers endorse a definition of family that deviates from the notion of chosen family. Interestingly, however, both of these mothers explained their definition of family *with reference to* chosen family. That is, they acknowledged the commonly invoked lesbian and gay construction first and then explained that it does not match their own definition. Thus, the mothers treated chosen family as a legitimate and valuable type of kinship arrangement that just happened not to resonate with them. As Mary Jane, a biological mother, explained: .

> I'm not one of those people who thinks my best friends are my family. And I know lots of lesbians do because they have no connection to their actual family. Or very limited connection. And they've done that family of choice, that stuff. Which I think is very important but I just don't think of it that way. For me, family means the people who we're related to.

It is clear from Mary Jane's comments that she understands chosen family as an important concept for the lesbian community, though she herself does not think about family in that way. Fortunately, Mary Jane and her partner Shannon have the support of their extended families, making reliance on non-biological family far less urgent. Interestingly, Shannon and Mary Jane also commented that they do not have much of a connection with the lesbian and gay community and have few lesbian friends, making it possible that they do not have people around them who are willing to engage in chosen family relationships.

At the same time that almost all of the mothers provided broad definitions of family, it was clear that at least some of them struggle to assert their own definitions in the face of the hegemony of traditional norms. In defining what family means to her, Diane listed a series of factors that are commonly attributed to the traditional family. However, she followed each factor with a self-questioning of what she had just said. The passage below reads as multi-layered dialogue with herself. She spoke with two voices as she moved back and forth between mainstream society and her own internal sense of what family means to *her*. Her obvious reluctance to engage with traditional familial ideology and simultaneous inability to just let it go perhaps epitomizes the struggle many lesbian mothers have in asserting their difference:

> [Family is] a place of care. A place of sort of committed connection to people. Um, you know. Support, common home, it's true that there's that too. I mean, *I don't know that that's my definition of a family,*

but that's the definition we're living by. You know I would allow for a lot larger definitions than that, depending on other people's arrangements. Common finances I guess is also true. *Again, is that part of my definition? I don't know.* But that's sort of a feature of it I guess, at least. Legal connection. I mean we've had to, you know, you do have to assert it at times, in connection with medical care, whatever. There is, I guess, a sense in which we also define ourselves in some kind of legal terms as a family. You know insisting on a sense of inclusion or right, or whatever. (emphasis added)

The hegemony of dominant traditions made asserting an oppositional position a very difficult task for mothers like Diane. This dilemma was perhaps further compounded by the fact that lesbian and gay families are increasingly being accepted by mainstream Canadians, particularly when their outward appearance resonates with heterosexual norms. While the dominant societal perception for centuries was that lesbians and gay men were exiles from family, in twenty-first-century Canada, at least some Canadians are willing to incorporate lesbians and gay men into the family fold. If they have children, acceptance as family is all the more likely. For mothers like Diane, this particular kind of acceptance can pose significant political problems. Put simply, some lesbian mothers do not want to be incorporated within the traditional family. In the following section, I discuss in detail the experiences of two families who sought to deviate quite dramatically from traditional norms. While each took a very different approach, neither found it particularly easy to assert an oppositional family life.

For Tracey and Helen, the growing acceptance of lesbian and gay families within wider society posed a significant political dilemma. Both women are extremely resistant to the traditional family, yet realize that as a well-educated, middle-class, home-owning couple who largely parented their infant son in a dyadic structure (his donor and his donor's male partner lived overseas), they are necessarily read as a traditional nuclear family. Their outward appearance belies their actual beliefs, but they can do little to change the perception. This is particularly difficult for Tracey, the non-biological mother, who was initially ambivalent about having a child for exactly this reason.[11]

In explaining what family means to her, Helen began by stating that "a family doesn't have to be this dyad and a child kind of thing. It can be many things and it can be defined and redefined over time." Helen had, in fact, co-parented a child in a communal setting a number of years earlier, and both mothers made it clear throughout the interview that they accept families that include three or more parents, as well as those that involve open relationships where multiple sexual partners might live in the same household. However, they feel that it is extremely difficult to assert alternative family forms within the current legal and social framework. The models they might want to adopt are completely absent from the public realm. As Helen explained:

> I mean the idea of, when people think of multiple marriages all they can think of is Bountiful.[12] And there aren't any models that are positive for more complex kinds of family relationships. Either, you know, intimate or sexual or whatever. And so I think we feel like we're trying to work within labels and within structures that don't really fit what it is we're trying to do.

While Helen and Tracey see themselves "as something other than a small nuclear family where [they] just happen to be lesbians," because they parent at a day-to-day level in a largely nuclear structure, they are usually understood through a very traditional lens. Helen explained:

> It's funny because I was reading an article recently about the way people define family. And the presence of children is almost invari-ably what makes a "family" for people. I guess in that sense, even though we have ideas about family that run counter to the ones that get perpetuated in mainstream culture and so on, I think I still have to remind myself that we, that people look at us and that we constitute something that looks more like a family than we used to.

In fact, when Helen and Tracey attempted to assert their own defin-itions of family, they were resisted by those around them who did not seem to understand why they might not want to take advantage of being allowed to assimilate into heterosexual norms. For example, when Helen told their lawyer that they wanted to complete a second-parent adoption but did not necessarily want to replace the biological father's name with Tracey's name on their son's birth certificate, the lawyer was surprised and confused. He could not understand why they would not want to make their son's birth certificate reflect his two-mother nuclear family. What Tracey and Helen actually wanted was to extend the boundaries of their family by providing their son with recognition of both his biological family (recorded on his birth certificate) and chosen family (secured through his adoption). This mingling of biological and chosen family seemed incongruous to the lawyer, as well as to the legal system, which is able to recognize both biological and social parenting, but only two legal parents.[13]

Helen and Tracey suggested that the difficulty of asserting alternative ideas about family is at least in part the product of active "mainstreaming" by the lesbian and gay community itself. Tracey feels that the argument that lesbian mothers are "just like everyone else" inevitably marginalizes those mothers who seek to express their difference:

> You know there are things to be critical [of] about the "lesbian baby boom." There are people for whom this is about mainstreaming and being just like everybody else and all that. And there is the sense that, you know, we're cops and lawyers and bankers and, um, but let's look at the parts of the queer community that are getting marginalized. And I think for those people who, you know, see themselves as radical queer activists and on the left, there are good reasons to be critical of some of this kind of shift. And that's one of the reasons that I think it took me a while to be comfortable with the idea that we were going to do this [have a child]. I mean this does feel like, I mean, all we need to do is go to our new house in East Van and paint the picket fence white. We do have a picket fence, it's just grey, that's all [laugh]. But, so, I'm uncomfortable in some ways about what the implications of all of that are.

At the same time that Tracey rejected the mainstreaming of some lesbian mothers, she also expressed a degree of uncomfortableness about her own decision to parent. While she wanted to make it clear to me that she and Helen take a progressive approach to parenting, she also recognized the creeping of the white picket fence into her life. She did conclude, however, by noting that she hopes her more radical views about family might change the perception of some lesbians and gay men who are automatically suspicious of lesbians who choose to parent.

While they clearly sought to assert their family's difference, Tracey and Helen recognized that being open about their views might put their family at risk. Mainstream society's acceptance of their family is predicated on the extent to which they masquerade as more traditional. As Helen explained:

> So it's only by not being open about those things [her acceptance of open sexual relationships] in certain circles that we get that sense of acceptance. And I think that's, that's true not just in the context of our family but in all kinds of contexts in our lives. Our families and sort of even our neighbours who, many of whom are, you know, many of the little old Catholic ladies, are quite caring and accepting of us. But [they] would be quite shocked if we said that we don't see any reason why a family of three or four adults couldn't be sexually intimate or that people could have open relationships or, you know, any number of things.

Not surprisingly, Tracey fears that her real views about family will result in backlash from those she perceives as hostile – religious fundamentalists, Albertans (her home province), and "rednecks" – who are "just as likely to dress up in white sheets at night as say their prayers." She feels, however, that even among more open-minded Canadians, there is a limit to what would be accepted; that as soon as her family moves away from "a sort of narrow triad of two parents and a child," acceptance among average Canadians will "drop pretty rapidly." As a result, and because they see their young son as vulnerable, Tracey and Helen have chosen to be careful about how they live their family life. They feel that they have to "pull back from the edge at a certain level" and cannot be the "radical social experimentalists" they were prior to their son's birth. Tracey noted that this is exactly why some more radical lesbian and gay activists argue that having children is not the "right thing" to do.

In many ways, Tracey and Helen epitomize the dilemma that Tracey highlighted: does having a child necessarily have a conservatizing effect on lesbian and gay family? In their case, the answer appears to be a tentative yes. While they want to be "doing family" differently, they feel that their options are limited. This reasoning is in part because their son was born premature and spent his first few months in hospital. This experience, not surprisingly, focused their priorities inwards, towards the challenges of their new family life. However, their need to "pull back from the edge" means that they now live their lives as a fairly traditional nuclear family. At one point Tracey noted, when comparing herself to a working-class lesbian friend who was raising her son as a single mother in a communal setting, that she and Helen also have "a lot to lose" by embracing an alternative family form. Their comfortable, middle-class, home-owning lifestyle would probably change if they were to embrace a non-nuclear family structure. It is thus not surprising that Helen and Tracey are often read as a traditional family by others. While their personal views belie their outward appearance, those views cannot erase their actual practice.

Elisha, a biological mother from Vancouver, shares many of the same views about family as Tracey and Helen, but takes a very different practical approach. Choosing to parent her daughter with three co-parents, none of whom are her conjugal partner, as well as various chosen family members, Elisha simply refuses to "pull back from the edge." Along with her eleven-year-old daughter, Akeela, she lives her radical politics openly. Elisha's commitment to alternative family began while planning Akeela's conception. Elisha knew she wanted to have a child and had been talking with a workmate for several months about her desire. However, she was not in a relationship at the time, and, while she did not expect to be with one partner for life, she was reluctant to have a child without additional support. Her workmate, Cassandra, eventually told Elisha that if she still wanted to have a child, Cassandra would be happy to co-parent. Cassandra did not want to be a full-time parent, but she was willing to commit to long-term involvement and financial support. Eleven years later, Cassandra's commitment remains the same. She is a fundamental part of Akeela's life and has overnight contact with her one night a week. Cassandra and Elisha have never been in a conjugal relationship, but both consider themselves Akeela's co-parents.

Once Elisha had arranged Cassandra's support, the two women went in search of a sperm donor. Elisha wanted a known donor who would be willing to be part of the child's life. Through various friends, she and Cassandra found Kyle and his partner, Nick. The four adults met, and after several months of talking, they drafted a donor agreement. Interestingly, Elisha felt protected by the fact that Kyle, whom she had not previously known, was heavily involved with the lesbian and gay community. She felt that this would produce "more accountability" or a kind of "wider accountability."[14] As she explained, "It just felt like there was a bigger community supporting us." Elisha returned to this feeling later in the interview when she explained why none of Akeela's parents have sought any kind of legal recognition of their relationships. In Elisha's mind, protection comes from the lesbian and gay community and its own internal rules of accountability rather than from the law. She speculated that this might be a naïve view, but she clings to it nonetheless.

During the months of inseminating that followed, Elisha began a relationship with Rosemary, who eventually moved in with her. Soon after, Elisha became pregnant. Elisha and Rosemary remained together until Akeela was almost one. After they separated, Rosemary continued to be involved in Akeela's life, and Akeela sees her as a very close friend. Kyle and Nick are also parents to Akeela. Soon after her birth, they began spending time with her together, though they were no longer partners. Their contact with Akeela increased over the years; at the time I interviewed Elisha, they were coming together to co-parent Akeela in the same home two days a week. Akeela saw both of them as her dads. Akeela and Elisha also lived with a friend – part of Elisha's chosen family – who had lived with them since Akeela was two. While this woman is not considered a parent, she has taken on a significant caregiving role in Akeela's life. Finally, Elisha has a significant family relationship outside of her immediate family. For the past few years, she has been engaged in a co-parenting arrangement with a heterosexual couple who see her as a third parent to their young daughter. She was present at the child's birth, provides regular caregiving, and, most importantly to Elisha, has "also helped think about [the child] in a bigger way." This latter responsibility meant that Elisha was involved in key discussions about how the child would be parented. Akeela has a relationship with the little girl, which Elisha sees as very important to Akeela's own developing sense of kinship. Elisha recognizes the unusualness of her relationship with the child and her primary parents, and tried to explain why it might have been so successful:

> I think the whole thing about possessiveness of children stops other people outside of, you know, the nuclear family – whether they be heterosexual or gay or lesbian – that, once you get two people having a baby they get all protective and it's hard for people to break in. You know, for people without children to feel like they have a right to other people's children, and it's hard for other people to feel like [they can] give the right to other people. But what's been really remarkable in my relationship with this couple, who are heterosexual, is that they've been very, you know, [they] let me interact with her as a parent would. It hasn't been that, "oh, she's upset. We have to take her back." You know. So I get to listen to her when she cries just like they do. And for me that's, I think, more about what being a parent is. That you're not just this accessory who doesn't really, really dig in there and, you know, wash the dishes or change the diapers, that kind of thing.

When asked whether she felt that she was a parent to this child, Elisha responded, "Yeah, yeah, I mean it's growing." She feels that her friends have been very open to her taking a parental role and, rather than having the attitude that "we're the unit and you're outside," the couple talks about Elisha as the baby's "third parent after the two of them." Because of the closeness of this relationship, Elisha has incorporated the parents and child into her own family.

Interestingly, Elisha and her various co-parents have refrained from seeking any legal recognition of their family relationships. Elisha stated that she does not want to live her life "depending on law" and prefers to rely on the accountability she perceives to exist within the queer community. She also feels that the "distance [that law] would have to travel to get to [her] family reality [is] so far" that it seems pointless to engage. However, rather than seeing her family's exclusion from law as a hindrance, Elisha sees strength in it existing outside of the legal framework. She feels that being outside law and, at least to some extent, the ideological framework it imposes gives her and her family more freedom to develop their own "systems and behaviours." The expansive network of chosen and biological family within Elisha's family illustrates exactly how freeing this can be.

Elisha noted that having such an unconventional family life is rarely easy. Sharing the parenting of her daughter with three other parents outside of any kind of conjugal relationships means that her family is rarely fully recognized. Unlike Helen and Tracey, who feel trapped by dyadic norms, Elisha's family is so incomprehensible to outsiders that it is never labelled "family." The non-conjugal nature of the parental relationships seems to make it hard for outsiders to view her as anything but a single parent. Ironically, this could not be further from the truth. However, as Elisha put it, "You don't get to call people 'family' that you're not having sex with." In many ways, the unintelligibility of Elisha's family stems from the lack of comparable images within public discourse. Elisha lamented the lack of stories about alternative forms of kinship; she feels that they are urgently needed by both the queer and heterosexual communities.

> It's hard that, that the stories we hear are the, the ones that are just like, just like the heterosexual model. And it doesn't really represent the, the scope of what we see. I think we really need more of the other stories. And, I think we need to hear more of the other stories from heterosexuals too that are raising kids with other people involved. There's still this illusion of the nuclear family that doesn't, isn't true, but somehow people don't see that.

Elisha is especially worried that the stories of queer families that are told by the lesbian and gay community (usually to outsiders) are rarely about people who are expanding the category of family. Rather, they are, as she put it, about lesbians who have been together for fifteen years, decide to have a child, and now live in the suburbs. While Elisha does not see this model as an inherently "bad thing," she does think it is a "narrow thing."

It is clear from the narratives that emerged from the interviews that, despite the enormous changes that have taken place with regard to the legal and social recognition of lesbian and gay kinship in recent years, chosen family and other non-normative family practices remain a significant part of kinship for many lesbian mothers. Almost all of the mothers I spoke to defined family through the concept of chosen family, and chosen family members were almost always incorporated into the lives of their children. If I had interviewed forty-nine heterosexual mothers, I may also have unearthed approaches to family that deviated from traditional norms; as the heterosexual family that invited Elisha to co-parent with them illustrates, the concept of chosen family is not unique to the lesbian and gay community. However, reflecting Judith Stacey's assertion that lesbian motherhood is "the pioneer outpost of the post-modern family, confronting most directly its features of improvisation, ambiguity, diversity, contradiction and flux," several of the mothers suggested that lesbians might be uniquely positioned when it comes to understanding the family outside of the traditional paradigm.[15] As Naomi explained:

> Being in a same-sex relationship, we are luckier than most. We can define family as what we would like it to be. So we don't have the same stereotypes, the roles.

Similarly, Toni attributed her broad concept of family directly to her identity as a lesbian. She argued that the process of coming out can sometimes create a dissonance between the individual and her family of origin that forces her to go in search of new forms of family – lesbian and gay family – and to rethink the uniqueness of biological family:

> It's interesting 'cause our sense of family is a bit different, because I think when you're gay, growing up, you're, you don't know really

what a sense of family is, because you have your immediate sense of family, but you know you're outside of this family. And until you sort of meet other gays and lesbians, you know, you don't know really who you are within your family. And then, you know, your friends really become your family. And I think that there's often, I find sometimes now, that there's that conflict between your immediate family and what you see as family. Because I see family as bigger and they see it a bit more insular, you know?

In these comments, Toni captures the unique process that many lesbians and gay men go through as they realize their difference in the context of their families of origin. The resulting search for lesbian and gay family, for people who share their outsider experience, often produces a much more expansive sense of family than their families of origin are willing or able to absorb.

While these mothers clearly have an expansive sense of family, because lesbian and gay families are now more widely accepted than they have been in the past, their own definitions of family are often silenced by the assumptions of those around them. That is, the presumption seems to be that if a lesbian family takes a certain form – for example, a conjugal couple with children – its members necessarily embrace the values traditionally associated with that form. This view is no doubt encouraged by the rhetoric of groups such as EGALE who have sought legal recognition largely through the assertion of the same-sex nuclear family.[16] It thus appears that with social acceptance comes a certain degree of mainstreaming, whether the individuals like it or not. Helen and Tracey epitomize this dilemma. Their nuclear family appearance works to mask their actual political beliefs, making it almost impossible for them to assert an alternative family model. What is interesting, however, is that when it came to discussing law reform issues, most of the mothers advocated for a legal model that resembles chosen family, independent of how their own family was arranged. It might, therefore, be expected that if the law were to embrace more fluid forms of family, more mothers might feel safe enough to follow Elisha's example and adopt an alternative model.

Defining Parenthood

Not surprisingly, given the expansive nature of their definitions of family, most of the mothers felt that the term "parent" should also be defined broadly so as to give the concept the flexibility needed to capture the vast array of possible configurations. This usually involved expanding the definition beyond the existing biological and legal framework. Ultimately, the mothers favoured a definition of parent grounded in both joint intention and practice. In other words, parents are the people who intend to parent a child and who, once the child was born, perform that intention through caregiving.[17] Thus, parenting was understood, as Edwards has argued in the reproductive technology context, more through relationship – socially realized caregiving ties – and less through relatedness, the abstract connections between people who are thought of as kin because of a biological connection.[18] While the initial conversations I had with the mothers about parental definitions focused on defining parenthood in the social context, when we turned to the question of how to define *legal* parenthood, they maintained their position. What I found, however, was that while the first element of the mothers' definition – intention – translated easily into a legislative drafting context where it could be used to establish presumptive parenthood, the second element – caregiving – was more difficult to capture in legislative provisions applicable at birth because caregiving can only be demonstrated over time.

Despite the mothers' clear belief that biological connection does not make one a parent without an additional relationship of care, the symbolism of biological relatedness was always present even as it was displaced. The biological asymmetry of lesbian families means that the meaning afforded to biology needs to be determined within each familial unit. First, the mothers had to decide how they would understand the role of biology vis-à-vis each other. If they chose to co-parent, how would they "tie in" the non-biological mother so that she felt secure in her role in the face of norms to the contrary? Second, what meaning, if any, would be given to the genetic tie of the donor? Would the donor's contribution be understood as purely biological or, in the case of a known donor, would his biological relatedness be used as the foundation for a social relationship? As noted above, while the discussions initially focused on defining parenthood in a social context, the mothers' views did not change when the conversation turned to defining legal parenthood.

Understanding Parenthood within the Lesbian Couple

While biological mothers were assumed to be mothers in all of the families (though this was not always as straightforward as it seemed),[19] the status of the non-biological mother needed to be negotiated. For the vast majority of the couples, the negotiations were brief. It was their intention to be co-parents and, recognizing the unfair advantage the biological mother would necessarily have, they set about making sure that the non-biological mother was somehow tied in to the role of parent.[20] The various mechanisms used to achieve this were legal (e.g., completing a second-parent adoption), social (e.g., non-biological mothers playing the role of equal caregivers), and symbolic (e.g., giving the child the non-biological mother's surname). Thus, becoming a parent was understood by the mothers as "a social process, or rather, the result of social practice."[21] In coming to this conclusion, the mothers did as much to expose the legally and socially constructed nature of biological parenting as they did to validate social parenting. Because parents were understood to be the people who intended to parent and did the actual work of parenting, both non-biological *and* biological mothers were awarded parental status on the basis of their active involvement in the daily care of their children. Sylvie, the non-biological mother of two daughters conceived with a known donor, explained her perspective:

> I like to use a term here which, I call myself the front-line parent. A parent is a front-line parent, is the parent who commits, who is available from the get-go to provide everything that is needed in the healthy raising of a child. And whatever sacrifice that that entails ... I'm the front-line parent. That means that I'm the parent who's there twenty-four hours. I'm there for the emergencies. I'm there for the heartache and the emotional, whatever. You know, to, to bear it all. I'm the one who has committed to doing that work and that has little to do with biology. Really little.

Sylvie clearly understands her parental connection to her daughters as stemming from the practice of "front-line" parenting, a practice that has little connection to whether she is biologically related to the children or not.

Some of the mothers drew on their own childhood experiences to further explain why they are so comfortable understanding parenting through a combination of intention and caregiving practice rather than through biology. Callie and Sam, each of whom had given birth to one of their two children, were both raised by their mothers and a non-biological father with whom each enjoyed a close relationship.[22] Neither woman had a relationship with her biological father. Callie could not even remember how to spell her biological father's name. In both instances, the women consider their non-biological fathers to be their fathers because they were the ones who had cared for them. As Callie said, "Put in the work, you get the label. That's about it." Michaela, the biological mother of an infant son, also drew on her childhood abandonment by her father to explain why she understands the title "parent" as something that needs to be earned through "work":

> My biological father took off, so it's like, you know, when he came back into our lives we were much older. And we're like well, you know, you're like biological Bob. Like you're not really, you got a lot of work to do before you're gonna be called Dad.

Like Callie and Sam, Michaela feels that her father's biological relationship was meaningless since it was not accompanied by the work of parenting.

In the same way that the non-biological mother was constructed through the social practice of caregiving, some of the mothers felt, or were surprised to find, that parenting by the biological mother was similarly constructed. Mary Jane and Shannon came to this conclusion only after Mary Jane, the biological mother, discovered that efforts to tie in non-biological mother Shannon had been so successful that Mary Jane did not feel like a mother herself. When their daughter was born, Mary Jane and Shannon were so conscious of ensuring that Shannon build a relationship with the child that Shannon was assigned almost all of the daily tasks of parenting. At one point, Mary Jane was doing little beyond breastfeeding. This situation left Mary Jane feeling that her "obvious" biological tie to her daughter lost its meaning when it was no longer accompanied by a caregiving relationship:

> It never occurred to me that I would feel insecure about my own mothering relationship to the baby. It never occurred to me that would happen and it did. Which was a total shock to me. You know, because I, I do, I guess sometimes in my head think, well, I have this biological connection to her, that's *so* obvious.

For Veronique, the biological mother of a ten-year-old boy, the constructed nature of biological parenting is something she recognized from the outset. Although she is a biological mother, she understands her status as a parent entirely through the activity of care. As she conceives it, the biological relationship she has with her son is only given meaning because she also has a social relationship with him:

> Like, for me, the biological tie between Nathan and I is obviously important. But, that said, I mean I really do think parenting is, is social. So, I mean there is a significance that I am Nathan's social parent as well. I think those two things have to come together.

Thus, while the tie between biological mothers and their children was seen by the mothers as conferring privilege, and was almost always understood that way outside the family, the relationship was not completely straightforward. Failure to activate an existing biological tie – that is, the failure to participate in at least some of the tasks of a "front-line parent" – may result in the individual losing or failing to acquire the title of parent.

Because the mothers equated being a parent with caregiving, their equal involvement in caregiving was understood as transforming them into equal parents. Thus, in thirty-three of the thirty-six families I interviewed, parenting was described as an equal endeavour. Rather than assuming that the biological mother would be the primary caregiver, the women engaged in what Sullivan labelled "shared primary mothering or caregiving."[23] This did not always mean that caregiving was divided exactly equally, or that one mother did not sometimes stay at home while the other mother worked outside the home.[24] What it did mean was that tasks were shared as evenly as possible between the mothers and that those tasks that might be associated solely with the female parent in a heterosexual family, such as feeding the child at night, were deliberately turned into joint endeavours. For example, Callie and Sam, who had each given birth to a child, talked about how parenting tasks were interchangeable between them, with little emphasis on who the child's biological mother was:

> *Callie:* We both work full-time so the children [aged two and four] are in day care during the day. But in the evenings in terms of who bathes the children, who cooks, who does ... its interchangeable.
> *Sam:* Yeah, I'm just thinking about that now from the children's point of view. It's a toss-up which mom you're gonna get.
> *Callie:* We didn't break into very traditional stereotypical roles. More like it was, "Okay you're home, you take them."
> *Sam:* It's been very balanced.

Many of the mothers described similar scenarios. Shared primary caregiving was clearly something they were committed to, both politically and as a way of diminishing the power of the biological link. While none of the mothers referred explicitly to feminism when describing the division of labour within their households, their views were clearly influenced by feminist arguments about the significance of dividing household labour evenly. Thus, while legal mechanisms such as second-parent adoptions were what ultimately secured the status of non-biological mothers as parents, psychically it was shared primary caregiving that made them *feel* like parents. It was also what made biological mothers understand their non-biological counterparts as parents.

This latter point is illustrated by the views of the three mothers who *did* draw a distinction between biological and non-biological parenting.

Each of these mothers had become their child's sole primary caregiver following the termination of their intimate relationship with the non-biological mother.[25] In one of these cases, the separation had occurred prior to the child's birth, and in the other two, it was during the first five years of the child's life. In these cases, the biological mothers saw themselves as the "real" mothers because they had been left, at least initially, to do the bulk of the caregiving work.[26] In other words, they continued to understand parenting through caregiving; a "real" parent is the one who does the work. However, each of these mothers speculated that they may have ended up being the primary caregivers because they were also the biological mothers. They suggested that some non-biological mothers may see themselves as having more freedom to limit their relationships with children that they have planned with their partners, particularly when they have not yet established emotional bonds with them. These three families are not necessarily representative, as other separated biological and non-biological mothers I spoke to had not had the same experience.[27] However, they do suggest that the traditional symbolic meaning attributed to biology will not always shift in the lesbian context.

Interestingly, given the belief by these three biological mothers that the non-biological mothers had less of a commitment to the child, in the two cases where the children had a relationship with their other mother, the biological mother felt committed to maintaining it.[28] This was the case even though neither of the non-biological mothers had any legal relationship with the children. In these two cases, the biological mother's decision stemmed from both a political commitment to the lesbian community and a commitment to the best interests of the child. Mischa explained the political component of her decision to maintain contact:

> *Interviewer:* You said that politically, you thought it was the right thing to do.
> *Mischa:* Yeah. Well politically because my allegiance to my beliefs is that, when you have a child within a lesbian relationship we have no other means of saying that what we're doing is two people having a child. And this is the only way we can do it. So, I have to

honour that and say if we break up, the fact that you didn't get to
have your biology in this mix doesn't mean I can walk away.
Shouldn't mean I can walk away.

Mischa's statement reflects Elisha's earlier comments about seeing
the lesbian and gay community as the source of accountability for her
parenting. For Mischa, being a lesbian mother means committing to a
model of parenting that protects non-biological mothers in the face of
their legal and social vulnerability. Interestingly, Mischa's maintenance
of the relationship between her daughter and her non-biological mother
has now led to a fairly amicable 50/50 caregiving arrangement. Yvonne,
the biological mother of a fifteen-year-old, takes a similar approach to
that of Mischa, though she articulates it through her commitment to
her daughter. Her daughter clearly sees her non-biological mother as a
mother, and this is how she was raised prior to her parents' separation.
Yvonne therefore refuses to take advantage of her superior legal position,
which would be particularly easy in this case as the non-biological
mother has a number of mental health issues. While these examples
may not be representative of all lesbian mothers, they do point to the
enormous commitment among at least some mothers to maintaining
the integrity of their community's understanding of family.

The only other crack in the mothers' narrative about the equal value
of non-biological motherhood came in the interview with Laurie and
Simone, a couple whose two daughters (aged five years and ten months)
were birthed by Simone but conceived using Laurie's eggs. In other
words, both mothers have a connection to their children that they described as "biological."[29] The way in which Laurie and Simone conceived
and birthed their children was the result of various medical complica-
tions and should therefore not be understood as a deliberate attempt
to create biological links between both women and their children. The
outcome, however, was that both women have a biological connection
to the children that makes them feel like they are both mothers in a way
that other lesbian mothers are not. Their views are largely based on the
fact that they feel they can see a difference between biological and non-
biological mothers in other lesbian families, with the biological mother
perceived to have "more of a connection" and "influence" with the

children. In contrast, they feel that this distinction does not exist in their own family. They also noted that in some families, the child call the non-biological mother by her first name. Laurie commented that it is perhaps a little judgmental of them to critique the parenting practices of other mothers, but they feel strongly that in some lesbian families, the non-biological mother has a less significant parenting role than the biological mother. When I delved a little deeper, however, it became apparent that at least some of their apprehension about these families is associated with family practices that have little to do with parenting. For example, they commented that some lesbian mothers do not share a bank account or are not otherwise economically intertwined, practices they view as a sign of "total commitment." It is therefore hard to know exactly what is at the heart of Laurie and Simone's belief that they are "*really* both the mothers." It does suggest, however, that the increased use of reproductive technologies that create biogenetic connections between children and *both* of their mothers may shift how biology is understood within the lesbian and gay community. In particular, it could signal a return to more traditional (and arguably heterosexual) understandings about who is a "real" parent than those currently espoused within the lesbian community.

Sperm Donors and Parental Status

The meaning to be attributed to the donor relationship in the context of the lesbian family is perhaps the most difficult issue that lesbian mothers face, not least because there is such a wide array of possibilities. When lesbian women decide to have a child, a decision must first be made about whether they will choose an anonymous donor, an anonymous donor with identity release (if available), or a known donor.[30] If a known donor is chosen, the mothers must also determine what meaning he will have in the context of their child's life. Will he be a symbolic father, an uncle-like figure, or "Dad"? The answer to this question necessarily presents a number of legal conundrums for lesbian mothers. Mothers must decide whether they will make a legal contract with the donor, whether any provision for access will be included within it, whether the donor's name will appear on the child's birth certificate, and whether the donor will consent to a second-parent adoption by the non-biological mother. Each of these decisions is made according to how the mothers and the donor understand his identity and role in the family.

While the mothers obviously play a significant role in determining the meaning attributed to the donor relationship within their family, the donor's role must also be understood in the context of the current (and widespread) moral panic about the prospect of "fatherless families." In fact, as suggested in Chapter 1, debates about lesbian use of donor insemination are part of a much larger debate about the meaning of fatherhood in contemporary society. Father absence has, in recent years, been constructed as unacceptable because of the perceived unique contributions fathers make to children's lives as gendered caregivers, disciplinarians, and economic providers. Drawing a connection between these "unique" contributions and outcomes for children, the lack of a father figure has been linked to lax discipline, criminal behaviour, teenage pregnancy, delinquency, youth suicide, poverty, and unemployment.[31] The response of politicians and the courts to this "crisis" has more often than not been to reinforce the heterosexual nuclear family and biological fatherhood by favouring liberal access arrangements, joint custody, and ongoing child support liability. In some cases, a father is imposed on a family independent of whether the man actually has a healthy relationship, or any relationship at all, with the child.[32] Unfortunately, lesbian families have not been immune to these trends.[33]

Given the current political discourse around fatherhood, which many of the mothers were keenly aware of, they felt quite vulnerable to the unplanned participation in their families of known donors. It was rarely because they rejected the idea of a father – whether active, symbolic, or semiotic – altogether. Rather, it was their sense that the symbolic weight attached to fatherhood would always prevail over their own conceptions of what it means to be a parent. In particular, they suggested that neither legal decision makers nor wider society were likely to agree with them that parental status was something that should be conferred only in the context of a caregiving relationship.

The Anonymous Donor
Twenty-four of the thirty-six families interviewed had conceived their children using anonymous-donor sperm. However, about half of this

group stated that they had initially wanted to use a known donor, and only after careful deliberation had they decided it was not the right choice. What made them change their minds, and what might it say about how they conceptualize the "known donor"?

The most common reason cited by the mothers for choosing an anonymous donor over a known donor was that while they would have liked their donor to be available to their child if needed, they did not want to share parenting with a third individual. That is, they wanted a father in name only – a symbolic father – who served little more than a semiotic function. Lisa and Sarah, who had unsuccessfully tried to find a man willing to fulfill such a role, actually used the term "deadbeat dad" to refer to the kind of donor they were looking for. While a couple of the mothers who had used known donors did in fact have a symbolic father arrangement, the mothers who wanted this arrangement but who eventually chose anonymous donors had trouble finding men willing to take on this secondary role. In most instances, the men they spoke to wanted to be actively involved in parenting and this was not the relationship the women envisaged. Maureen and Gillian explained:

> *Maureen:* Yeah, we spoke to a couple of men. There was somebody that we knew fairly well. And he considered it. We sort of had the uncle analogy in our mind. And as he sort of started thinking more about it he had questions like well what if I, what if I wanted to have a say in what preschool the child went to? Or what if I wanted to stop ...
> *Gillian:* In on my way home from work? And ...
> *Maureen:* And so it was clear that he wanted more of a parent role.
> *Gillian:* And he did. He would love to have been a parent.
> *Maureen:* Yeah.
> *Gillian:* And so in fairness to him, because that wasn't what we envisioned, we said no.

Sam and Callie, who had also spoken to prospective donors and described themselves as being "very close to picking someone," had similar concerns. They see known donors as having the ability to wield a great deal of power and control, and the scenarios they described had a slightly more fearful edge than those mentioned by Maureen and Gillian. Callie explained their fears:

> We were the ones who were gonna be doing the parenting. And we didn't want to risk someone in the future coming and saying, "Hey, you can't move because, you know, I won't be able to see my child." Or, uh, "No, I don't want my child to go to a school like that." Or whatever. To influence any kind of parenting. We just wanted it to be simple and uncomplicated.

Going one step further than Callie, a number of the mothers expressed a very real fear that the donor might ignore the parties' original intentions and demand custody of or access to the child. Recognizing that donor agreements were "not worth the paper they were written on," these mothers felt that choosing a known donor was simply too big a risk to take. Delia, a biological mother who also happens to be a lawyer, explained:

> We talked very briefly about the donor being somebody we knew and quickly realized that we didn't really like that plan ... It doesn't matter what people say. You know when they're signing a contract and they're agreeing to something. Then they get a little baby in their hands. Hearts melt and people change their minds. And that's just something we didn't want to deal with.

Janet, the biological mother of two children born using anonymous-donor sperm, experienced exactly the situation Delia described. Fifteen years ago, she and her partner had a son with a known donor who was to be a symbolic father only. The little boy was born with significant medical problems, however, and was hospitalized for much of his short life. While the child was in hospital, the donor became very involved and asserted his right as a father to take part in the boy's medical care. With no legal protection available to them, Janet and her partner had little ability to assert their understanding of the donor relationship. As a result, the hospital staff treated the donor as the boy's parent. When it came to having her other children, Janet stated that while "idealistically" she wanted a known donor, given her earlier experience, she felt it was just "too risky."

It is obvious from the comments made by these mothers that the limitations of the law, coupled with the social power that biological fathers were clearly understood to possess, were significant factors in their decisions to choose an anonymous donor. Given the various legal disputes that have emerged over the years between lesbian mothers and their donors, it is not surprising that the mothers doubted that their familial definitions would be upheld.[34] What is interesting is that the presence of laws in their favour, albeit limited ones, did not always allay their fears. Even in British Columbia, where the array of post-birth legal protections available is wide (though certainly not complete), many of the women still felt that choosing a known donor made them too legally vulnerable. They simply did not trust the legal system to protect the interests of themselves or their children over those of the donor. Rochelle, who had an identity-release anonymous donor, stated:

> We thought about having a known donor, but we just don't think that the laws in Canada worked to protect the children. And that's the biggest reason why we decided not to have a known donor.

Mary Jane and Shannon, an Edmonton couple with an anonymous donor, expressed a similar sentiment:

> *Mary Jane:* Yeah, we were both really, well I shouldn't speak for you, but I was really uncomfortable with the idea of a known donor. Just because of worries about claiming paternity at some point.
> *Shannon:* Yeah, that was our biggest thing. Losing the baby in a legal battle was actually our biggest concern.

Alluding to the influence of the fathers' rights movement within family law, Rosie and Toni saw the courts as pro-father, making them even more vulnerable to the claims of a known donor. The decision as to whether to choose an anonymous or known donor had been very hard for them as Rosie had really wanted a man who could be a caring, gentle, and loving male figure in their child's life. In the end, however, their fear of the courts, and particularly what they perceived as its bias towards fathers, made them change their minds:

> *Rosie:* I think that the legal system doesn't allow for it [having a known donor]. I mean you can just see a judge sort of going, [banging her hand on the table] "The father has rights!" What, because he donated sperm? I don't think so. You know, like, I don't. You know all of a sudden like these people come back into their lives and say, "Well, I'm his dad!" Well, no you're not a dad!
> *Toni:* Uh huh.
> *Rosie:* Because being a father and a dad has a lot more responsibility than just claiming that that's what you are.

The known donor emerged from these conversations as a slightly sinister figure with the law on his side. The mothers' perceptions of the existing law meant that they did not feel safe choosing a known donor, even though at least half of them favoured known donors as the option they otherwise felt most comfortable with. Their main reason for shying away from known donors derived from a fear that their definitions of parent would not be accepted by the legal system or society at large. Thus, in choosing an anonymous donor, they traded "their knowledge of biological connection for protection from ... potential kinship claims and from the very basis of such claims: paternity."[35] In doing so, they exposed the ongoing legal vulnerability felt by many lesbian mothers even as the law expands to include them. Rosie and Toni's comments are perhaps the most salient on this issue. As they understand it, legal mechanisms for parental recognition offer little security when the law itself operates within an ideological framework characterized by patriarchy and heterosexism.

Known Donors

By choosing anonymous donors, and thus removing the donor from the family context, the twenty-four families who used anonymous donors were able to avoid many of the more difficult questions around parental definitions. In contrast, the twelve families with known donors were constantly confronted with the question "What makes a parent?" Breaking this question down into smaller pieces, many of them grappled with whether their sperm donor could be involved in the child's life but not a father, or a father but not a parent. Approaches to these issues were not necessarily consistent across the group.

In defining the role of known donors, the mothers emphasized, as they had when defining "family," the importance of the freedom to self-define within each family unit. However, within this broad process of self-definition, and mirroring the categories developed in Sullivan's study of lesbian families in the San Francisco Bay Area, three categories of donor identity emerged.[36] The most common identity attributed to donors, with seven of the families falling within this category, is that of a "flexibly defined male figure" with whom their children have a relationship but to whom no parental status is imputed. While some of these men are referred to as the child's father, most are known by their first name. In this first category, the men are regular visitors in the child's life, though some are far less involved than others. The second category is made up of two families who see their donors as symbolic fathers. A symbolic father is "someone the family can hang the label 'dad' on – an embodied human referent that the child may identify as his or her progenitor."[37] In other words, it is, as Sullivan notes, "a purely sign-driven, semiotic arrangement."[38] Though their identities are known to their biological children, donors who fall into the second category have almost no relationship with their progeny. The final category is made up of two families whose donors are active, practicing parents with all of the rights and responsibilities implied by that status, though without legal custody.[39] However, in both of these families the mothers are still considered to be the primary parents.

The two families with donors who are considered active parents understand the men in this way because of the significant caregiving roles they play in the lives of their children. The men provide overnight care for the children on a weekly basis and also take part in at least some of the day-to-day caregiving. In both instances, the children view the men as fathers. This was not necessarily the plan when the women first considered having a child with a known donor. For example, biological mother Rhona initially wanted only herself and her partner to be her children's parents and did not want the donor to be "too involved." However, soon after her first son's birth, the donor, Ian, began visiting on a weekly basis. Within months, Ian was spending time alone with his son, and by the time the boy was three years old, Ian had him for overnight visits with him and his same-sex partner, Rick. Rhona and her partner separated when her first son was an infant, and she decided to have a second child without a partner. Ian was unable to act as a donor by that time for health reasons, but his partner, Rick, agreed to take on the task. Rhona was comfortable with this idea because Rick was already a significant part of her eldest son's life. When her second son was born, the two men remained heavily involved with the children, though their own intimate relationship eventually ended. Because of limited space and financial difficulties, for a period of three years, Rhona, Rick, and the two boys shared a house. During that time, Rick played a pivotal caregiving role. Rhona described both men as the "boys' dads" and considered Ian also to be a "parent" to both of them. Rick, on the other hand, is understood by Rhona to be a parent only to his biological son on the basis that he does not make "the same effort" with regard to caregiving for his non-biological son. Despite the parental role the two men play in their sons' lives, Rhona stated that she and her partner of seven years are the boys' "primary parents." However, Ian and Rick continue to see the boys, aged thirteen and eight at the time of the interview, for overnight visits every weekend. In addition, they alternate spending one evening a week with them. Rhona described the arrangement:

> One night a week one or the other of them picks the kids up from school, brings them here. Like tonight, Rick took them to his place. Ian would pick them up and bring them here. Do dinner for them. Get homework done. Put them to bed kind of thing. And then Liz [her partner] and I get that one night out a week.

There is no doubt that in the case of Rick and Ian, the semiotic, biological, and social elements of parenting were brought together in each of the men in relation to his own biological child. In Ian's case, these three elements were also fused in relation to his non-biological son. The crucial element that made these men parents was the fact that they provided regular care for their children. The only aspect of parenting missing was legal custody. That remained the sole domain of the mothers.

The remaining families – those who see their donors as symbolic fathers or significant male figures in their children's lives – are faced with a very different set of issues, primarily because there is such a range of degrees of donor involvement available. Those who see their donors as symbolic fathers have perhaps the easiest decision-making process. These mothers never intended their donors to be anything more than peripheral figures in their children's lives, available for consultation only at the request of the child. It is thus not surprising that these men were referred to as the child's "donor" and have had little to no involvement in the child's life. Mothers who see their donors as significant figures in their children's lives have a more complex set of issues to address. The most common concern of the mothers in this group was whether they would choose a "donor," "father," or "uncle-like" identity for their donor and how this might work in practice. Defining the donor's identity often proved to be difficult, particularly given what the mothers often described as the "utter failure" of language to capture the identities created.

The one thing that all of these mothers were clear on was that a biological connection does not make a donor a parent. Thus, no donor can simply by virtue of his genetic contribution claim the identity of parent. Such a title requires an additional caregiving relationship. This was explained succinctly by a number of the mothers. For example, Rochelle noted that "genetics is genetics and parenting is parenting. They're different. Genetics does not make one a parent." Michaela argued in a similar fashion that "an eighth of a teaspoon of biological matter is not a parent." While none of the donors in this category were understood as parents, some of them were given the title "father." In fact, one of the concepts the mothers took great pains to explain to me was that a donor can be a father without being a parent. Antonia's donor lives with his male partner and visits his two sons once or twice a year from another province; he is understood to be a father (as is his partner), but neither man does enough caregiving to be considered a parent. As Antonia explained:

> I think you can be a dad but not a parent. I think that's maybe kind of the area where it's a bit grey. I mean one of their [her sons'] dads came out for spring break and he and I and the kids went skiing together. And the whole time he was there he was a dad and a parent, but that was a week out of the whole year. You know, he's not there at three in the morning when they're sick and I think it brings up that whole question of, you know, who's really doing the parenting? Can you parent one week a year? Or two weeks a year?

Tracey explained how her son's donor, who is a very close friend but lives overseas, is also a father but not a parent:

> He's a father but he's not a parent. So he fathered the child in a biological sense, but he's, he's not a parent. And I think that, that [her son] will refer to John as "John." But we want to be clear that John is his father. So we're working so that, what we really want to do is not have secrets. Not have things that can't be said.

In these two families, the men are clearly understood to be fathers but lack the depth of caregiving relationship and responsibility necessary to acquire parental status. The children know they have "a dad," but they do not relate to him through a parental paradigm.

In a slightly different category are those mothers who acknowledge the biological tie between donor and child, but do not consider their donors to be either fathers or parents. In trying to describe their identities, they sometimes referred to them as "like uncles" or "somewhere between a donor and a father." Without the language to truly describe the relationships these men have to the children, some of the mothers fell back on the term "father." The terminology they chose, however, was seen to have important ramifications, particularly outside of the home, causing many of the mothers to switch terms depending on the situation. Carey, for example, struggles with what to call her donor, who sees his son once a fortnight, since none of the terms "donor," "father," or "parent" really capture his role. She also wants to avoid people outside of the family thinking that he has more caregiving responsibility than he actually has. Ultimately, she chooses her terminology on the basis of the specific situation she is in, though it is clear from the pauses and stuttering in the following discussion that she finds this a difficult issue to resolve:

> *Carey:* It [the term she uses] depends on who I'm talking to. I always define Nora and I as [his] parents and sometimes, um, I will include Roger [donor], depending on who I'm talking to. But, I don't consider, he's not a hundred percent parent. He's very much a part-time parent. And I don't think he even completely gets what it is like to be a full-time parent. So a lot of times, I don't consider him to be a parent.
>
> *Interviewer:* You said that in some circumstances you would refer to him as a parent. Which people would you be talking to when you make that distinction?
>
> *Carey:* I guess people who are kind of already familiar with the situation. I'll talk about [my son's] "dad." Whereas other times I'll say [my son's] "donor." Just, it's 'cause neither is completely accurate. He's really in between.
>
> *Interviewer:* When you said you would use "donor" when you're speaking to people who maybe don't understand the situation, is that out of a fear that Nora will somehow be negated?
>
> *Carey:* No, no, no. Not at all. Because I don't, I don't want them to think that [my son] has three full-time caregivers when really it's Nora and I, we're really doing it. To professionals, Nora and I are the parents. I don't, I don't bring his dad into it at all. Because I don't want people to start thinking that he has responsibilities that he doesn't have.

Carey's reference to the inability of language to fully capture the nature of the donor's relationship to the child was a common concern. In many instances, the mothers complained that language simply can not grasp the complexity of the relationship between donor and child. Paternal terminology was also perceived by the mothers as carrying a great deal of "social power," especially in light of the rise of the fathers' rights movement and the ongoing legal vulnerability of non-biological mothers. For example, in describing the role of her donor in the life of her seven-year-old son, Jasmine noted how difficult it is to assert their lesbian family in the face of the enormous symbolic meaning that attaches to the designation "father":

> *Jasmine:* Chris [her son] and [his donor] do see each other and Chris knows him as his father. But we don't define him as part of our family. Chris is starting to think maybe he might be sort of part of the family, but in a distant sort of uncle-like way or something. But not immediate family. We'll see, we maintain to both of them that whatever relationship they develop we'll support. It hasn't been easy.
>
> *Interviewer:* What's been difficult?
>
> *Jasmine:* The words are wrong. Like to call him "father," and yet he hasn't been there at all, in any way. And he can show up and take Chris out to McDonalds and be a wonderful hero once every few weeks. Uh, I guess it is sort of the plight of a lot of single moms. That's been difficult, especially in the beginning where Bianca doesn't have the biology and it was really important to make sure that she's the one acknowledged and not him. We had, we were really cautious to not include him ... Today there's no more issues around who's the parents, but you know it's more in public. As far as Chris goes, I mean he knows that Bianca and I are his parents. But if Neil [the donor] comes to something like one of his performances or something and he introduces him as "father," they will defer to him. And that kind of stuff. 'Cause we don't have the right words for it. Yes, he's the biological father and yes he may be important in Chris's life, but don't defer to him.

In this discussion, Jasmine captured the difficulties of negotiating donor identity in the public sphere. Despite it being clear to Jasmine's son who his parents are, in public situations, the mere presence of her son's "father" results in outsiders deferring to him. This says as much about the patriarchal role fathers continue to play within the heterosexual family structure as it does about society's inability to acknowledge alternative families. Working within a heterosexual paradigm in which the contribution of sperm equals "father" and being a father means having authority, outsiders defer to Jasmine's donor without thought. This dilemma points to something mentioned by a number of the mothers: the ease with which men are awarded the title "father" in the heterosexual domain. Trying to work through this issue for herself, Helen commented that "for many heterosexual fathers, [sperm donation] is the largest part of their contribution. They've never had to think about whether that means they're really fathers or not." Helen seems to be suggesting that because the semiotic and biological aspects of fatherhood are fused (and the social aspect largely ignored) in the heterosexual context, there is a profound lack of thought about what makes a man a father beyond the contribution of sperm. This is perhaps at the heart of the problem lesbian mothers have in asserting their own definitions. Because they *do* think about what makes a man a father or a parent – and they have largely come to the conclusion that the single most important feature is participation in caregiving – they do not necessarily extend fatherhood to men who might traditionally be understood as fathers in heterosexual families.

Should Parenting Be Limited to Two People?

While many of the mothers were fearful of courts imposing "fathers" on their families, only a small number felt that parenting should be limited to two individuals. This was the case even when their own families resembled the nuclear model.[40] In fact, over three-quarters of the mothers supported the idea of a child having three or more parents *if that was what the parties had agreed to*. In most instances, they envisaged the recognition of a known donor (and perhaps his partner), provided that the men were playing a caregiving role to which the parties had all agreed prior to the child's birth. The mothers' reasons for favouring a non-dyadic parenting model varied, but most of them argued that where the parties had intended such a family arrangement, the child could only benefit from the love and attention of additional adults. Elisha, who parents her daughter with several co-parents and sees communal parenting as the optimal model, explained:

> It's not healthy for Akeela [her daughter] or for me, for me to be the only person that she can go to. You know the world is big and you need more than one person with their little rigidities and strengths. You need different strengths and they kind of help you be more well balanced if you can get different things from different people, and have different struggles with different people too. That you don't think that, you know, this is the only way to act.

Sylvie also endorsed a flexible parenting model, emphasizing the isolating effects of nuclear parenting:

> You know, I really do believe what I said when you first came in. The more parents the better. You know. And that's where we need to go legally, is to be in a position where we can prove that that is a benefit. That the old saying of "it takes a village to raise a child" really is true. That forcing people by legislation to be isolated in their parenting is a recipe for disaster. It really is! To open that up would be most beneficial, I think, for all involved. And for society as a whole.

Sylvie, whose known donor is largely uninvolved, went on to express some frustration with not being able to invite her donor to play a more significant parenting role. Had the law been open to a three-parent configuration, that is what she and her partner would have chosen. However, Sylvie's legal vulnerability as a non-biological mother, coupled with the legal power she and her partner feel the donor has as the biological father, forced them to be exclusionary in their parenting:

> We've organized ourselves in this way mostly because [of] the way the law currently is and because we feel that we have to do this to protect ourselves and our children. To be exclusionary. Otherwise we would be quite open to, to the idea of having the sperm donor thought of as a "parent." It's just not wise legally for us. It's a *big* mistake to ever use that word.

Sylvie's comments help explain the apparent contradiction between many of the mothers' reluctance to share parenting with a third parent and their overwhelming support for multiple-parent families and a law reform model that provides legal recognition to such families. Sylvie seems to suggest that if the law gave them more security, lesbian mothers might be more open to both known donors and regular donor involvement.

A final reason for extending parentage beyond the dyadic model came from Lisa, who suggested that recognizing multiple parents might be beneficial because it would make "more visible the invisible work of parenting." Lisa argued that if more than two parents could be recognized, it would challenge the assumption that two parents should be able to provide everything that is necessary to raise a child. It might also highlight how many parents actually find it difficult to achieve this "norm" and how isolating it can be. By recognizing that a three- or four-parent family might offer a more balanced family life, multiple-parent recognition would make "visible the real work of raising a child." Lisa also suggested that the recognition of multiple parents might shift what she sees as the patriarchal nature of the nuclear family:

> It seems to me that recognizing that third person could just shift the, the patriarchal duality of it. Like there's one head and one not, a subordinate. So that might work in a kind of subversive way. And I think it would be good for the kids as well, just teaching them about different possibilities. And then that's a valid option and it just kind of expands what's possible. Takes us out of a kind of stereotypical expectation.

While not all of the mothers had such a nuanced political stance towards non-dyadic parenting as Sylvie and Lisa, the vast majority of them believed that the two-parent model lacks sufficient flexibility. As a result, they favoured the possibility of multiple parents, provided that their own role as mothers was legally protected. They did acknowledge that the legal recognition of multiple parents might increase the complexity of disputes between parents but felt that this was not sufficient reason to deny recognition altogether.

Severing the Link between Marriage and Parenting

A final definitional theme to emerge, and one that was somewhat unexpected given the availability of same-sex marriage in both British Columbia and Alberta at the time the interviews were conducted, was that few of the mothers made any link between marriage and parenting. In fact, in many cases the mothers expressed deep concern about the legal recognition of their parenting relationships but dismissed legal marriage as something they were "not interested in." This severing of the traditionally positive link between becoming a parent and being married was unexpected given the frequency with which proponents of same-sex marriage had used the fact that lesbians and gay men are now parenting to support their legal claims.[41]

Despite the fact that most of the women represented in the study had been in a relationship with their same-sex partner for over a decade, in only nine of the thirty-six families were the mothers married and in only two others did the mothers have any intention of getting married. Of those who were married, in only three cases did they make a link between their desire to marry and a sense of it being important for their children and parenting relationships. In one of those families, the mothers married prior to the birth of their daughter because, although they felt it was a "weird conservative thing" to do, they thought it would be best for the baby to be born to a married couple. In the other two cases, the mothers thought it would "solidify" their families and make their children feel more "secure" because they would be "just like everyone else."

The remaining seven couples married for purely practical reasons and were often quite insistent in their need to get across that their decision to marry was not because they believed that parenting is best performed within a legal marriage. For example, Emily and Lesley married because their donor approached them about whether he could tell his parents about his son. The fear this created for Emily and Lesley was what eventually "drove" them to get married. They felt that being married would give them greater legal protection against claims from their donor's extended family. Their attitude to the marriage itself was quite revealing and certainly did not reflect any reverence for it as a fundamental institution of Canadian society. As Emily recounted, "I guess it means I'm sticking around for a while! I mean, it was a joke. It had no bearing on anything." While few mothers were quite this flippant about their marriage, most of them cited reasons for marrying that reflected those of Emily and Lesley. Finally, some of the mothers who were married had a simultaneous critique of the institution that sat uncomfortably alongside their decision to marry. Veronique, for example, noted that she is "very skeptical" about the assumption that having married parents is "good for kids." However, she does feel that her marriage made her relationship with her partner, which began when her son was six, "very real" to him.

A large number of the mothers who were not married expressed strong resistance towards the institution and saw no positive connection between being legally married and parenting. While I did not question them explicitly about their reasons for rejecting marriage, it was apparent that at least some of their views derived from feminist critiques of marriage as a patriarchal institution. In fact, talk of marriage elicited heated responses about how the same-sex marriage campaign had not adequately represented women's interests. Sylvie, for example, sees same-sex marriage as harmful to women and wants nothing to do with it:

> We're not impressed. What can I say? [laugh] I never wanted marital rights. I don't believe the institution of marriage has served women well. I do not believe in it and I do not want to participate in it.

Tracey and Helen, who had grappled with the idea of getting married but eventually rejected it in favour of an informal "un-wedding," expressed similar concerns about what same-sex marriage means for queers and women with more radical politics. In telling the story of how they came to reject marriage, they explained how they had shifted from seeing the "potentially radical implications of marriage" to feeling that it was more productive to seek change from outside the institution. This shift stemmed in large part from their developing belief that legal marriage will inevitably conservatize the lesbian and gay community and "mark as illegitimate" those who refuse to participate.

When the same-sex marriage debate emerged in Canada, Helen and Tracey's first impulse was that "something that makes George Bush that angry [had] to be good." However, they quickly began to resent the fact that the advocates of gay marriage were treating marriage as somehow capable of making their relationship "more real." Tracey explained their discomfort:

> We didn't want to allow the state to sanction us and for that to change what our relationship was. We had already been as committed as two people can be for nine years and we resented any implication that this was changing our relationship or making it more real. So we, we had a lot of ambivalence about it.

Their distrust of the marriage campaign grew when they realized the "very conservative standpoint" the main advocates were arguing from. They had hoped that gay marriage might "blow up the family" and that lesbian and gay participation in the institution could provide some "radical political valence." As Helen explained, EGALE wanted to argue for marriage on the basis that "we are just like everyone else" and she wanted to argue "from the point of, no, we're not just like everyone else." Ultimately, Tracey and Helen rejected the capacity of marriage to be a progressive institution. Instead, they sought to destabilize the notion of what marriage means, and one of the ways in which they could do that was to reject the idea that children are best raised by married parents.

Continuing in a similar vein to Tracey and Helen, Kinwa and her partner, Ruth, suggested that the marriage campaign may actually have been damaging to the interests of lesbian mothers. As a working-class Aboriginal woman, Kinwa perceived the marriage campaign as dominated by the interests of elite gay men who ignored what she saw as the more critical needs of lesbians with children:

> You know, marriage wasn't an issue for the lesbians. And we kept standing up at the [EGALE] meeting and saying, "That's not our issue." And the rich gay men stood up and said, "We want to be able to marry each other." So legal recognition of parenthood? Yes. Legal recognition in terms of marriage? I don't think so. That wasn't the hill I was prepared to die on.

There is nothing in Kinwa's comments that might suggest that she sees any positive connection between gaining marriage rights and parenting. This severing of the traditionally positive link between parenting and being married marks these lesbian families as remarkably distinct from mainstream ideology. Furthermore, it suggests that any law reform related to lesbian parenting should not be centred around the marriage relationship.

Conclusion

It is clear from the definitions provided by many of the mothers that their ideas about, and practice of, family do not conform to traditional legal or social norms. While none of them completely abandoned all elements of the traditional family, they had, as Strathern suggests, "pressed old ideas into new service."[42] This often involved redefining family in a way that incorporated chosen family and recognized the choice about whether to treat biological relatives as kin. While the mothers spoke confidently about the ways in which they had put their expansive and relatively non-traditional familial definitions into practice within their own immediate families, they returned frequently to the fact that their views were not reflected within wider society or the law. There was a strong sense among the mothers that non-nuclear, non-conjugal, and non-biological families are not ones which the law was currently able to accommodate. As Christy noted, "[The laws] are very oriented towards nuclear families. They don't seem to take into account the complexities of the families that are coming up today." While the mothers did not unquestioningly endorse pursuing law reform, there was a relatively uniform consensus that law is an important component of their bid for change. In the next chapter, the possibility of legislative reform is explored, giving specific attention to the issue of whether the diversity that is clearly present among the lesbian parenting community is capable of being captured within a legislative framework.

Engaging with Reform   **4**
Legal Mechanisms for the Recognition of the Lesbian Family

One of the most significant challenges posed by law reform directed at lesbian parents is how such a heterogeneous array of parental and family arrangements can be contemplated by a single legal regime. The diversity of parenting practices within the lesbian community suggests the need for a flexible legislative framework, capable of providing a variety of recognition mechanisms for a broad array of family forms. On the other hand, the need for flexibility cannot be met at the expense of lesbian family security. For example, law reform that enables lesbian parents to co-parent with a donor should not create a presumption that all lesbian parents intend such an arrangement. These are issues that scholars, legislatures, and law reform bodies have grappled with for several decades. Initial contributions tended to focus on the security of the lesbian nuclear family through the use of parental presumptions applicable in situations where a child has been conceived via donor insemination. In more recent years, however, a growing number of law reform commissions have sought to combine nuclear family security with a degree of flexibility that would enable known donors to play a legally recognized role in their children's lives.

In this chapter, I begin my exploration of parenting law reform designed to meet the unique needs of planned lesbian families. The chapter begins by taking an initial step back from the law reform debate to consider the attitudes of the mothers towards law and legal engagement. As noted in earlier chapters, while developing a law reform proposal was a goal of the research, I did not want to presume that the mothers whole-heartedly supported engaging with the law. In fact, given the current tendency among many of Canada's most vocal lesbian and gay rights organizations to focus almost exclusively on achieving social change through legal mechanisms (primarily litigation), I felt it was important that the mothers have an opportunity to express their views about the vigorous pursuit of law. Given the tentative willingness on the part of most of the mothers to pursue a law reform agenda, particularly a legisla-tive one, the second half of the chapter explores already existing, as well as proposed, law reform. It focuses primarily on legislative efforts in other jurisdictions and on proposals for reform that have emerged from legal academics and a variety of law reform commissions.

Attitudes towards Law

Law is very much a part of the lives of all the mothers I interviewed. In fact, all but two of the thirty-six families have engaged with law in one way or another, and almost all of the mothers rated legal recognition of their parental relationships as a high or medium priority in their lives. In most cases, the mothers' legal engagement involved entering into a second-parent adoption. In a significant number of families, however, mothers have engaged further with law by entering into donor, guard-ianship, and separation agreements, or by completing wills or powers of attorney. Because of the significance of law as a social institution in Western societies, the mothers understand legal recognition as capable of conferring both legitimacy and rights on their families, something that many of them desire. What I found, however, was that the mothers' relationships with and attitudes towards law are far more complicated than might have been presumed in this era of frequent lesbian and gay engagement with legal strategies. Despite the potential benefits offered by law, few of the mothers understand law to be solely positive. For example, many of them are distrustful of the legal system and those who administered it, particularly when it comes to dealing with lesbian families. They therefore doubt whether legislative reform would necessarily lead to more favourable decision making by judges. Others view existing law reform strategies – primarily those based on equality-seeking litigation – as assimilationist or incapable, on their own, of creating any real understanding or acceptance of their families within wider society. Thus, the mothers' concerns about law relate primarily to their perceptions of what goes on in court. They have reservations about both the process of legal decision making and the nature of courtroom strategies. The mothers were far less critical of legislative reform, though they still worry about judicial interpretation of any legislation that might be introduced. What is clear, however, is that the mothers' concerns about law, broadly defined, are sufficient to make them reluctant to put all of their hope, time, and resources into law reform.

"Legitimacy" through Legal Recognition

Whether or not they see it as entirely desirable, a significant number of the mothers understand the legal recognition of their parenting relationships as capable of conferring upon them a certain "legitimacy" or "normalcy," particularly outside of the home. Because they assume that members of the public are more supportive of familial relationships that are legally recognized, they expect legal recognition of lesbian parental relationships to produce greater overall acceptance. Antonia, a non-biological mother, explained this expectation:

> I think that people tend to see the law as sort of God. You know if you're legally their parent. And I think people even use those terms. "Are you *legally* their parent?" You know, so I think that that's why the same-sex marriage thing I think will change attitudes. 'Cause I think if it's legal, then people, I don't know. I'm making an assumption but I think that there are people who kind of sit on the fence and if the law is such then they'll say, "Oh, okay, then it must be okay." It's law. So I think the same thing with parenting. If there's legal things in place that say this is the definition of a family and these are legally parents then I think there might be some more acceptance [by] people who are kind of on that edge.

The social support that might come with the legal recognition of their parental relationships is also viewed by the mothers as important to their children. For example, the mothers feel that legal recognition might give their children an additional tool when confronted about their families in the playground or elsewhere in life. As Paula explained, the legal recognition of her son's two mothers would give him a "right to be" when "out there [in public]." Paula does not think that parental recognition would change the nature of their relationships within the home but that it would make the family feel more secure in its dealings with outsiders.

Many of the mothers also see the legal recognition of their parental relationships as capable of making those relationships more real to extended family members, though they emphasized that within their own homes, their parental relationships are solidified through caregiving, not legal documentation. However, recognition *outside* of the immediate family unit remains important, particularly for non-biological mothers whose parents often do not consider their daughter's non-biological children to be their grandchildren. Paula, a biological mother, explained this with reference to her partner's family:

> I think [the second-parent adoption] is important symbolically. Like, I think it helped Belinda's parents arrive at the fact that she actually was a parent. That she, it gave them something they could understand. If someone adopts a child then they have an official capacity, right?

Similarly, Antonia, who had her children before any form of legal recognition was available, stated that she thinks her parents "would have been way more on board had there been some legal things in place." Thus, there is something about the officialness of the law – the "law as God" perception – that gives extended family members permission to overlook biology and treat their daughter's non-biological children as their grandchildren.

Legal recognition of their parental relationships, particularly if immediate and automatic, is also understood by the mothers to afford them a level of family security they do not feel they currently have. By far the biggest concern of the mothers, with almost all of them citing it as their most significant legal issue, is the precarious status of the non-biological mother. This concern is exacerbated by the lack of clarity around the legal status of known donors. While various forms of legal recognition are available to the non-biological mothers, they are not without problems. Second-parent adoption involves delays, fees, and legal representation, as well as the consent of the biological mother (and biological father, if known), while birth certificate registration for both mothers is not available in all provinces and its legal value is uncertain. Furthermore, neither second-parent adoption nor the gender-neutral birth certificate adequately addresses the legal status of known donors. By contrast, presumptive legislative provisions that, given certain circumstances, automatically confer legal status on the non-biological mother are expected by the mothers to offer them a level of family security that is, at present, beyond their reach.

Reservations about Legal Engagement and Law Reform

Despite the advantages legal recognition is seen to confer, the vast majority of the mothers expressed at least some reservation about the prospect of legal engagement. As noted in Chapter 3, their concerns focused primarily on the quality of judicial decision making and the litigation process. They expressed far fewer concerns about legislative reform, perhaps because it avoids what they see as the highly discretionary nature of the courts. While almost all of the mothers have reservations about law, their concerns do not prevent them from supporting a law reform agenda. However, they approached the prospect of reform with caution and a healthy dose of cynicism. Significantly, the mothers refuse to put all of their faith in law, preferring to see it as one part of a much larger strategy for change.

The most consistent reservation the mothers expressed about law relates to their profound distrust of what they described as "the legal system." Their distrust centres largely on judges who are seen as unrepresentative, pro-father, and able to make decisions based on their personal biases. These concerns about judges prevent them from seeing legal engagement, particularly via litigation, in an entirely positive light. The following conversation with Emily and Lesley, whose known donor is largely uninvolved, was a common interaction. It emerged in the context of Lesley, a social worker with considerable courtroom experience, feeling very unsafe about the potential power of their donor, despite the fact that they have several legal measures in place.

> Interviewer: So in a sense you don't trust the legal system.
> Lesley: Oh, I do not trust the legal system. Actually, I can tell you that for sure. I do not trust it.
> Interviewer: Don't trust it for anything?
> Lesley: No.

Lesley's distrust of the legal system, which is shared by her partner, has not been overcome by having a donor contract, a legal marriage, and both of the mothers' names on their son's birth certificate. The driving force behind Lesley and Emily's distrust appears to be what they see as the bias of judges, coupled with the enormous amount of discretion they enjoy. In Lesley and Emily's view, parental recognition achieves little if there is no simultaneous attention to the ideological biases of judges. Emily explained:

> It depends on who the judge is, in terms of their own biases. They are not unbiased. And they're usually in their sixties or seventies. So right now I'm guessing ... [they] have been in the legal system for their entire lives, quite sheltered frankly. So how can they actually have any sense of what society is actually like for the people they represent?

Lesley and Emily's views are shared by a number of the mothers, particularly those who feel vulnerable to the legal incursions of known donors. There is a strong perception among the mothers that sex, sexuality, class, age, and values separates judges from the lesbian experience of parenting and that the chasm between a judge's experiences and their own may be too wide to cross. Elisha, for example, decided to avoid law altogether on the basis that the legal system is far less likely than the lesbian and gay community to hold the members of her large and diverse family accountable. As she explained, "I felt like if anyone is gonna be able to say [to the donor], 'What are you doing being an asshole?', you know, it was gonna be the gay and lesbian community. It wasn't gonna be anybody in the legal system." Mothers like Elisha, therefore, do not see the legal recognition of their parenting relationships as any great panacea because they do not expect that once incorporated into the legal framework, their families will necessarily be understood or respected.

A second reason for the mothers' reluctance to engage with law seems to stem from the fact that the dominant approach to law reform adopted by lesbian and gay rights organizations involves arguing that lesbians and gay men are "the same as" heterosexuals. Thus, in the mothers' eyes, legal engagement often has the effect of forcing lesbian and gay families to submit to heterosexual norms. In Christy's mind, this is unacceptable and will ultimately lead to exclusions:

> It annoys me that there's all this, like heterosexual kind of rules that have developed over the years from heterosexual history. And it's just put on couples that are gay and lesbian. I think there's some people that are gonna slot in, but in the end gay and lesbian relationships do not slot into the heterosexual mould.

Christy resists the notion that lesbian and gay relationships are "the same as" heterosexual relationships, and is uncomfortable with the existing law's "heterosexual rules" being applied to same-sex couples. Ultimately, she supports law reform only if it displaces the heterosexual framework. Thus, her concern is not with law per se, but rather with the litigation strategies adopted (whether by choice or necessity) by various gay rights advocates. Expressing a similar sentiment, Sylvie argued that she could only "believe in" law reform if it involves a complete rethinking of family law. Moulding the current framework to fit lesbian and gay needs – the strategy most commonly adopted – is insufficient to break down what she sees as the ideological assumptions embedded within the system. She explained her perception of family law as outdated:

> The [current family law system] is archaic. It no longer applies. Hasn't for centuries. We need to scrap it already. We need to acknowledge

the fact that, that our times have gone beyond what the law can handle and we need to actually reinvent a body of law that, that [reflects] reality, not delusion.

Sylvie went on to note that reform strategies that accept the existing family law framework will only ever involve assimilation for lesbian parents or, for those who cannot or refuse to assimilate, exclusion.

Finally, over half of the mothers refuse to put all of their energy and hope into the law reform process because they feel that parenting law reform – whether achieved via litigation or legislation – will not, *by itself*, produce significant or immediate progressive social change, which they defined as a change in societal attitudes towards lesbian mothers and their families. In other words, this group of mothers distinguished between being granted legal recognition and being accepted, supported, and understood by those around them. As Sam noted, even after laws are passed and legal recognition is granted at a "face-to-face, individual, at-the-moment level," discrimination and a lack of acceptance may prevail. In fact, many of the mothers anticipate that societal acceptance and understanding will take a considerable amount of time and feel that for many members of the public, it will not be until they have some direct contact with same-sex families that their attitudes might begin to change. As Julia noted, "I don't know that you can just change the laws and expect it [social change] to happen." Some of these mothers speculated that social change might even take several generations after a law is passed to emerge, though they were encouraged by the speed with which attitudes towards same-sex relationships have improved in Canada since the legislative reform of recent years. There was also a general consensus among this group that law reform is only one part of a much larger process of social change that includes ongoing political activism, public visibility, education, and public awareness campaigns. Thus, legal engagement is not understood by these mothers as a means to an end but rather as a single tool within a much larger strategy. As Christy put it, "You gotta do political activism and legal work *together*." Thus, while legal recognition is seen by some of these mothers as providing them with the foundation of legitimacy often necessary to carry out these additional political activities, most feel that legal recognition alone is not enough.

Thus, while the mothers support law reform in general, many of them do not regard it as capable, on its own, of solving all of their familial recognition concerns. Furthermore, they feel that if law reform is to be pursued, a complete rethinking of the current system is required. Simply mapping lesbian families onto the heterosexual norm is an inadequate solution. Sylvie noted that "[law reform] cannot be built on what we have right now. What we have right now has to be dismantled first."

Existing Legal Trends: Law Reform Initiatives Elsewhere
This section discusses lesbian parenting law reform initiatives to date, particularly those that have focused on building new legislative models that do not take existing norms as their starting point. These models provide the backdrop to the practical law reform discussions outlined in Chapter 5.

The Academic Debates
Some of the earliest attempts to develop a law reform strategy designed to recognize the parenting relationships found within planned lesbian families emerged among legal academics in the United States in the 1990s. Pioneered primarily by Nancy Polikoff, and later taken up by Fred Bernstein and Paula Ettelbrick,[1] the debate was triggered by a series of US court decisions involving both intra-lesbian disputes and disputes between lesbian mothers and their donors.[2] In all cases, biological parenthood triumphed over the planned lesbian family: biological mothers were favoured over non-biological co-mothers and (often distant) relationships between donors and children were preferred over social relationships between lesbian co-mothers and their children.

With little legal or social support for creating a new legal regime to determine parentage within planned lesbian families, Polikoff initially focused on ways in which the existing law could be utilized by lesbian mothers to protect their parenting relationships. Her early offerings included proposals based on equitable estoppel, *in loco parentis,* the concept of third-party status, and a form of step-parent adoption.[3] Underlying each proposal was the belief that "courts should redefine parenthood to include anyone in a functional parental relationship that a legally recognized parent created with the intent that an additional parent-child relationship exist."[4] In other words, legal parentage should be awarded to those who intentionally take on the responsibilities of parenthood ("functional parenthood") rather than those who share a biological relationship with the child. Polikoff's initial proposals were, however, limited by the parameters of the existing legal principles she sought to expand. In her subsequent work, she attempted to break free of the existing legal framework, focusing instead on the possibility of drafting new laws that would enable lesbian couples and single women – whether through private contracting, second-parent adoption, or legislative presumptions grounded in the intentions of the parties – to shape legal parentage in ways that would meet their unique needs.[5]

Polikoff's most provocative contribution, and the one that perhaps resonates most in the current climate, is the suggestion that statutory presumptions, supplemented by the enforcement of private agreements, should be introduced to counteract the biological assumptions that typically inform the assignment of legal parentage.[6] Not restricting its application to situations in which the child is conceived through donor insemination, Polikoff's proposal included two key elements: (1) that where the legally recognized parent intends to create a functional parent relationship, and the functional parent consents, a parental relationship should be presumptively established; and (2) that conception through donor insemination confers no parental rights on the donor. Corollary to the second element, Polikoff proposed that courts should specifically enforce agreements made by sperm donors to forego parental status. At the same time, courts should uphold agreements that provide donors with a limited "non-parental" relationship with the child on the basis that family structures beyond the nuclear family should be accommodated.

Polikoff's work was built upon by Fred Bernstein, though Bernstein's proposal reflects his additional concern with the rights of donors.[7] While Bernstein generally endorsed Polikoff's desire to expand the traditional concept of family through the legal recognition of lesbian co-mothers, he was concerned that her analysis did not give significant weight to the relationship between an involved known donor and his child. In Bernstein's view, donors who are regularly involved in their children's lives occupy a significant space between father and stranger that is also worthy of legal protection. He thus argues that any law reform proposal designed to respond to the unique circumstances of lesbian and gay families must address three primary needs:

> (1) involved sperm donors need to know that their relationships with their children (even if initially unintended or only periodic) will be preserved; (2) lesbian mothers need to know that the law will protect the families they create; and (3) children of donors and lesbian mothers need to know that relationships with adults they have come to view as important – including relationships with involved biological progenitors – will be protected.[8]

Bernstein translates these three needs into a legislative "model presumption" that would provide a right of contact to involved donors who have developed a healthy relationship with a child and who are subsequently barred from continuing that relationship by the child's legal parents.[9] Thus, Bernstein's model is retrospective: it applies only when already established access is later denied. The model includes three presumptions: First, a known donor who currently exercises access with his child is deemed an "involved donor." Second, absent unfitness, permitting an involved donor contact at a level that approximates his involvement in the child's life prior to the conflict is presumed to be in the child's best interests. Third, permitting the involved donor access (or any other) rights beyond those that are already being exercised is presumed not to be in the child's best interests.[10] While Bernstein's model is designed to apply only in situations of conflict and thus fails to facilitate legal certainty at the time of a child's birth, it represents one of the first attempts to draft legislation that permits deviation from the nuclear family model without simultaneously undermining the planned lesbian family (where one exists).

Since Bernstein's attempts to deal with the legal status of known donors, there has been increasing interest in creating reform proposals that protect the core nuclear unit, whether a lesbian couple or single mother, but do not preclude the possibility of recognizing additional adult/child relationships, whether parental or something less. For example, while not dealing specifically with donor recognition or lesbian parenting, American family law scholar Martha Fineman has proposed a parentage model that prioritizes the core unit of caregiver and dependant, but simultaneously allows for various opt-in relationships, including non-parental ones.[11] Fineman argues that the fundamental familial unit deserving of the protection of law is the nurturing unit of caregiver and dependant, exemplified by the mother/child dyad.[12] Her choice of the mother/child dyad is based on her argument that this unit, because of its dependent nature, is inherently vulnerable.[13] By drawing the family boundary around the mother/child dyad, Fineman demands that it, rather than the marital unit, attract the special and preferred treatment of the state.[14] However, any additional familial arrangements, whether parental or not, could be secured through private contract.[15] Thus, biological mothers would have the option of creating contractual relationships with conjugal partners or other adults that give those parties some form of legal recognition within the family. Fineman's proposal is designed to maintain the integrity of, and draw attention to, the vulnerability of the mother/child unit while simultaneously allowing for additional familial relationships to be legally recognized.

A similar proposal was suggested by Alison Harvison Young, who argues that the law should protect the "core unit" of the family, however that might be defined, in order to allocate support obligations, testamentary issues, and decision-making authority.[16] However, this identification should not "preclude the development of supplementary roles which could be legally recognized and which could generate significant links and support systems for children."[17] Fineman is also not alone in suggesting that private contracting might have an important role to play in family construction, particularly when conception is achieved through some form of alternative conception method. Writing about heterosexual families who conceive using artificial insemination or in vitro fertilization, both Marjorie Maguire Schulz and Janet Dolgin suggest that private contracts, because they indicate the parties' intentions, would reduce the legal confusion surrounding intention-based, or non-biological, parenting.[18]

The most comprehensive, and recent, academic foray into the legal recognition of lesbian-headed families comes from Australian scholar Jenni Millbank, who rejects Polikoff's reliance on the concept of the functional family in favour of legislative presumptions grounded in what she argues are the *most likely* intentions of lesbian-headed families.[19] In other words, her model is grounded in intentionality but does not require parties to produce private agreements or evidence of their conduct as proof of their intention. Millbank's argument is premised on the failure of "functional family" – the claim that rights should attach to, or flow from, the way a relationship functions rather than being limited to its legal form – to protect lesbian parenting relationships. She argues that while lesbians and gay men have had enormous legal success utilizing the functional family model when seeking rights from the state, particularly with regard to adult-relationship recognition, the concept has had limited utility in the intra-parenting context. In fact, the notion of functional family has often been misused by birth mothers or completely ignored by courts in disputes between lesbian mothers and known sperm donors.

Millbank attributes the failure of functional family in the lesbian parenting context to the ideological trends that currently dominate both Australian and international family law. Drawing on cases from Australia, the United Kingdom, the United States, and New Zealand involving intra-lesbian disputes or disputes between lesbian mothers and donors, Millbank argues that "the rise of the fathers' rights movements and increasing emphasis on biological family gives both discursive and legal authority to essentialised, gendered and symbolic status claims by biological parents, valorizing distant biological fathers over mother-led family units, and separated biological mothers over non-biological mothers."[20] While she does not directly reference Canada, the concerns Millbank raises clearly resonate in a Canadian context.

Given the misuses and marginalization of functional family in the parenting context, Millbank turns to the concept of intentionality as an alternative method for ascribing legal parentage. However, unlike Fineman and Polikoff, she shies away from an emphasis on intention gleaned through private contracting, preferring some form of "automatic, universal and stable legal recognition for co-mothers" based on what she *presumes* to be their pre-conception intentions.[21] Her rationale for creating what is essentially a presumptive model of intention is that the attempt to conceive within a lesbian relationship is more often than not a shared enterprise between the two women, marked by consent to the conception taking place within the women's relationship. In other words, Millbank argues that conceiving a child within a lesbian relationship *implies* an intention on the part of the two women to be equal co-parents. She prefers such an approach over one that attempts to "discover" the intentions of the parties based on pre-birth or post-birth practices for a number of reasons. First, she points to the fact that while lesbians often define the donor's role prior to conception via some sort of agreement, they rarely address the co-mother's role in writing, possibly because they assume that the donor has some existing legal status while the co-mother does not. Thus, although most lesbian couples intend to parent together, they rarely have any documentation to suggest that this is actually the case. Second, while donor agreements are becoming more common, many arrangements are never formalized. Even when they are, once conflict arises, it often becomes clear that although the parties may have appeared to agree on paper, the written words meant very different things to each individual. For example, numerous cases have demonstrated that agreeing to "donor involvement" without further explanation of what that might entail can result in dramatically different views as to both the amount and nature of donor access. Finally, even when intention is "clearly expressed, mutually understood and evidenced," it is not given even attention or appropriate weight by judges. In donor versus mother(s) cases, courts frequently apply a "but for" test to determine the donor's intention, asking whether the man would have agreed to donate if his role was to be confined to that of a donor rather than a traditional father. By contrast, a "but for" analysis is never applied to the mothers, with no court considering whether the mothers would have agreed to conceiving with that particular donor if they thought he would be a traditional father rather than an occasionally involved known donor. In other words, some intentions are privileged over others, with biological parents generally taking precedence over social parents.

For the reasons discussed above, Millbank argues that "privatized binding pre-conception contracts placing the burden of consciously negotiating individual agreements onto each and every lesbian-led family should not be contemplated."[22] Instead, legal presumptions of parental status that embody the *likely* intentions of most lesbian-headed families should apply automatically. However, the presumptions may need to be tempered by discretionary powers and by the ability to "opt in" to additional recognition mechanisms for those families who do not conform to the nuclear model. Ultimately, Millbank develops four presumptions, with the first two serving as "bright line" presumptions and the last two being informed by a "child's best interests" inquiry:[23]

1 If two women are in a committed cohabiting relationship (whether or not formalized) and the non-birth mother consents to her partner's attempt to conceive through assisted conception, she is the second parent of the resulting child or children.

2 The biological father (whether known or unknown) is not a parent if assisted conception is used.

3 Additional parents can be added through an opt-in process (with the consent of the birth mother and co-mother).

4 The recognition of other adult-child (non-parental) relationships can still be achieved if necessary through a functional analysis.

While Millbank acknowledges that her presumptions may be both under- and over-inclusive in their purview, she favours a presumptive approach, grounded in assumed intention, because it provides a "starting point, a relatively level, predictable and lesbian-centred point from which disputes can be addressed." In particular, it would likely shift judicial understandings of family such that "if and when a functional family analysis is undertaken regarding other adults, the reification of genetic ties and gendered parenting ... would not continue."[24]

The Legislative Trends

While there has been significant academic debate over the years about the ways in which the law might be reformed to reflect the realities of non-biological, intention-based parenting, few legislatures have taken up the issue. Those that have tend to focus exclusively on the legal parentage of children born via assisted conception to heterosexual parents. For example, while several Canadian provinces have legislated with regard to parentage in cases of assisted conception within heterosexual families,[25] the only province to do the same for lesbian families is

Quebec.[26] Introduced in 2002 as part of the province's civil union legislation, Quebec's reformed filiation laws determine legal parentage in situations in which a child is born to either an individual or spouses (either opposite or same sex) through some form of "assisted procreation."[27] At the heart of the Quebec legislation is the concept of a "parental project," which "exists from the moment a person alone decides or spouses by mutual consent decide, in order to have a child, to resort to the genetic material of a person who is not party to the parental project."[28] Where a parental project is found to exist, the parties to it are presumed to be the child's legal parents.[29] At the same time, any parental rights of the donor of the genetic material, provided the donor is not a party to the parental project, are extinguished.[30] Read together, these provisions protect the intending parents from unwanted donor involvement while also ensuring that donors avoid any unintended obligations, such as child support liability.[31] The Quebec model differs from most presumption-based legislation addressing assisted conception by including the additional concept of a parental project. In doing so, it places the focus on the joint intention of the parties to the project rather than simply the consent of the non-biological parent. It thus captures the importance of joint intention explicitly in a way that other models, such as Millbank's, may not.

Although the Quebec law is by far the most comprehensive and inclusive presumption-based parenting law available in Canada, it remains a limited model. While able to accommodate the needs of both same-sex couples and single mothers, it continues to limit parenting to two legal parents. For example, there is no possibility of a parental project between three or four individuals. It also does not envisage a known donor playing any legally recognized role in a child's life, except in circumstances where he or she is a party to the parental project and thus a legal parent. Finally, the Quebec provisions limit parenthood to single women or spouses. Article 538 of the *Civil Code* makes it clear that a parental project can only be undertaken by "spouses" or by a woman alone, preventing a birth mother and a non-conjugal partner from agreeing to parent together.

Beyond Quebec, there is little by way of legislative recognition for planned lesbian families in Canada. As noted in Chapter 1, although a number of provinces have legislation governing birth registration for children born to lesbian couples, only Quebec addresses legal parentage directly or the implications for parentage of using a known donor. It is worth noting, however, that at least one province, British Columbia, is in the process of reviewing its legal parentage laws and has given specific attention to planned lesbian families.

As part of its review of the provincial *Family Relations Act*, the Ministry of Attorney General in British Columbia produced a White Paper that contains significant reforms in the area of legal parentage.[32] The proposed legislation includes a presumption of parentage in favour of a lesbian co-mother in situations where the co-mother's female partner conceives via assisted reproduction. The legislation also includes a presumption that a sperm donor has no legal status with regard to a child born via his donation, though it does not explicitly address the status of known donors. Finally, the proposed reform permits the legal recognition of three-parent families. If the latter is part of the final legislation, British Columbia will become the first jurisdiction in the world to expressly recognize through legislation the possibility of a three-parent family. The White Paper proposal has not yet been debated in Parliament and it is therefore difficult to know whether all of the provisions will receive parliamentary support.

Outside of Canada, a wider variety of parental recognition models are available to lesbian-headed families. One of the most recent and comprehensive examples can be found in the state of Victoria, Australia. Introduced in 2008 following several years of public consultation through the Victorian Law Reform Commission, the *Assisted Reproductive Treatment Act* represents some of the most cutting-edge parentage legislation in the world.[33] While the act covers numerous topics, from surrogacy to posthumous conception, it explicitly clarifies the legal status of both non-biological mothers and donors. First, it includes a presumption that donors are not the legal parents of any child born as a result of their donation.[34] This presumption applies to children conceived by heterosexual and same-sex couples as well as single women. Second, the non-biological mother is presumed, providing she consents to the procedure, to be the child's legal parent and can appear on the child's birth certificate.[35] Both presumptions apply whether the child was conceived at a fertility clinic or via self-insemination at home, ensuring that known donors are treated identically to anonymous donors for the purposes of legal parentage.[36] Finally, the presumptions are irrebuttable, preventing an individual judge from interpreting the situation differently. Similar legislation exists in other Australian states, though none explicitly includes known donors or single mothers within the framework.[37]

The only other jurisdiction to address the legal status of known donors is New Zealand. Unlike the Victorian legislation, the New Zealand law, the *Care of Children Act* 2004 (NZ), acknowledges that in some families, known donors play a significant, albeit non-parental, role in their child's life. It thus allows a known donor, in a discrete set of circumstances, to opt in as a non-parental figure with the presumptive parents' consent. It does so through the recognition of written parenting agreements. Section 41 of the *Care of Children Act* expressly sanctions formal agreements that address the role of a known donor in a child's life, including the amount of contact the donor will have with the child.[38] The agreement itself cannot be enforced under the act, but a court may, with the agreement of all parties to it, make a consent order that embodies some or all of the terms of the agreement.[39] That order, insofar as it relates to contact with the child, can be enforced under the act as if it were a parenting order relating to contact.[40] Importantly, neither an agreement nor an order has any impact on the donor's legal status with regard to the child. Neither enables him to become a legal parent, nor on their own do they produce guardianship status. Although the terms of the agreement can be varied by a court and the "best interests of the child" principle will always prevail, section 41 permits lesbian women and their donors to carve out a role for the donor prior to conception that will, in most cases, be respected by a court.

Law Reform Commissions

A number of law reform bodies have also addressed legal parentage within planned lesbian families, producing some of the most radical solutions. For example, the reform proposals put forward in a position paper of the Victorian (Australia) Law Reform Commission (as part of a larger reform process) were much more progressive than the eventual legislation, which focused on recognizing the lesbian nuclear family only. In fact, both the New Zealand Law Commission (NZLC) and the Victorian Law Reform Commission (VLRC) proposed legislative frameworks that would enable the planned lesbian family to extend beyond the nuclear unit to include, with the consent of the presumptive parents, known donors with parental status.[41] For example, in its *Position Paper Two* on parentage in the context of assisted reproductive technology, the VLRC recommended that in addition to parental presumptions in favour of a single mother or couple who conceive via alternative insemination, a donor be permitted to "opt in" as the legal parent of a child.[42] However, a donor could only do so with the consent of the birth mother and her partner (if she has one), and the application to opt in must be made as early as possible in the child's life. Thus, in circumstances where the birth mother, her partner, and the donor *intend* the donor to be recognized as one of the child's parents, the donor should be able to secure all of the legal rights and responsibilities of parenthood.[43] It was expected that only a few families would adopt such a model and that in most instances, it would be lesbian mothers who were co-parenting with a known donor. The VLRC felt, however, that this model should be equally available to heterosexual parents. In making its recommendations, the VLRC supported the possibility of a child having three legal parents. Responding to suggestions that this may increase family law disputes, the VLRC noted that an opt-in model might actually reduce potential conflict "because the opt-in process would assist the parties to reflect on and clarify their roles and expectations in respect of the child from the outset."[44]

The VLRC did not recommend in its position paper the extending of any kind of *non-parental* recognition to known donors. The commission considered the issue, noting that many donors are involved in their children's lives without being legal parents, but concluded that the legal protection of non-parental donor/child relationships is best achieved through existing legal frameworks. For example, it was suggested that known donors could apply for a parenting order, which could include access, under section 65C of the federal *Family Law Act* 1975 (Cth). This section allows "any other person concerned with the care, welfare or development of the child" to seek a parenting order.[45] The VLRC did express some concern about the use of this provision by donors, particularly in circumstances where the donor was not intended to play a role in the child's life.[46] Because the Australian *Family Law Act* does not require a parenting order applicant to be a legal parent, donors could easily frustrate the intentions of a lesbian family through a section 65C application. However, because the VLRC could not recommend amendments to federal laws, it was unable to suggest a more appropriate framework. The VLRC ultimately recommended that the most effective method by which to reduce uncertainty in this area was through the provision of legal information, counselling, and advice to women and their donors.[47]

The NZLC also addressed the possibility of multiple-parent families, but it was far more specific about the process for "opting in" than the VLRC. Though ultimately rejected by the government, the NZLC proposed a two-stage process for a donor of genetic material to become a legal parent in situations where the donor and mothers had agreed to such an arrangement.[48] The first stage involved three elements: (1) filing with the court *prior to the child's conception* a sworn statement by the lesbian couple that the donor will be the child's genetic parent and that they want the donor to be a legal parent, along with a sworn statement from the donor that he will be the child's genetic parent and wants to be a legal parent; (2) evidence that all parties received independent legal advice, as well as counselling, about issues raised by their planned family; and (3) an agreement between the couple and donor about contact between the donor and the child or the role of the donor in the child's upbringing. If satisfied that the evidence is in order, a Family Court registrar would give interim approval to the appointment of the donor as a legal parent. The second stage of the process would occur after the child's birth, at which point proof of the donor's genetic parentage would be furnished and the registrar would approve the appointment. The donor would then be registered, along with the couple, as a legal parent. Like the VLRC, the NZLC did not address the possibility of non-parental recognition, perhaps because such an arrangement is already provided for in the *Care of Children Act*.

Conclusion

While few jurisdictions have explicitly addressed legal parentage in the context of lesbian parenting, the models that do exist, whether actually in force or still at the proposal stage, provide an excellent starting point for Canadian reform. The existing models not only address the legal issues raised by nuclear family parenting, but also seek to grapple with multiple-parent families and the legal status of known donors. The consistent theme that runs through all of them is the emphasis on pre-conception intention, whether explicit (as in the case of donor agreements) or implicit (as Millbank proposes). Thus, legal parentage in the context of alternative insemination should be determined not by reference to biology but by the intentions of the parties involved in the conception process. The key then becomes how intention is determined: via donor agreements, non-birth parent consent, behavioural patterns, or presumption.

Largely absent from the more recent proposals is any consideration of caregiving, a fundamental element of parenting identified by the mothers I interviewed, though Millbank's reliance on presumptive intention is grounded in the assumption that lesbian couples intend to share caregiving. The absence of any reference to caregiving in the proposals is probably a result of the fact that each model is designed to apply at birth, making an analysis of caregiving patterns impossible. Excluding caregiving from the analysis also limits the ability of a court to abuse such a provision, as Millbank argues they often do when applying functional family arguments. In other words, a judge cannot use occasional access visits by a donor as evidence of parental caregiving or argue that because a non-biological mother is engaged in paid work, she is not as committed to caregiving as a biological mother who works within the home.

The proposals discussed in this chapter formed the backdrop to the discussions I had with the mothers about law reform. Having determined that they were tentatively open to the reform process, the next stage was to consider which model resonated most with their lives. This was achieved by presenting the mothers with a variety of reform models derived from the existing literature. Chapter 5 considers their responses.

(Re)forming Law's Family   **5**

Having established that the mothers were interested in pursuing a law reform agenda, the next task was to determine what that reform might look like. The discussions I had with the mothers about law reform built on the earlier, more general, questions about familial definitions, with the key issue being how the mothers' often broad definitions might translate into a practical law reform context. The conversation tended to be twofold. First, the mothers addressed some of the "big picture" questions posed by law reform. Two issues dominated these discussions. The first was whether the mothers' endorsement of multiple-parent families could be appropriately translated into a legislative model capable of recognizing multiple parents or non-parental figures, such as an involved known donor, without jeopardizing the security of the lesbian family. The second issue was what form legislative recognition should take: Is it preferable to have a presumptive model that provides automatic legal recognition to the lesbian couple or single mother (like the Victoria, Australia, model), an "opt-in" registration model that requires a positive action on the part of all parents (similar to the NZLC model), or some combination of both? Once these more philosophical issues had been resolved, the mothers were asked to respond to three specific law reform proposals. Based on their discussions of these models and their broader philosophical concerns about what they hoped law reform might achieve, a final proposal was created. Given that most of the children in these families were too young to express their own views as to how their families might be defined, the final proposal reflects solely the needs and views of their parents. As the children get older, they may define "family" in ways that cohere *or* contrast with their parents. At the same time, it can be argued that it is in a child's best interests to enjoy the certainty and stability provided by laws that extend legal recognition to the individuals who bear primary responsibility for their care.

The chapter begins by discussing the first of the "big picture" questions: Should the law be able to recognize multiple-parent families? The discussion focuses on the mothers' approach to this question once it was framed directly in the context of legislative reform. The chapter then turns to the form legislation might take, discussing the mothers' responses to three specific law reform models, each of which represents a different approach to legal inclusion. Finally, drawing from the mothers' recommendations as to both form and content, I present a comprehensive law reform proposal.

Expanding the Legal Family: The Recognition of Multiple Parental and Non-Parental Figures

The vast majority of the mothers interviewed (twenty-nine of the thirty-six families) felt that parenting should not be limited to a two-parent model. When asked to reflect on this position in a legal context, the mothers maintained their conviction, though not without certain qualifications. The mothers' support for the legal recognition of multiple parents tended to derive from the fact that for some families this was the reality of their lives. Multiple-parent recognition was therefore the only legal model that was, as Rhona put it, "truly descriptive of [their] circumstances." In most instances, the mothers were referring to families that included two mothers and an actively involved "donor dad" (and maybe his partner), though a number of them also mentioned blended families, Aboriginal families, and the extended family networks of certain immigrant groups within Canada.

Given the fact that at least some Canadian families already include three or more parents, and the vulnerability of these families to having contrary legal understandings imposed upon them, the mothers felt that the law should be reformed so that it has the capacity to extend legal recognition to multiple parents if that is what the parties agree to. To do otherwise, especially in the face of actual parental responsibility being exercised, seemed "wrong." Paula reflected on a particular family in this situation:

> I can think of one, one family that I know [that] has made an impact on me, where it's two mothers and a father who co-parent. I think just seeing their family and how, how that works, it just seems wrong to me that they can't have that [legal recognition]. And it totally seems plausible to me that other families would become formed that were similar to that. So I think, yeah, that the law should recognize the parents who are active in taking responsibility.

In advocating for the multiple-parent model, Sylvie also focused on the importance of giving legal recognition to all of the individuals who are "taking responsibility" for a child. Expanding on her earlier discussion of the concept of the front-line parent, Sylvie explained her commitment to multiple (as well as single) parent recognition:

> I think that, again, if we come back to my definition of the front, who the front-line parent is. That could be one, two, three, it depends. There are circumstances where the front-line parents are a handful of people and that works very well for everybody. And in that context full legal rights should be accorded to each and every one of those people. The definition of the nuclear family right now does not serve anyone and within that definition it is very well ingrained that it can only be two. Even one is considered quite outlandish. You know, so I think we need to scrap that altogether.

Mothers like Paula and Sylvie endorse the multiple-parent model even though their own families resemble the two-parent structure. This possible contradiction between belief and practice was explained by a number of the mothers, who indicated that they might have chosen a known donor or encouraged their known donor to be more involved had the law provided some protection for the two-mother family. However, the lack of legal clarity meant that they did not feel safe making such a choice. A number of the mothers who supported multiple-parent recognition also feel that their own parenting practices should not limit the options available to others. Maureen is one of these mothers:

> Yeah, I mean certainly for us the two-parent model would work but I don't think everybody should be limited to our model. I don't know a lot of three- or four-parent models that have ... I mean I just don't have a lot of experience with that but I, I know there are some out there. And I think they should have the right to have legal protection as well.

While the vast majority of the mothers supported the abandonment of the two-parent model, there was some concern about how a more fluid model might work in the context of law. A number of the mothers, including the seven who expressed serious reservations about adopting a multiple-parent model, regarded its legal application as "really complicated." Most frequently, they noted the increased potential for conflict once three or four adults are legally involved in a child's life. As Delia, who preferred the two-parent model, argued, "It's hard enough to get two people to agree on parenting. You throw in a third person. Oh!" Others noted the additional challenges of day-to-day decision making when multiple parties have a legal right to have their views taken into account. As Michaela put it, making sure everyone has an equal say in parenting decisions could "just get out of hand." There was also some fear among mothers, including several who supported abandoning the two-parent model, that permitting the legal recognition of multiple parents might result in donors being given rights in circumstances where they are not actually parenting. Emily, for example, endorsed the application of the multiple-parent model in situations where all of the adults are actively involved in parenting. However, she expressed considerable concern about the potential for donors who are not actually caring for a child to assert their right to be recognized as a legal parent on the basis of biology alone. She feared that if such a situation were to arise, the donor would succeed in his claim:

> I think it should be flexible but if it came to the court system and [the donor] says, "Hey, I could be a parent. I'm here, why are you not letting me be?" That would set up a system where he'd, that would be a very good fight in court. Where in fact he'd win. He'd win, he'd get that guaranteed, hands down. So, yes, I agree it should be flexible. Do I still worry about that? Absolutely. 'Cause I could see that being the avenue for our justice system to allow for the donor to become a parent. A father. I have reservations about that.

Emily was not alone in worrying about how a multiple-parent model might apply with regard to a known donor who had only limited involvement in the child's life. As noted in Chapter 3, a known donor was understood by the mothers to be a parent only when he plays a significant (and intended) caregiving role. Thus, while all of the mothers who supported multiple-parent recognition saw it as the perfect way by which to recognize a three- or four-parent family in which the donor (and possibly his partner) is genuinely parenting, if such a model were to be implemented, various safeguards would need to be included.

A possible solution to this dilemma is the creation of a secondary legal category, less than a parent, which would recognize the non-parental relationships some known donors develop with their children. Creating a new legal category for non-parental secondary figures in a child's life would hopefully reduce the tendency to see these individuals as parents and thus create more security for the lesbian family. Support for this concept was widespread among the mothers, many of whom viewed the relationship that an involved donor might develop with a child as non-parental but worthy of some kind of legal recognition. In fact, several of the mothers invoked the "best interests of the child" principle to explain their commitment to maintaining the relationships children develop with their donors as well as with other significant adults. It was thus not surprising that in grappling with the issue of how the law might respond to an involved donor (while simultaneously protecting the lesbian family from unwarranted intrusions), thirty-one of the thirty-six families indicated that they would support the creation of a new legal category to capture the familial contributions of secondary figures who might have regular contact with the child but who are not engaged in parenting relationships.[1] While these secondary figures could be dealt with through existing access laws, a separate legal category has several advantages. First, existing access laws are designed for separating heterosexual parents, apply most frequently to heterosexual fathers, and are grounded primarily in the biological link between access parent and child. This is exactly the kind of legal framework lesbians mothers are trying to avoid. Secondly, because the secondary figure category would come with clearly defined rights and responsibilities attached, it would provide a clarity that access law cannot. Finally, as will be discussed below, unlike existing access laws, the secondary figure category can only be realized with the consent of the primary parents.

A number of the mothers grappled directly with how these secondary non-parental figures might be understood. Michaela, for example, sees them as occupying a grey area between mere donor and parent that warrants some kind of legal recognition:

> I wonder if there's some grey area in between where you can recognize [an involved donor relationship]. Especially, you know, if a lesbian couple chooses to have a guy in the family and call him "Dad," right, then you know he should have some rights. And he wouldn't have any rights [in the current system]. And, I think that that's kind of unfortunate even though it makes me queasy thinking about it. [chuckle] Because what rights would he be getting, you know what I mean? But I still think that if he's being a good dad and, and, all's going well, so, yeah. So, I, I think that there should be like a grey area. And maybe that's just, just that he could be named as a guardian.

Similarly, Mischa supported both a multiple-parent model and a secondary legal category for non-parental figures such as involved known donors. She noted that such a system would protect relationships between the child and non-parental figures in the event of unforeseen events, such as parental death:

Mischa: Well, if I were going to design a program, I think I would say that that you should be able to opt for whatever you choose. So I don't think you should say there can only be two primary [parents], but maybe there could be categories. There could be primary caregivers, two or more, and there could be secondary or whatever you want to call them. Additional. And so for instance, in our case, maybe we could have two primary [parents], and then a secondary could be her biological father, who is in some form, a, a parental figure I guess. But he doesn't really have much [responsibility]. But if I were to die I would want him to continue to have a right to see her. I would be very upset if I died and this wouldn't happen. So that would be a lesser category. A right to access and maybe some minimal responsibility to contribute if she fell on hard times or something. I mean, I don't know. Some, sort of, lesser ...

Interviewer: Lesser responsibility and lesser rights, but still recognition of some sort?

Mischa: Uh huh.

The struggle that both Mischa and Michaela experienced in explaining the nature of the secondary, non-parental category occupied by involved donors indicates the challenge involved in transforming a theoretical concept into a legal principle. While they know how these relationships work in practice, it is difficult for them to imagine how an involved donor's identity might be captured in law and what restrictions would be necessary to ensure that the primary parents remain secure. Attempts to resolve some of these more technical concerns were explored when the mothers moved to discussing more concrete law reform proposals.

While the vast majority of the mothers I interviewed were eager to embrace multiple-parent families, their views may not be entirely representative of the lesbian parenting community. As noted in the Introduction, the vast majority of the women I interviewed were white, middle class, and well educated. Their societal privilege may have provided them with the confidence to deviate from existing norms. In contrast, more marginalized women may feel less confident about abandoning the nuclear family model. It is also possible that the mothers, as members of a community that is typically (though perhaps mistakenly) presumed to be open minded and forward thinking, may have felt some pressure to appear "progressive." While I do not have any evidence that this was the case, when presented with a number of reform models that could be described as ranging from more progressive to more conservative, interviewees may have been reluctant to choose a conservative option. Unfortunately, it is impossible to know exactly what influences shaped the mothers' responses to my questions. However, the relative uniformity of their responses indicates a fairly high level of agreement.

What Form Should Legal Change Take? Presumptions versus Registration

The second issue that dominated the mothers' discussions about practical law reform was what practical form the changes might take. Recognizing that to this point, the mothers may not have thought much about practical legislative models, the interviewer invited them to respond to three proposals that, if implemented, would apply to both same-sex and heterosexual families who conceive using some form of alternative insemination. That is, the favoured model would replace any existing legislation. The three models, described below, were developed through an analysis of various existing law reform discussion proposals considered in Chapter 4. Ultimately, the models reflect an array of approaches to parental recognition and respond to many of the desires and concerns already identified by the mothers. For example, two of the models allow for the legal recognition of multiple parents as well as other significant non-parental figures. All three of the models respond to the mothers' need for legal security, especially vis-à-vis donors. Deliberate effort was made, however, to keep each of the models loosely defined so that mothers could shape them in ways that suited their own needs. The mothers were also encouraged to develop their own models for reform.

The first model presented to the mothers was referred to as the "presumption model." This model would extend to the same-sex context the existing legal framework, in which the parties to an intimate heterosexual relationship are presumed to be the parents of a child born into the relationship or within nine months of the relationship ending, provided that the non-biological parent consented to the conception procedure. Thus, if the biological mother's partner consents to a conception procedure, both members of the couple would be deemed legal parents without any need on the part of the non-biological mother to take any other action, such as adopting the child. In the case of a single mother who conceives through donor sperm, she alone would be the child's legal parent. Parental status would therefore continue to be limited to one or two individuals, and donors would immediately and permanently be denied the status of legal parent.[2] The presumption model would obviously involve making certain assumptions about the lesbian couple themselves. If they are in a conjugal relationship and the non-biological mother consents to the procedure, the presumption is that both parties to the relationship intend to parent the child. It would therefore not be possible for the parties to a relationship to agree that only one of them would actually parent. It would also not be possible for a non-conjugal couple to take advantage of the presumption.

The second model, the "opt-in model," is based largely on intention. Rather than relying on biology or adult-relationship status, as the current system tends to do, the opt-in model would require adults who intend to parent a child to register as the child's parents. The one exception would be the child's birth mother, who would be presumed to be the child's parent.[3] Being permitted to register as an additional parent would not require a biological connection to the child or a conjugal relationship with the child's biological mother, and would not be limited to one other individual. In other words, several individuals, whether involved in conjugal relationships or not, could opt in as parents, creating a three- or four-parent family. The opt-in model would also permit significant non-parental figures, such as an involved donor, to opt in to the legal family. The status that might extend to such an individual was not defined in the scenario presented to the mothers, but it was made clear that it was something other than parental. The issue of when individuals might be allowed to opt in and whose consent would be required was left to the mothers to decide.

The final model combines the presumption and opt-in models to produce a framework that would grant automatic parental status to the conjugal couple (or a single mother) while also allowing for additional parents and non-parental figures to opt in to the legal family. This "combination model" was designed to provide presumptive legal security for the couple or single mother while simultaneously creating space for an additional degree of fluidity in family formation. The model has many of the benefits of the opt-in model, but not at the expense of the conjugal couple. It would protect the non-biological mother in a way that the opt-in model would not, while still allowing for donors to play a legally defined role. The questions of when individuals might be allowed to opt in and how consent might be dealt with were once again left to the discretion of the mothers.

The most popular model, with twenty-one of the thirty-six families preferring it, was the combination model. The opt-in model was favoured by twelve families, and only three families endorsed the presumption model. These responses suggest that the vast majority of the mothers want the security of a presumption-based model, but only if accompanied by an additional more fluid framework grounded in intention. The mothers' responses to the three models will be discussed in order of their preference, beginning with the highly favoured combination model.

The Combination Model

The twenty-one families who favoured the combination model viewed it as capable of achieving the best of both worlds. While it would grant the parties to a conjugal relationship (or a single mother) automatic and full legal protection as parents, it would also allow additional parents or non-parental figures to be legally recognized. This latter point reflects the mothers' strong commitment to both multiple-parent families and the limited legal recognition of significant non-parental figures in a child's life. It also demonstrates the extent to which the mothers rejected an either/or approach to parental recognition. Ultimately, their preference was for a reform proposal that appeared to capture the benefits of both formal and substantive equality. Paula's simple comments sum up the views of many of the mothers who favoured this model:

I think, I think there is an importance of someone opting in and saying that they're committed [to] the process. But I think if you're conceiving a child in a relationship that there should be some kind of presumption as well.

Thus, there was a sense that the parties to the relationship were making an active choice to parent and that the choice should be respected by the law, but not to the exclusion of other individuals who were invited and committed to playing a role in the child's life.

For mothers whose families actually resemble the combination model – a conjugal couple with an involved known donor – it was particularly attractive. They could see their own families reflected in the model and realized how it would have benefited them if it had been in place when their children were born. For example, Antonia, a non-biological mother who had to negotiate a joint custody arrangement with her ex-partner as well as an (informal) access agreement with the donor and his partner, explained why she favoured the combination model:

> Because I think for us it would have been nice to have just the automatic [presumption] when [the] kids [were] born. 'Cause we didn't even have that. I mean I, you know, here we were going to the hospital to have our kids that we had planned and had conceived together. You know, really, I mean it's interesting 'cause my partner says, or my ex-partner, that she and I really conceived the kids. We just didn't do it biologically. And so I would like when the kids are born that whoever conceives them in whatever way are the parents. And that didn't happen. So we had to actually get that in place. Then we moved on to, so now the dads are, we want them to have some status and they haven't had any. Other than, you know, [what] we've given them. But they haven't had any legal status at all.

Antonia's attraction to the combination model was based on the security it would give the couple (or a single mother) while also allowing the primary parent(s) to open up the family to other parental and non-parental figures. This arrangement was perfect for her family given the active, but only occasional involvement, of her sons' "dads," who lived in another province.

While the majority of the mothers supported the combination model, they were willing to do so only if a number of concerns were addressed. The most significant concern related to consent: Would consent be required before an additional party could opt in, and who would have the power to exercise it? This concern obviously related to opt-in provisions in general and was voiced by mothers who favoured both the combination and opt-in models. All of the mothers who raised the issue of consent argued that a consent provision is necessary and that whether an additional individual could opt in should depend on the consent of the couple (or single mother) protected by the parental presumption. If it does not, the presumption becomes meaningless. The mothers' need for a strong consent provision was based largely on their perceived vulnerability vis-à-vis donors. The following interaction with Jasmine, who ultimately favoured the combination model after the consent issue was resolved, captures the nature of the mothers' concerns around consent:

> *Jasmine:* Okay, so in my case Bianca and I decide we're going to, um, be the parents. Neil [the donor] wants some involvement. He has a, he chooses to opt in? Or we chose to opt in? And those are the parts, like, so I wouldn't want to say. I wouldn't think of a blanket, yeah, like let's have opt-ins. And I wouldn't want to make it any more confusing in that now we have to get his permission to opt him out for instance. So, I would, I would, I would keep my final decision on that combination to see what the combination is.
> *Interviewer:* Okay, would you feel more comfortable if, in order to opt in, you had to get the consent of the primary parents?
> *Jasmine:* Yeah, they're the ones that get to decide who else comes in. That makes me feel better.

Paula similarly noted the dangers of opting in not being regulated by some form of consent. She argued that without a consent provision, a donor who was not intended to be part of the family could opt in at his own discretion:

> So the ability for other persons to opt in ... you'd need consent so
> that you don't have a sperm donor who's not going to be acknow-
> ledged. Like if there's a "contract" that's developed, you don't want
> someone in violation of that contract to just opt in without the
> consent of the other parties.

Thus, building a consent provision into the combination model would
permit those mothers who want to extend legal recognition to other
parents or non-parental figures to do so but would also protect those
mothers who do not intend to make such a choice.

A number of other concerns related to the combination model were
raised by individual mothers who wondered about its practical application. For example, some speculated about when opting in might take
place (when planning the child? at conception? at birth?) and how the
rights and responsibilities of those who opted in might be defined and
recorded. Others wondered whether birth certificates would change to
include the names of the additional parents or significant non-parental
figures who had been invited to opt in. Not enough of the mothers
commented on these questions to gain any sense of what their shared
perspective might be, but they are issues that would need to be resolved
if the model were to be transformed into a legislative framework.

The Opt-In Model

The twelve mothers who favoured the opt-in model were attracted not
only to its flexibility, but also to its direct link to intention. They emphasized the importance of parenting being a conscious act. As Sam
noted, "By having to go through some sort of pro-active action you're
making, you're consciously making a commitment." Some of the mothers
speculated that adding a level of consciousness to the act of becoming
a parent might benefit the institution of parenting itself. More fore-
thought would inevitably be given to the enormous responsibility
parenting entails. The mothers who favoured the opt-in model were also
attracted to its rejection of presumptions, particularly presumptions
based on relationship status. Gillian noted that an opt-in framework
would allow the parties themselves to consciously shape their family

rather than having the law impose the framework from above. She felt that this would be particularly helpful in times of conflict:

> If people disagree later on and it does have to go to court, at least there is the, the stated intentions of all of the parties from, at the outset. And, and then, you know hopefully decisions really can be made sort of in the best interest of the child at that point rather than, "Well, unfortunately the law says that these are the primary parents."

The mothers who favoured the opt-in model were also attracted to the fact that by avoiding presumptions based on biology or relationship status, the opt-in model would allow partners to choose whether they both intend to be parents.[4] This level of fluidity was particularly attractive to the mothers who did not necessarily make a link, as Millbank does in her proposal, between a woman having a child and her partner being a parent.[5] As Sally noted, the biological mother and her partner may have agreed that the partner would not actually be a parent; the opt-in model would allow for this intention to be given legal form:

> For example, there's a couple of women that I know that are in a relationship, and yet the child is not her, the partner's child. She is an aunty and [partly] a care-giver, but [is] not considered a parent. And that's certainly not within [the current law], but that's how they decided to do it. And that's fine. And so I think that you need to make [that a] serious consideration. Is that her child? Am I making that commitment?

In Elisha's family, this is exactly what happened. Elisha chose to co-parent with a non-conjugal partner, while Elisha's conjugal partner, whom she met while pregnant, was not considered a parent. This model, therefore, was one that Elisha found attractive:

> The opt-in one sounds more kind of appealing. I mean, especially like my situation of living with [my partner], like she was very clear

that she didn't, you know, wasn't opting in ... She was willing to be around and be supportive and be somewhat involved but she was like, totally, you know freaked out by the idea of commitment and financial responsibility. And all those things. She, she would not have opted in and would not have necessarily even been in the relationship if, if it was gonna be like a given that she would then have to take that on.

For Elisha, the opt-in model would provide exactly the fluidity she needs to adequately parent her daughter. Because her family was framed around the concept of intention rather than biology or adult-relationship status, the opt-in model is the only framework capable of capturing the nature of her family relationships.

Ironically, the opt-in model's complete rejection of presumptions was also understood to be its most significant weakness. Those who opposed the opt-in model but who favoured the opt-in provisions in the combination model were worried that adults would avoid responsibility for children by not opting in. They were particularly concerned about this possibility in the heterosexual context but noted that it could also occur within lesbian relationships. Their concern revolved around birth mothers being left to care for and financially support their children in the event of a partner refusing to opt in. Veronique, who ultimately favoured the opt-in model, recognized this weakness:

> The problem though with that, with that kind of a system [an opt-in system] would be where people have committed to taking on a set of responsibilities around a child and then decide that they no longer want to opt in. And so, so the person who, the other person who's involved in that arrangement, might be left having to do everything when they didn't expect that that would happen. So I mean, and obviously too, we have to be, cognizant of the fact that in, in terms of heterosexual relationships, that, that often happens to women.

Veronique went on to suggest that a possible solution to this dilemma would be to separate economic issues from parenting. If biological mothers were not fearful of the economic and lifestyle ramifications of partners failing to opt in – because state assistance was adequate and quality child care was affordable and available, for example – then they may have fewer concerns about the prospect.

Not surprisingly, the mothers who favoured the opt-in model also raised issues of consent and timing, and came to many of the same conclusions as those who favoured the combination model. Most of the mothers advocated for strong consent provisions that placed the power to give consent solely in the hands of the birth mother. This approach was understood to protect the birth mother's autonomy as a parent while still allowing for the recognition of additional parental relationships. The few mothers who raised issues of timing tended to prefer that those who opt in do so very early in a child's life.

The Presumption Model

Only three families favoured the presumption model, and in each family, their commitment to it derived from a belief in formal equality. The presumption model was seen as extending to lesbian couples the same parenting framework that heterosexual couples who conceived through donor insemination already enjoyed. In other words, these families felt that the presumption model would treat them identically to heterosexuals, and this was what they wanted. Rochelle was one of those who favoured the presumption model:

> I think we should, I think we should be treated as heterosexuals. And equal. There's, there's no reason why Angie and I should not have been. I mean, we've been together a long time. You know, we were married. There's no reason why we're not any different than [them].

Not surprisingly, these same mothers, earlier in their interviews, had already expressed their rejection of the idea of multiple-parent families, as well as the legal recognition of significant non-parental relationships. They therefore saw no need to extend the presumption model to cover other family structures.

While few mothers chose the presumption model, much can be learned from considering the reasoning of those who rejected it. The most common reason for opposing the presumption model was that it does not capture the multiple parental and significant non-parental relationships that can be found within lesbian and gay families. Rather, it limits parenting to two people in a conjugal relationship, and for many mothers, such an approach seemed like a step backwards. It was not that they completely rejected formal equality; rather, it was that formal equality was understood as insufficient. Their preference was for reform that *combines* equal treatment with additional provisions grounded in a more substantive vision of equality.

The presumption model was also understood to be inadequate because it limits the possibility of intention-based, self-conscious parenting. Mothers such as Veronique saw this as a problem for both heterosexual and lesbian and gay parents:

> I mean I just think we need to be more self-conscious about what it means to raise a child. And so the, the more self-conscious we can be, the more conscious of what that means to everyone, the better. And so that's why I think the, the problem around you know, automatic presumptions, well I mean, in terms of lesbian couples it really does just simply mimic what happens in a heterosexual relationship. And maybe what needs to happen in heterosexual relationships is more consciousness about the negotiation of relationships.

The presumption model was thus rejected by the vast majority of the mothers on the basis that it mimics an inadequate status quo. It was seen to serve neither lesbian mothers nor heterosexual parents particularly well.

From Law Reform Proposals to a Legislative Model

Drawing from the mothers' responses to the law reform models presented, as well as from the wider definitional frameworks they employed, a law reform proposal was developed. The proposed legislation comprises two parts and applies to both heterosexual and same-sex couples, as well as to single women, who conceive a child through some form of alternative conception method. The proposal applies only in the assisted-reproduction context and addresses specifically the need in such a situation to provide legislative (intention-based) presumptions contrary to those based in biology. Part 1 addresses the assignment of legal parentage at birth. The first three sections of Part 1 focus on establishing a parental presumption in favour of the intending parent(s) derived from their pre-birth behaviour. This is done through the concept of a parental project, which is introduced in section 1. Adapted from the *Civil Code of Quebec*, the term "parental project" is used in the proposal to refer to a situation in which an individual or couple *mutually consent* to conceive a child via alternative conception.[6] While the term "parental project" is somewhat clinical, I chose to adopt it because it does not resemble any pre-existing family law terminology in common law Canada. It is therefore clear that the legislation is not invoking an already existing concept.

While the Quebec legislation does not specifically define the term "parental project," other than to state that such a project "exists from the moment a person alone decides or spouses by mutual consent decide, in order to have a child, to resort to the genetic material of a person who is not party to the parental project,"[7] I felt it would be helpful to provide some legislative guidance as to the meaning of the term. Such guidance would clarify the factors relevant to establishing the pre-birth intention and encourage judges to apply the legislation uniformly and in accordance with its purpose. Thus, in section 2 of the proposed legislation, decision makers are provided with a non-exhaustive list of criteria that might indicate participation in a parental project, beyond the requirement in section 1 that both parties have consented to the insemination. The list includes whether the non-biological parent consented to the insemination, participated in pre-conception planning (including but not confined to the choosing of a donor), was present during some or all inseminations, attended pre-natal appointments, and was present at the child's birth.

Once it has been established that a parental project exists, the parental presumption contained in section 3 applies. Thus, in circumstances where a couple has agreed to participate in a parental project, the partner of the woman who gives birth is presumed to be the child's legal parent. In the case of a single mother, the presumption applies solely to her. The effect of these sections is twofold. First, they give automatic parental status to couples who mutually agree to parent, whether both individuals are biologically related to the child or not. Second, they allow single parents, as well as individuals who do not intend to parent with their conjugal partner, to achieve sole parental recognition in circumstances where they make it clear that the parental project is theirs alone. Although sections 1 through 3 prioritize the conjugal couple (where one exists), the opt-in provisions in Part 2 ensure that a non-conjugal parent could also be granted legal recognition.

Although sections 1 through 3 ensure that the intentions of a non-biological parent are given legal force, section 4 permits the partner of a woman who gives birth to a child to *contest* the partner's presumptive parentage of a child on the basis that the partner was not a party to a mutual parental project. This section is designed to protect those women (or men) who are partnered to the birth mother but who do not intend to parent. Finally, section 5 extinguishes the parental rights, as well as any non-parental right of access, of a donor in relation to a child born via his or her genetic contribution, except in the narrow circumstances described in Part 2.[8] Section 5 makes it clear that a genetic link created via donor insemination does not make the donor a legal parent. At the same time, the exceptions described in Part 2 ensure that where there is a mutual intention to involve the gamete provider in the child's life, that intention can be given legal force.

The goal of Part 1 is to presumptively protect the intentional (lesbian or single mother) family as the child's central family unit. Rather than viewing such a family as lacking a father, it solidifies the lesbian or single mother family unit as complete. Part 2 of the proposed reform addresses the opt-in procedures that enable the presumptive family to extend beyond the one- or two-parent model in circumstances where the primary parent(s) *mutually consent* to such an arrangement. The opt-in procedures enable known donors, or other non-biologically re-lated parties, to be granted legal rights in circumstances where all of the parties intend the individual to play a role. Section 7 permits an additional party to apply to opt in, with the consent of the legal parent(s) as established in Part 1, to the status of parent. Such an application must be made within one year of the child's birth and, if granted, would extend all of the rights and responsibilities of parenthood to the second or third parent, without limiting the parental status of the intending parent(s).[9] This section is designed to meet the needs of those families that include, from the outset, three or four actively involved parents. Section 8 permits an additional party to apply, with the consent of the legal parent(s), to opt in to the status of "non-parental adult caregiver." Absent unfitness, a non-parental adult caregiver will have a right of access to the extent determined, in writing, by the child's legal parent(s). The written agreement will be registered alongside a successful opt-in application and will be enforced as if it were a parenting order. An application to be a non-parental adult caregiver must be made within one year of the child's birth.

The provisions in sections 7 and 8 are designed to protect the rights of the presumptive parents while still allowing for a donor to be involved in a child's life if the presumptive parents have consented to the arrangement. The existence of sections 7 and 8 will hopefully encourage women to choose donors carefully. These sections, and specifically the requirement that access arrangements be put in writing, will force parents and non-parental adult caregivers such as donors to discuss their intentions at the outset. If the donor wants to play a role in the child's life that exceeds what the presumptive parents are comfortable with, these provisions should encourage them to find another donor. Section 8(e) makes it clear that granting non-parental adult caregivers additional rights beyond those agreed to in writing is presumed not to be in a child's best interests. This provision is designed to deter a judge from presuming that because an individual shares a biological link with a child, or because a child does not have a male or female parent, it is in the child's best interests to have a relationship with that individual in excess of what had been originally agreed upon. The provisions in sections 7 and 8 are likely to be used by families that include a known donor who is involved in the child's life but does not play the role of parent, arguably the most common form of known-donor family.

As noted above, the draft legislation that follows is designed only to highlight the issues that need to be contemplated by any future legislative regime and to serve as a catalyst for further discussion.

PARENTAGE OF CHILDREN BORN
OF ASSISTED REPRODUCTION

Part 1: Parental Presumptions

Section 1

A parental project involving assisted procreation exists from the moment a person alone decides, or spouses or common-law partners by mutual consent decide, in order to have a child, to use for the purpose of conception the genetic material of a person who is not party to the parental project.

Section 2

1 Subject to section 1, in determining whether a parental project exists between two parties, the court shall consider whether the spouse or common-law partner of the woman who gave birth to the child

    a participated in pre-conception planning, including but not confined to the choosing of a donor of genetic material;
    b was present during inseminations;
    c attended pre-natal appointments;
    d was present at the child's birth.

2 The failure of the partner of the woman who gave birth to the child to participate in any of the activities listed in subsections (a)-(d) is not conclusive evidence of the absence of a parental project.

Section 3

If a child is born of a parental project involving assisted procreation between two spouses during their marriage or common-law relationship or within three hundred days after its dissolution or annulment, the spouse or common-law partner of the woman who gave birth to the child is presumed to be the child's parent.

Section 4

No person may contest the parentage of a child solely on the grounds of the child being born of a parental project involving assisted procreation. However, the spouse or common-law partner of the woman who gave birth to the child may contest parentage if there was no mutual parental project or if it is established that the child was not born of the assisted procreation.

Section 5

The contribution of genetic material for the purposes of a parental project does not create a parental relationship between the contributor and the child born of the parental project or entitle the contributor to access with a child, except in the circumstances described in Part 2.

Section 6

For the purpose of this Part, a woman's common-law partner is the person who, not being married to the woman, is cohabiting with her in a conjugal relationship of some permanence.

Part 2: Opt-In Procedures

Section 7

a Upon the birth of a child and the consent of the legal parent or parents of that child, any person can apply to the court to opt in to the status of legal parent.
b An application to opt in as a legal parent must be made within one year following the birth of a child.

Section 8

Upon the birth of a child and the consent of the legal parent or parents, any person can apply to the court to opt in to the status of non-parental adult caregiver.

a An application to opt in as a non-parental adult caregiver must be made within one year of the child's birth.

b Absent unfitness, a non-parental adult caregiver has a right of access at a level determined by the child's parent or parents.

c Access agreements must be in writing and filed with the opt-in application.

d Access agreements will be enforced as if they were a parenting order relating to access.

e Absent unfitness, permitting a non-parental adult caregiver access at the level determined by the child's parent or parents is presumed to be in the child's best interests.

f Permitting a non-parental adult caregiver rights beyond those determined by the child's parent or parents is not presumed to be in the child's best interests.

g A non-parental adult caregiver shall have no child support liability unless otherwise agreed.

In addition to the provisions included above, subsequent amendments would need to be made to any provincial or federal legislation that addresses legal parentage, particularly laws that limit parental status to two legal parents. A number of other issues would also need to be clarified, such as whether and how opt-in parents or non-parental adult caregivers might appear on a child's birth certificate, whether opt-in parents would be liable for child support, and how custody and access disputes should be addressed in the event that the child has more than two legal parents. These issues are not minor but would require further consultation to address.

Conclusion

Recognition of the lesbian family requires a creativity that has rarely been evident in litigation-based law reform efforts to date. The approach that has tended to prevail – tinkering with the pre-existing framework and then requiring lesbian families to mould themselves to it – provides little more than a band-aid solution. This is not to say that these efforts have had no impact. To the contrary, they have radically changed the legal circumstances within which lesbian mothers parent. Lesbian mothers today experience a level of family security that could hardly have been imagined two decades ago. Unfortunately, however, the reforms that have occurred have done little to challenge the traditional ideological assumptions underlying the legal family. For example, reforms such as the introduction of second-parent adoption have simply added a same-sex twist to the conjugal, two-parent unit. While this might be sufficient for some lesbian families, the vast majority of the mothers I interviewed demanded a more flexible system, whether their own families resembled the traditional model or not.

Recognizing planned lesbian families in all their diversity requires a significant rethinking of how we assign legal parentage, particularly in the context of assisted conception. The usual signifiers of parenthood – biology and/or adult-relationship status – are simply insufficient in the lesbian context. In fact, many of the mothers I interviewed suggested that these rules are also increasingly problematic for heterosexuals who conceive via a method other than intercourse. What is needed is an alternative approach to the assignment of legal parentage in situations of assisted conception that recognizes that "parent" is an expanding concept capable of taking on a multiplicity of new forms. Yet lesbian families must not fall victim to a new fluidity in which the boundaries of their families are manipulated in an effort to "find fathers" for already complete family units. Rather, planned lesbian families are entitled to the same baseline of recognition as heterosexual couples who conceive via donor insemination. What is therefore needed is a model of parental recognition that provides a level playing field for lesbian mothers while simultaneously expanding the field to encompass families that extend beyond the two-parent model. The combination model – capable of protecting the intending parent(s) at the same time that it opens up the family to include multiple parents and non-parental adult figures – is the model most suited to this task.

Some Concluding Thoughts on Law Reform and Progressive Social Change

6

A considerable amount of thought, time, and effort goes into creating a planned lesbian family. With little guidance from the law, parental and non-parental relationships must be defined and agreed upon from within, often in terms that are contrary to societal norms. Existing legal mechanisms, such as second-parent adoptions, can be drawn upon by the lesbian family to help support its internal family decisions, but the existing law fails to address the underlying need for legal security at the time of birth. Nor does it accommodate lesbian mothers who parent outside of a dyadic norm. Legislative reform is clearly needed. The challenge is determining how change might be achieved and what form it should take.

What this study has shown is that any law reform that is pursued cannot simply map the existing legal framework onto lesbian families, as formal equality is likely to do. Such an approach will only lead to exclusions. Instead, reform must be grounded in empirical research that directly engages planned lesbian families. Ultimately, what might be needed is a series of provincial government committees that are directed to facilitate public consultations on same-sex parenting, consider the research that already exists, and commission additional research on parenting issues that have not yet been adequately explored. A reform process that does not engage directly with the lesbian parenting community and those who work within it is unlikely to capture the diversity of needs and the complexity of the family relationships that exist.

While a parenting law reform agenda is urgently needed in Canada, a consistent theme to emerge from the study was a reluctance on the part of the mothers to put their complete faith in law. Many of them expressed a mistrust of legal institutions, particularly judges and the courts, as well as a belief that law alone cannot change societal attitudes. Lesbian mothers are not alone in questioning the capacity of law to achieve progressive social change for marginalized groups. Law is often presented as a great panacea, but in reality, it provides only limited solutions. Same-sex marriage has not rid Canada of homophobia, and improved parenting laws will not automatically transform society's attitudes towards two-mother families or non-biological mothers in particular.

Law and (Progressive) Social Transformation

While this study has focused primarily on achieving law reform, it is perhaps important to conclude by considering whether legal change can realistically be expected to effect progressive social change for lesbian mothers. In other words, what are the strengths and weaknesses of using law – particularly litigation, which has thus far dominated the parenting reforms – as a tool for positive social transformation? "Positive social transformation" can, of course, mean different things for different people. In the context of this study, I understand it to refer to two related factors. First, progressive social transformation for lesbian mothers would involve a significant increase in the level of social acceptance experienced by lesbian families with children. Acceptance would extend beyond the law itself to incorporate public and private institutions such as schools, hospitals, community organizations, parenting groups, sporting associations, and the media, as well as ordinary members of the general public who simply encounter lesbian mothers in the course of their daily lives. Acceptance would be measured not by the degree to which individuals and institutions comply with the law, but rather by the extent to which they embrace and validate the relationships between lesbian mothers and their children.

Second, and significantly more ambitious, progressive social change for lesbian mothers would involve a fundamental shift in the ideological paradigm through which both "family" and "parenthood" are understood. In other words, the legal recognition of lesbian motherhood, and the debates that would necessarily accompany it, would become a catalyst for the rethinking of family relationships more generally. For example, extending parental status to non-biological lesbian mothers on the basis of their pre-conception intention and post-birth caregiving practices may challenge wider society to rethink the assumption that parental rights should always stem from a biological relationship. Treating known donors as parents only in circumstances where the parties have agreed to such an arrangement is likely to encourage similar debates. By introducing the prospect of three- or four-parent families, the legal recognition of lesbian motherhood may also produce new societal narratives about the permissible boundaries of the family unit. For example, the presence of three- or four-parent queer families may encourage heterosexuals to rethink the units around which they erect their family boundaries.

Some scholars have questioned the ability of law, particularly judicial decision making, to elicit either of the types of social change I have described. While law is often regarded by marginalized groups as a key site of social struggle, several factors inhibit its capacity to contribute to progressive social change. First, because law is not the sole site of social power, a singular pursuit of legal strategies, whether litigation or legislation, is unlikely to completely transform existing relations of power.[1] For example, while a lesbian non-biological mother might secure legal parental status via a second-parent adoption, she may still experience discrimination at the hands of public institutions, such as schools or hospitals, who view her status as secondary to that of the biological mother. In fact, a number of the non-biological mothers interviewed told stories of teachers who asked them which woman was the "real mother," directed all of their attention to the biological mother, and sought information about the child's "father." In all of these cases, the non-biological mother was one of the child's legal parents. These stories point to the presence of non-legal sites of regulatory power that continue to impact negatively on lesbian mothers even in situations where they have obtained legal recognition as parents.

Law's inbuilt conservative tendency, particularly in the family arena, also limits its ability to produce progressive social transformation. The conservative nature of law is the product of a number of factors. First, the role of precedent in the positivist common law tradition means that case law tends to be backward looking. As Ngaire Naffine explains, "[The doctrine of precedent] means that like cases are treated alike; judicial decisions are made by reference to previous judicial decisions in analogous cases; the present is bound by the past."[2] Thus, incorporated within legal decision making and adjudication is a preference for the status quo. It is possible, therefore, as we have seen in Quebec, to have progressive legislation interpreted through a very traditional lens, ultimately excluding a lesbian mother from the status of legal parent. Naffine does go on to argue that *in practice* the doctrine of precedent can be fairly flexible: only a small part (the *ratio decidendi*) of each judgment is binding on subsequent decision makers, the *ratio* can often be interpreted in multiple ways, and judges can limit the effect of previous decisions that they consider "unsound" by interpreting their *ratios* narrowly. Thus, precedent does not always prevent judges from breaking new ground. However, it does place significant limitations on what can be achieved through litigation, and it certainly encourages the re-assertion of the (typically conservative) normative position. In the context of the family, the normative position tends to prioritize the hetero-normative, two-parent, biological family.

The second factor contributing to law's conservatism is the inextricable and mutually perpetuating link between law and ideology, which means that law is both constrained by and reproduces dominant social values: ideas, beliefs, and practices that are treated as natural, inevitable, and necessary to the proper functioning of society.[3] In the context of lesbian parenting, the importance of analyzing law as ideology is perhaps best illustrated by considering how law articulates "the family." Shelley Gavigan notes that

> "the family" is presented in law ... as the basic unit in society, a sacred, timeless and so natural an institution that its definition is self-evident. Its privacy is sought to be protected and its sanctity proclaimed. That it is the fittest place to raise children is again so self-evident as to not

merit question, and the hold of the family is strong despite the knowledge that large numbers of individuals live in households which
bear no resemblance to the ideal family.[4]

The "common sense" nature of law's understanding of the family
makes the detection of law's ideological content and prejudicial effect
a somewhat difficult task. In fact, as Gavigan notes, looking for blatant
manifestations of discrimination will rarely expose the role of ideology
in law. Such an approach tends to miss "the subtle processes" by which
legal doctrine and judicial interpretation and decision making repro-
duce and reinforce traditional (biological and heterosexist) norms.[5] The
subtlety of the relationship between law and ideology makes it very
difficult for lesbian mothers to tackle with any specificity the nature of
their exclusion, particularly in situations where legislation appears to
be in their favour.

Despite the complex and often complicated relationship between
law reform and progressive social change, marginalized groups such as
lesbian mothers rarely have the luxury of giving up on law altogether.
As demonstrated throughout this book, lesbian mothers and their children continue to experience the very real harm of existing outside of
the current legal framework. Thus, engaging with law in order to secure
some of its practical benefits is arguably a necessity, even if legal change
makes only a limited contribution to progressive social transformation.
Law therefore remains an important strategic tool and site of affirmation for lesbian mothers. The question that remains is how they might
engage with law so as to increase the possibility of progressive social
transformation and minimize law's assimilationist tendencies.

Positive Engagement with Law

As noted in Chapter 4, many of the mothers approach law cautiously,
alert to its deficiencies. In fact, while a number spoke positively of the
"legitimacy" and practical benefits that legal recognition of their families offered, few understand legal engagement – particularly with the
courts – as solely positive. The mothers cited a number of reasons for
their position, the majority of which focused on litigation and judicial
decision makers. First, many of the mothers are distrustful of the legal

system and those who administer it. Somewhat echoing the argument made above about the relationship between law and ideology, the mothers feel that the law and those who interpret it embody a certain set of norms such that even in situations where lesbian mothers are legally protected, the law will not always be applied in a way that honours or respects their families. Second, many of the mothers view the current approach to law reform – a court-based strategy grounded largely in formal equality – as assimilationist and incapable on its own of creating any real understanding or acceptance of their families within wider society. They are particularly skeptical of law reform efforts that simply map the current framework onto their families. Finally, a significant portion of the mothers feel that reform – even legislative reform – of the current parenting laws will not, in itself, produce significant or immediate progressive social change. In fact, many of the mothers expect acceptance and understanding to take time and believe that for many members of the public, it will not be until they have some direct contact with same-sex families that their attitudes might begin to change. The vast majority of the mothers therefore feel reluctant to put all of their hope, time, and resources into law.

While most of the mothers made at least some reference to law's limitations, most had engaged with law in one way or another and they almost universally favoured further law reform. Not surprisingly, given their reservations about the courts and judges, the mothers spoke particularly favourably about legislative reform. Thus, despite their reservations, law is understood as a necessity and even of some positive value. It extends practical benefits and provides the mothers with a sense of family security. Those mothers who parented during times of minimal legal recognition understand the enabling power of law particularly well. Because they experienced what it was like to have no legal status, this particular group of mothers can see with the greatest clarity the benefits the new forms of recognition could provide.

What most of the mothers refused to do, however, was to engage with law uncritically. This finding is worthy of attention, not only because it suggests that many lesbian mothers are cognizant of the limitations of law as a tool for progressive change, but also because it suggests that the lesbian and gay voices that are often heard in the courts are neither fully representative nor universal. In fact, unlike so many of those who have participated in marriage and parenting litigation, most of the mothers I interviewed refuse to accept that their entitlement to legal recognition rests on the extent to which their families reflect traditional norms. Rather, most of the mothers understand their entitlement to derive from society's obligation to reflect family diversity. Further evidence of this critical edge emerges upon examination of the legislative proposals ultimately favoured by the mothers. The reform model that most of the mothers favoured would alter some of family law's most entrenched norms and severely diminish the significance of the biological, two-parent family. Notably, the least popular model was one that simply maps the existing legal framework onto lesbian mothers. While introducing the reform model proposed above may not produce immediate social change (and may even result in backlash), its contribution to the gradual fracturing of the ideological framework within which the existing law operates may be a first step towards greater social acceptance of lesbian families and of alternative families more generally.

The critical edge demonstrated by many of the mothers I spoke to was, of course, enabled by the context in which the conversations took place. In talking to me, they enjoyed the rather utopian possibility of being able to ask for exactly what they want. They did not need to grapple with courtroom strategy, the trends within section 15 equality rights jurisprudence, or the conservative media. Rather, they were able to imagine freely, and what they imagined is revealing. The mothers did not start from a position of formal equality or an idealized vision of what family life should look like. Rather, they identified their own family practices and worked backwards. They argued that their families, like many of those headed by heterosexuals, come in diverse forms and that *diversity* should be the value that underlies family recognition. Thus, rather than seeking to equate their families with existing conceptions, they demanded that the concept of family be rethought.

Rethinking family is not an easy task, and some portions of Canadian society will undoubtedly attack the reform model proposed in this book for its lack of "real world" practicality. Whether the mothers' proposals are understood as realistic or utopian, what is important is that they illustrate a critical engagement with law that has the potential to maximize the possibility of progressive social transformation. In the wake of the same-sex marriage debate, it is perhaps exactly the kind of approach to legal engagement needed by the lesbian and gay communities of Canada.

Conclusion: Moving Forward

From the first successful second-parent adoption case in 1995 to the recent three-parent decision in 2007, many courageous lesbian mothers in Canada have been willing to subject their families to judicial scrutiny in the hope that their parental relationships might be recognized. Significant legal victories have been won through the litigation process, and many lesbian-headed families have benefited from favourable judicial decisions. In fact, recent cases, such as the three-parent decision of *A.A. v. B.B.*, suggest that at least some judges are willing to go to significant lengths to lend legal support to lesbian-headed families. What I learned from the mothers I interviewed, however, is that the time has come for a new legal strategy. While litigation has served lesbian mothers well in the past, it cannot produce the broader conceptual changes that this research supports. The solution is thus likely to lie in the legislative process. Unconstrained by the existing legal framework or precedent, the statutory reform process provides an environment in which creative responses are more likely enabled: new conceptual frameworks can be debated, experts and their research can be consulted, and multiple voices can be heard.

Generating legislative change is not a simple or straightforward task. While court action can be initiated by individuals, legislative reform requires extensive campaigning, public education and support, and, ultimately, government agreement. Lesbian mothers might therefore need to take a two-pronged approach. First, they will need to garner the support of already existing advocacy groups that might have the resources, political connections, and media savvy that are often necessary to run a successful reform campaign. The most obvious organization from which to seek support is EGALE. With the backing of a well-known and increasingly well-respected organization such as EGALE, lesbian mothers might be able to generate the kind of public and government interest that a successful reform campaign requires. In fact, now that the same-sex marriage debate has concluded, EGALE is likely to be looking to launch its next campaign. Given the organization's recent focus on queer-family issues, the legal recognition of parenting relationships seems like an appropriate choice.

Second, while lesbian mothers may benefit from aligning themselves with a pre-existing organization, they may also need to form their own lobby groups. Ultimately, this was the strategy adopted in other jurisdictions, such as Victoria (Australia) and New Zealand, and it has been remarkably successful. For example, by forming grassroots organizations that then lobby government for legislative change, the lesbian parenting community in Victoria was able to convince the government to refer the issue to the Victorian Law Reform Commission. Over a four-year period, the VLRC carried out public consultations, issued three discussion papers, and ultimately published a report that recommended legislative changes very much in line with what lesbian mothers had requested. In 2008, legislation was finally passed. The success of the Victorian experience illustrates what can be achieved even by small lobby groups committed to change. Whether lesbian mothers in Canada choose to align themselves with a large organization like EGALE, create their own grassroots lobby groups, or both, they will need to look for strategic opportunities to raise their concerns. If their campaign for reform is successful, lesbian mothers will not only secure legal recognition for themselves, but will also make a significant contribution to the ongoing debate about what it means to be a legal parent.

Appendix
Participant Profiles

Note: All participants are identified using a pseudonym.

Anna is the non-biological mother of Neil and Hazel, aged seven and four, whom she co-parents with her partner, Anne-Marie. The children were conceived via known-donor insemination. Their donor, Edgar, sees the children approximately once a week, and for two weeks during the summer, they travel with him to visit his family in eastern Canada. The family lives in their own home in Vancouver.

Antonia is the non-biological mother of twin boys, Craig and Taylor, aged eleven. Antonia co-parents the boys with her former partner, with whom she shares a joint custody arrangement. The boys were conceived via known-donor insemination, and their donor, Roger, as well as his male partner, Rory, are considered to be their "dads." The boys spend several weeks a year with Roger and Rory, who live in Atlantic Canada.

Brigid and Coral, whom I interviewed together, are the parents of Cailyn, aged one. Cailyn was born via anonymous-donor insemination. The family lives in their own home in suburban Calgary.

Callie and Sam, who were interviewed together, are the parents of Aiden and Lara, aged one and three. Each woman is the biological mother of one of the children. The children were conceived via anonymous-donor insemination. The family lives in co-operative housing in Vancouver.

Carey is the biological mother of Simon, aged three, whom she co-parents with her partner, Nadia. Simon was conceived via known-donor insemination. His donor, Tim, sees him twice monthly and is understood to be somewhere between a father and an uncle. The family was renting an apartment in Vancouver when I conducted the interview, but was about to move to co-operative housing, also in Vancouver.

Christy is the biological mother of Macy, aged three. Macy was conceived via anonymous-donor insemination. When Christy was pregnant, she formed a relationship with Deidre. While Deidre was not considered to be Macy's parent at first, as the relationship developed, Deidre took on a parental role. Christy and Deidre are now separated, but Deidre continues to play a significant role in Macy's life and is considered to be her second mother. The family lives in Calgary.

Delia is the biological mother of Casey, aged two, whom she co-parents with her partner, Paige. Casey was conceived via anonymous-donor insemination. Delia and Paige are married. The family lives in their own home in suburban Vancouver.

Diane is the biological mother of Pamela, aged two, whom she co-parents with her partner, Celia. Pamela was conceived via anonymous-donor insemination. The family lives in Vancouver.

Elisha is the biological mother of Akeela, aged ten, whom she parents with three other co-parents: a non-conjugal parenting partner (Cassandra), Akeela's biological father (Kyle), and Akeela's biological father's former partner (Nick). Akeela was conceived via known-donor insemination. Kyle and Nick are considered to be her "dads." Akeela sees Cassandra as her second mother, though Cassandra and Elisha have never been in a conjugal relationship. Akeela spends time with all of her parents, though she lives primarily with Elisha. The family lives in a rental property in Vancouver.

Emily and Lesley, whom I interviewed together, are the parents of Maddox, aged three. Maddox was born via known-donor insemination. Maddox's donor, Ryan, sees him twice a month. Ryan is understood to be a donor, but not a parent and is known to Maddox by his first name. Emily and Lesley are married. The family lives in a rental property in suburban Vancouver.

Jacky and Carly, whom I interviewed together, are the parents of Dana, aged two. Carly was pregnant with their second child at the time of the interview. Dana was conceived via sexual intercourse with a donor. The donor plays no role in Dana's life. The second child was conceived via anonymous-donor insemination. The family lives in a rental property on the edge of Edmonton.

Janet is the biological mother of Mia and Caleb, aged seven and three, whom she co-parents with her partner, Felicity. Mia and Caleb were conceived via anonymous-donor insemination. The family lives in their own home in suburban Vancouver.

Jasmine is the biological mother of Christopher, aged six, whom she co-parents with her partner, Chloe. Christopher was conceived via known-donor insemination. Christopher's donor, Terry, sees Christopher twice a month and is considered to be his "dad" but not a parent. The family lives in their own home in Vancouver.

Julia and Virginia, whom I interviewed together, are the parents of Kieran, aged eighteen. Kieran was conceived via anonymous-donor insemination, though the donor's identity is known by a third-party intermediary. The family lives in a rental property in Calgary.

Laurie and Simone, whom I interviewed together, are the parents of Maggie and Hailie, aged five years and ten months. Maggie and Hailie were born via in vitro fertilization using an embryo created with Laurie's egg and anonymous-donor sperm. Simone carried both children. The family lives in their own home in suburban Calgary.

Mary Jane and Shannon, whom I interviewed together, are the parents of Britt, aged eight months. Britt was conceived via anonymous-donor insemination. The family lives in their own home in Edmonton.

Maureen and Gillian, whom I interviewed together, are the parents of Brandon, aged seven. Brandon was conceived via anonymous-donor insemination. The family lives in their own home in a small community within an hour of Vancouver.

Michaela is the biological mother of Richard, aged one, whom she co-parents with her partner, Ellen. Richard was conceived via anonymous-donor insemination. The family lives in their own home in Vancouver.

Mischa is the biological mother of Jade, aged nine, whom she co-parents with her former partner, Janice. Jade was conceived via known-donor insemination. She sees her donor, who also has an adopted son, once a week. He is understood to be Jade's "dad," but not one of her parents. Mischa and Janice separated when Jade was eight months old, and while the separation was initially conflictual, they now enjoy a fairly amicable 50/50 custody arrangement. Mischa lives in her own home in Vancouver.

Naomi is the non-biological mother of Ahava, aged two, whom she co-parents with her partner, Chaya. Ahava was conceived via anonymous-donor insemination. She is being raised to be aware of her Jewish heritage. The family lives in their own home in Edmonton.

Nic is the non-biological mother of Katrina, aged seven. Nic and her ex-partner, Lucy, separated when Katrina was four. The two mothers have a joint custody agreement and Katrina shares her time equally across the two households. Nic also has two adopted teenage daughters, who continue to have a relationship with Lucy. Katrina was conceived via known-donor insemination. Her donor cares for her regularly and is considered to be her father. The family lives in co-operative housing in Vancouver.

Nicole is the biological mother of Clarissa, aged nineteen, whom she co-parents with her partner, Talia. Clarissa was born via known-donor insemination but has no contact with her donor. Nicole has three adult children from a previous marriage who, when they were children, lived with Clarissa and Nicole. The family lives in a small community in British Columbia's Fraser Valley.

Paula is the biological mother of Dakota, aged two, whom she co-parents with her partner, Jana. Dakota was born via anonymous-donor insemination. The family lives in co-operative housing in Vancouver.

Penny is the biological mother of Melody, aged twenty-nine. Melody was conceived via anonymous-donor insemination. Penny was a single mother for most of Melody's childhood and considers herself to be Melody's sole parent. Penny lives in an apartment that she owns in Vancouver.

Rhona is the biological mother of Caden and Max, aged thirteen and eight, whom she co-parents with her partner of seven years, Doris. Caden and Max were born via known-donor insemination while Rhona was unpartnered. Each boy has a different donor, but the two men were once partners. Caden and Max see their dads on a weekly basis, and little distinction is drawn between which man is the biological father of each boy. Both men are considered to be parents, as is Doris. Rhona and Doris are married. The family lives in a rental property in Vancouver.

Rochelle is the biological mother of Madison, aged one, whom she co-parents with her partner, Abigail. Their daughter was conceived via anonymous-donor insemination. Rochelle and Abigail are married. The family lives in their own home in Vancouver.

Rosie and Toni, whom I interviewed together, are the parents of Liam, aged six. Liam was conceived via anonymous-donor insemination. The family lives in their own home in a small town approximately a hundred kilometres from Calgary.

Ruth and Kinwa, who were interviewed together, are the parents of Bailey, aged ten. Bailey was conceived via anonymous-donor insemination. Kinwa is a member of a local Aboriginal band and, although Kinwa is Bailey's non-biological mother, Bailey is being raised to be aware of his family's Aboriginal heritage. Ruth and Kinwa have been trying to adopt a child from the child protection system for several years. The family lives in their own home in Edmonton.

Sally is the biological mother of Owen, aged one, whom she co-parents with her partner, Mae. Owen was born via anonymous-donor insemination. The family lives in their own home in suburban Calgary.

Sara and Lisa, whom I interviewed together, are the parents of Riley, aged one. Riley was conceived via anonymous-donor insemination, though her donor is part of the "identity release" program. The family lives in a rental property in Vancouver.

Sophie and Catherine, whom I interviewed together, are the parents of Alain, aged three. Alain was born via anonymous-donor insemination and is being raised in a francophone household. The family lives in their own apartment in Vancouver.

Sylvie is the non-biological mother of Leesa and Miriam, aged five and three, whom she co-parents with her partner, Carissa. Leesa and Miriam were conceived via known-donor insemination. Their donor, Edward, sees them occasionally and plays a very minor role in their lives. He is understood to be a donor and not a father. The family live in co-operative housing in Vancouver.

Tracey and Helen, whom I interviewed together, are the parents of Jayden, aged four months. Jayden was conceived via known-donor insemination. His donor, Brian, lives overseas with his male partner but has visited Jayden since his birth. The family lived in an apartment in Vancouver when I interviewed them but was moving to a recently purchased home.

Veronique is the biological mother of Nathan, aged ten, whom she co-parents with her partner, Edele. Nathan was born to Veronique at the end of a previous relationship, and it was not intended that her partner be Nathan's co-parent. Nathan was born via anonymous-donor insemination. Veronique and Edele are married. The family lives in their own home in Edmonton.

Yael is the biological mother of Aaron, aged twenty-one, and the non-biological mother of Freya, aged twenty-eight. Both Aaron and Freya were conceived using anonymous-donor insemination. Yael separated from her partner when Freya was seven and Aaron was one month. She co-parented Freya with her former partner after their separation, but raised Aaron primarily on her own. Yael lives in a rental property in Vancouver.

Yvonne is the biological mother of Kayla, aged fourteen. Yvonne separated from Kayla's non-biological mother when Kayla was a toddler. They now share custody of Kayla, though she spends most of her time with Yvonne and her partner of eight years, Sheila. Sheila is considered to be Kayla's stepmother. Kayla was conceived via anonymous-donor insemination. The family lives in a small town about an hour from Calgary.

Notes

Introduction

1 Kath Weston was the first scholar to refer to the lesbian and gay "baby boom." Kath Weston, *Families We Choose: Lesbians, Gays, Kinship* (New York: Columbia University Press, 1991).

2 Statistics Canada, *Family Portrait: Continuity and Change in Canadian Families and Households in 2006, 2006 Census* (Catalogue no. 97-553-XWE2006001) (Ottawa: Statistics Canada, 2007). The Canadian statistics appear to reflect an international, albeit Western, trend. For example, research from Australia, the United States, and New Zealand has confirmed that between 15 and 20 percent of lesbian women in those countries are raising children. See Jenni Millbank, *Meet the Parents: A Review of the Research on Lesbian and Gay Families* (Sydney: Gay and Lesbian Rights Lobby [NSW], 2002), 20-21.

3 Statistics Canada, *Profile of Canadian Families and Households: Diversification Continues* (2001 Census Analysis Series, Catalogue no. 96F0030XIE2001003) (Ottawa: Statistics Canada, 2002).

4 This figure was provided by a Genesis Fertility Centre employee who testified before the BC Human Rights Tribunal in the two-mother birth certificate case of *Gill v. Murray*, 2001 BCHRT 34, para. 8. There is no data on the number of single lesbian women using Genesis's services.

5 The first sperm bank in the world to actively market itself to lesbian women, The Sperm Bank of California in Oakland, notes on its website that two-thirds of the children born through its services are parented by lesbian couples. The Sperm Bank of California, http://www.thespermbankofca.org/pages/page.php?pageid=1.

6 For a discussion of the experiences of these women, which were markedly different from the experiences of many lesbian mothers today, it is helpful to read Ellen Lewin's groundbreaking work. Lewin's interviews with 135 lesbian mothers were conducted between 1977 and 1981. Her accounts of the mothers' experiences reveal the enormity of the legal and social changes that have occurred since that time. Ellen Lewin, *Lesbian Mothers: Accounts of Gender in American Culture* (Ithaca: Cornell University Press, 1993).

7 Many of these women faced considerable opposition from their former male partners, and some found themselves involved in custody disputes. Others decided that they could never win in court and reluctantly withdrew from their children's lives. While most of the mothers who went to court were successful in gaining custody, judges often placed limitations on them, including prohibitions on their new female partners living in the home. For a discussion of some of these early cases see Katherine Arnup, "'Mothers Just Like Others': Lesbians, Divorce and Child Custody in Canada," *C.J.W.L.* 3 (1989): 18; Katherine Arnup, "'We are Family': Lesbian Mothers in Canada," *Resources for Feminist Research* 20 (1991): 101; Jenni Millbank, "Lesbians, Child Custody, and the Long Lingering Gaze of the Law," in *Challenging the Public/Private Divide: Feminism, Law, and Public Policy*, ed. Susan Boyd (Toronto: University of Toronto Press, 1997), 280; Susan Boyd, "Lesbian (and Gay) Custody Claims: What Difference Does Difference Make?" *Can. J. Fam. L.* 15 (1998): 131.

8 The National Youth Advocacy Coalition, an umbrella organization for gay and lesbian youth in the United States, found that between 1995 and 2000, the average coming out age dropped from nineteen to fifteen. Sarah Wildman, "Coming Out Early," *The Advocate*, 10 October 2000, 39. A more recent study found that the average age a teenager in the United States now comes out is thirteen. See Marilyn Elias, "Gay Teens Coming Out Earlier to Peers and Family," *USA Today*, 7 February 2007, http://www.usatoday.com/news/nation/.

9 While it is difficult to accurately ascertain how many lesbian women actually conceive in the context of heterosexual relationships and then subsequently come out, Millbank has argued, based on her review of the international literature on lesbian and gay parenting, that it is "fair to estimate that between 50-70% of the children being raised in lesbian households are now children born into lesbian families rather than from previous heterosexual relationships. This proportion will likely increase in the next ten years." Millbank, *Meet the Parents*, 24n2.

10 For some exceptions, see Fiona Nelson, *Lesbian Motherhood: An Exploration of Canadian Lesbian Families* (Toronto: University of Toronto Press, 1996), and Arnup, "'We Are Family'"; Katherine Arnup, ed., *Lesbian Parenting: Living with Pride and Prejudice* (Charlottetown, PE: Gynergy Books, 1995).

11 Fiona Kelly, "An Alternative Conception: The Legality of Home Insemination under Canada's *Assisted Human Reproduction Act*," *Can. J. Fam. L.* 26 (2010): 149.

12 *Civil Code of Quebec,* S.Q. 1991, c. 64, arts. 538-42. In Canada, the assignment of legal parentage at the point of birth is addressed in provincial legislation.

13 Though designed to address the specific needs of planned lesbian families, for the sake of consistency the model would apply to both same-sex and opposite-sex couples who rely on assisted reproduction.

14 Judith Stacey and Timothy Biblarz, "(How) Does the Sexual Orientation of Parents Matter?" *American Sociological Review* 66 (2001): 159; Raymond Lee, *Doing Research on Sensitive Topics* (London: Sage, 1993); Kenneth Plummer, *Documents of Life* (London: Allen and Unwin, 1981), 214.

15 Robert Burgess, *In the Field: An Introduction to Field Research* (London: Allen and Unwin, 1984), 57-58.

16 The lesbian "nuclear family" refers to an intact two-mother family. The mothers in these families may have conceived using the sperm of a known donor, but he is not included within their family structure.

17 Stacey and Biblarz, "Sexual Orientation of Parents."

18 While it impossible to know exactly how many lesbian women become parents via alternative conception as opposed to adoption, the fact that Canadian fertility clinics are experiencing a rise in the number of lesbian clients seems to suggest that the former is becoming an increasingly popular choice.

19 Burgess, *In the Field,* 108; Plummer, *Documents of Life;* Gillian Dunne, *Lesbian Lifestyles: Women's Work and the Politics of Sexuality* (London: MacMillan, 1997), esp. 29.

20 Millbank, *Meet the Parents.*

21 In one family, the birth mother was not the child's genetic mother. The child was conceived using an embryo created using anonymous-donor sperm and the non-birth mother's egg.

22 As will be discussed in Chapter 4, the three donor categories mirror those identified by Maureen Sullivan in her study of lesbian mothers living in San Francisco. Maureen Sullivan, *The Family of Woman: Lesbian Mothers, Their Children, and the Undoing of Gender* (Berkeley: University of California Press, 2004), 49-50.

23 Ibid., 50.

24 See, e.g., Dunne, *Lesbian Lifestyles;* Sullivan, *Family of Woman;* Renate Reimann, "Does Biology Matter? Lesbian Couples' Transition to Parenthood and Their Division of Labour," *Qualitative Sociology* 20 (1997): 153; Ruth McNair, Deb Dempsey, and Sarah Wise, "Lesbian Parenting: Issues, Strengths and Challenges," *Family Matters* 63 (2002): 40; A. Brewaeys et al., "Lesbian Mothers Who Conceived after Donor Insemination – A Follow-Up Study," *Human Reproduction* 10 (1995): 2731.

25 Sullivan, *Family of Woman;* Reimann, "Does Biology Matter?"

26 Stacey and Biblarz, "Sexual Orientation of Parents," 166.

27 Ibid.

28 One couple who conceived through in vitro fertilization admitted to spending almost $20,000 on fertility services.

29 Sullivan, *Family of Woman,* 242.

30 Statistics Canada, *Income of Individuals, Families and Households: Highlight Tables, 2001 Census* (Catalogue no. 97F0024XIE2001014) (Ottawa: Statistics Canada, 2003), http://www12.statcan.ca/english/census01/.

Chapter 1: The Legal and Social Context

1 The federal *Divorce Act* does address parentage, though only in the context of parental separation and primarily for the purposes of child support liability. It contains no provisions addressing the assignment of parentage at the time of birth. Furthermore, the *Divorce Act* can only be used by parents who have been party to a legal marriage, an institution only recently made available to same-sex couples in Canada. *Divorce Act,* R.S.C. 1985, c. 3, s. 16(10).

2 Malina Coleman, "Gestation, Intent and the Seed: Defining Motherhood in the Era of Assisted Human Reproduction," *Cardozo L. Rev.* 17 (1996): 497.

3 Roxanne Mykitiuk, "Beyond Conception: Legal Determinations of Filiation in the Context of Assisted Reproductive Technologies," *Osgoode Hall L. J.* 39 (2001): 781, 786.

4 *Vital Statistics Act,* R.S.B.C. 1996, c. 479.

5 Ibid., s. 1.

6 Mykitiuk, "Beyond Conception," 779.

7 Selma Sevenhuijsen, "The Gendered Juridification of Parenthood," *Soc. and Leg. Stud.* 1 (1992): 74.

8 *Family Relations Act,* R.S.B.C. 1996, c. 128, s. 95; *Children's Law Reform Act,* R.S.O. 1990, c. 12, s. 8; *Child, Youth and Family Enhancement Act,* R.S.A. 2000, c. C-12, s. 1(1)(a); *Family Law Act,* S.A. 2003, c. F-4.5, s. 1(f), s. 8(1); *Family Maintenance Act,* C.C.S.M. c. F20, s. 23; *Family Services Act,* S.N.B. 1980, c. F-2.2, s. 103; *Children's Law Act,* R.S.N.L. 1990, c. C-13, ss. 7 and 10; *Children's Law Act,* S.N.W.T. 1997, c. 14, s. 8; *Maintenance and Custody Act,* R.S.N.S. 1989, c. 160, s. 2(j); *Child and Family Services Act,* S.N.S. 1990, c. 5, s. 3(1)(r)(vii); *Custody Jurisdiction and Enforcement Act,* R.S.P.E.I. 1988, c. C-33, s. 3(1); *Child Status Act,* R.S.P.E.I. 1988, c. C-6, s. 9(1); *Civil Code of Quebec,* S.Q. 1991, c. 64, art. 525; *Children's Law Act,* S.S. 2002, c. C-8.1, s. 45; *Children's Act,* R.S.Y. 2002, c. 31, s. 12.

9 This fact is acknowledged in provincial family law legislation, which allows a court to order, in situations where a man denies paternity, that the man and child undergo a DNA test to determine genetic paternity. Such a test can then be introduced as evidence in child support proceedings. See, e.g., *Family Relations Act,* s. 95.1; *Children's Law Reform Act,* s. 10.

10 Research has suggested that as many as 10 percent of children have a different father from the one listed on their birth certificate. See Kermyt Anderson, "How Well Does Paternity Confidence Match Actual Paternity? Evidence from Worldwide Non-Paternity Rates," *Current Anthropology* 48 (2006): 511.

11 Marjorie Maguire Schulz, "Reproductive Technology and Intent-Based Parenthood: An Opportunity for Gender Neutrality," *Wis. L. Rev.* (1990): 297.

12 *Fraess v. Alberta (Minister of Justice and Attorney General)*, [2005] A.J. No. 1665.

13 In a constitutional challenge in Saskatchewan to the exclusion from the presumptions of paternity of women who cohabit with female partners, the court rejected the application, holding that extending the presumption to women would be impossible "simply because a woman could not have provided the seed." *P.C. v. S.L.*, 2005 SKQB 502, para. 17.

14 As will be discussed below, some provinces allow a non-biological mother to be listed on a child's birth certificate at birth. However, birth certificates, while important legal documents, are not proof of legal parentage.

15 Recognition of lesbian legal parenthood at the point of family formation (i.e., when the child is born) should be distinguished from recognition in situations of conflict, particularly conflict with donors. In most provinces, the law is now able to recognize two legal mothers (provided some positive action is taken by the non-biological mother), but the legal weight accorded to non-biological motherhood appears to diminish in situations of conflict, whether that conflict is with a donor or with the biological mother. See, e.g., *K.G.T. v. P.D.*, [2005] B.C.J. No. 2935 (SC); *S.G. v. L.C.*, [2004] Q.J. No. 6915.

16 For the Ontario litigation, see *Re K* (1995), 15 R.F.L. (4th) 129 (Ont. Prov. Ct.). As of July 2009, same-sex second-parent adoption is permitted in all Canadian provinces and territories except Prince Edward Island and Nunavut. See *Re K; Re A* (1999), 181 D.L.R. (4th) 300 (Alta. Q.B.); *Re Nova Scotia (Birth Registration No. 1999-02-00420)* (2001) 194 N.S.R. (2d) 362 (S.C.) (Nova Scotia); *Adoption Act*, C.C.S.M. 1997, c. A2, s. 10 (Manitoba); *Adoption Act*, S.N.L. 1999, c. A-2.1, s. 20 (Newfoundland and Labrador); *Adoption Act*, S.S. 1998, c. A-5.2, s. 23 (Saskatchewan); *Adoption Act*, R.S.B.C. 1996, c. 5, ss. 5, 29 (British Columbia); *Adoption Act*, S.N.W.T. 1998, c. 9, s. 5 (Northwest Territories).

17 In all but two provinces (Quebec and Manitoba), the availability of the gender-neutral birth certificate has been the result of litigation. The provinces that permit two same-sex parents to appear on a child's birth certificate from birth are British Columbia (*Gill v. Murray*, 2001 BCHRT 34), New Brunswick (*A.A. v. New Brunswick (Department of Family and Community Services)*, [2004] N.B.H.R.B.I.D. No. 4), Manitoba (*Vital Statistics Act*, R.S.M. 1997, c. V60, s. 3(6)), Quebec (*Civil Code of Quebec)*; Ontario (*M.D.R. v. Ontario (Deputy Registrar General)*, [2006] O.J. No. 2268) and Alberta (*Fraess v. Alberta)*.

18 *A.A. v. B.B.*, [2007] O.J. No. 2. (C.A.). The interveners at the Court of Appeal level, the Alliance for Marriage and Family, recently sought to be added as a party to the case in order to seek leave to appeal the decision to the Supreme Court of Canada. The application was rejected on the basis that the Alliance did not have standing to be added as a party. *Alliance for Marriage and Family v. A.A.*, 2007 SCC 40.

19 In Quebec, Newfoundland and Labrador, Alberta, and the Yukon, the male partner of a woman inseminated with donor sperm is deemed to be the legal father of the child if he consented to the insemination. *Civil Code of Quebec*, arts. 538-42; *Children's Law Act*, R.S.N.L., s. 12; *Children's Act*, s. 13; *Family Law Act*, S.A., s. 13(2).

20 These new provisions in the *Civil Code of Quebec* were introduced in June 2002 alongside Quebec's civil union laws, which apply to both heterosexual and same-sex couples.

21 *Civil Code of Quebec*, art. 538.3.

22 For a detailed discussion of these broader family law trends in the parenting context, see Susan Boyd, "Gendering Legal Parenthood: Bio-Genetic Ties, Intentionality and Responsibility," *Windsor Y.B. Access to Justice* 25 (2007): 63.

23 Judith Stacey, *In the Name of the Family: Rethinking Family Values in the Post-Modern Age* (Boston: Beacon Press, 1996), 142.

24 Two-thirds (65.7 percent) of Canada's 5.6 million children aged fourteen and under live with married parents. The remaining one-third live with unmarried cohabiting parents (18.4 percent) or with a single parent (15.9 percent). Statistics Canada, *Family Portrait: Continuity and Change in Canadian Families and Households in 2006, 2006 Census* (Catalogue no. 97-553-XWE2006001) (Ottawa: Statistics Canada, 2007).

25 The term "functional family" refers to families that do not meet the legal definition of "family" in any given jurisdiction, but who operate or "function" in the same way as legally recognized families. For example, same-sex couples with children are often said to "function" in the same way as opposite-sex couples with children, and are thus entitled to equal treatment under the law.

26 For a discussion of the emergence of fathers' rights groups in Canada and their role in family law reform, see Susan Boyd and Claire Young, "Feminism, Fathers' Rights, and Family Catastrophes: Parliamentary Discourses on Post-Separation Parenting, 1966-2003," in *Reaction and Resistance: Feminism, Law and Social Change*, ed. Dorothy Chunn, Susan B. Boyd, and Hester Lessard (Vancouver: UBC Press, 2007), 198.

27 For a discussion of the role of both neo-liberalism and neo-conservatism in shaping Canadian family law, see Brenda Cossman, "Family Feuds: Neo-Liberal and Neo-Conservative Visions of the Reprivatization Project," in *Privatization, Law and the Challenge to Feminism*, ed. Brenda Cossman and Judy Fudge (Toronto: University of Toronto Press, 2002), 169.

28 For example, fathers' rights advocates were extremely well represented during both the Special Joint Committee on Child Custody and Access hearings in 1998 and the Federal-Provincial-Territorial Report on Custody and Access and Child Support hearings in 2001. Both committees were tasked with proposing reforms to the custody and access provisions of the federal *Divorce Act*. See Boyd and Young, "Family Catastrophes."

29 Linda Neilson, *Spousal Abuse, Children and the Legal System: Final Report for the Canadian Bar Association, Law for the Futures Fund* (Fredericton, NB: Muriel McQueen Fergusson Centre for Family Violence Research, UNB, 2001).

30 Dawn Bourque, "'Reconstructing' the Patriarchal Nuclear Family: Recent Developments in Child Custody and Access in Canada," *C.J.L.S.* 10 (1995): 6.

31 Susan Boyd, "Is There an Ideology of Motherhood in (Post)Modern Child Custody Law?" *Social and Legal Studies* 5 (1996): 502.

32 Linda Neilson, "Partner Abuse, Children and Statutory Change: Cautionary Comments on Women's Access to Justice," *Windsor Y.B. Access Just.* 18 (2000): 115; Helen Rhoades, Reg Graycar, and Margaret Harrison, *The Family Law Reform Act 1995: The First Three Years* (Sydney: University of Sydney and the Family Court of Australia, 2000), 78-82.

33 Neilson, *Spousal Abuse*, 80.

34 Female lawyer quoted in ibid.

35 Ibid., 84.

36 Similar findings were reported in Melanie Rosnes, "The Invisibility of Male Violence in Canadian Child Custody and Access Decision-Making," *Can. J. Fam. L.* 14 (1997): 31.

37 Neilson, *Spousal Abuse*, at 59. This is despite research evidence indicating that patterns of abusive behaviour often indicate poor parenting skill and ability, that between 30 and 50 percent of men who physically abuse their partners will also physically abuse their children, and that the rates of child abuse increase with the severity and frequency of the pattern of partner abuse. Peter Jaffe, David Wolfe, and Susan Wilson, *Children of Battered Women* (Newbury Park, CA: Sage, 1999); Marlies Sudermann and Peter Jaffe, *A Handbook for Health and Social Service Providers and Educators on Children Exposed to Woman Abuse/Family Violence* (Ottawa: Health Canada, National Clearinghouse on Family Violence, 2000); M. Pagelow, "Effects of Domestic Violence on Children and Their Consequences for Custody and Visitation Agreements," *Mediation Quarterly* 7 (1994): 347.

38 Jaffe and Geffner, cited in Grace Kerr and Peter Jaffe, "Legal and Clinical Issues in Child Custody Disputes Involving Domestic Violence," *C.F.L.Q.* 17 (1999): 1.

39 Children who witness violence are at risk for a number of significant emotional and behavioural problems such as aggression, bullying, anxiety, destruction of property, insecurity, depression, and secretiveness. Almost 60 percent of children who are exposed to violence show symptoms consistent with a DSM-IV diagnosis

of post-traumatic stress disorder (Lehmann, cited in Kerr and Jaffe, ibid.). Children who witness violence are also at risk of developing inappropriate attitudes about the use of violence to resolve interpersonal conflicts. Boys who are exposed to violence are more likely to end up being abusers in an intimate relationships. For example, in a Statistics Canada study, women were three times more likely to be assaulted as well as suffer repeat, severe and injurious abuse if their father-in-law was violent towards their mother-in-law (Rodgers, cited in Kerr and Jaffe, ibid.).

40 *Johnson-Steeves v. Lee* (1997), 29 R.F.L. (4th) 126 (Alta. Q.B.); *Johnson-Steeves v. Lee* (1997), 33 R.F.L. (4th) 278 (Alta. C.A.).

41 *Johnson-Steeves v. Lee* (Alta. Q.B.), para. 6.

42 Ibid.

43 *Johnson-Steeves v. Lee* (Alta. C.A.), para. 16

44 Ibid.

45 *Johnson-Steeves v. Lee* (Alta. Q.B.), para. 42.

46 Ibid., para. 41.

47 *Trociuk v. British Columbia (Attorney-General)*, [2003] 1 S.C.R. 835. *Trociuk*, a unanimous decision, was the first Supreme Court of Canada decision in which section 15 equality rights were successfully invoked by a father.

48 Darrel Trociuk rejected the hyphenation option and continued to argue that the children should bear his name only. *Trociuk*.

49 *T. (D.W.) v. British Columbia (Attorney-General)* (2001), 90 B.C.L.R. (3d) 1, para. 172.

50 *Family Relations Act*, s. 1.

51 In fact, as Boyd notes, the Supreme Court judgment repeatedly emphasizes fathers' rights, while making only one reference to parental responsibilities. Boyd, "Gendering," 15.

52 *Trociuk*, para. 16.

53 Ibid., para. 31.

54 Hester Lessard, "Mothers, Fathers and Naming: Reflections on the Law Equality Framework and *Trociuk v. British Columbia (Attorney General)*," *C.J.W.L.* 16 (2004): 165.

55 *Civil Code of Quebec*, arts. 538-42. The new articles were introduced in June 2002 by the *Act Instituting Civil Unions and Establishing New Rules of Filiation*.

56 *S.G. v. L.C*, [2004]. Unfortunately, a media publication ban was put on the case, making it difficult to know anything about the dispute other than what is included in the interim judgment: *S.G. c. L.C.*, [2005] J.Q. No 7407.

57 The two mothers did not file affidavits, so it is not known whether they accept or challenge this evidence: *S.G. v. L.C.*, [2004], para 7.

58 It should be noted, however, that even Quebec's law appears to maintain as its underlying premise the father/mother dyad. In article 539.1 of the code, it is stated

that where the spouse of the birth mother is a woman, that woman takes up the rights and obligations that would otherwise accrue to the father. While this provision was probably included to ensure that the law of succession could apply smoothly, it also illustrates that even when two women are parents, the basic starting point is the heterosexual father/mother model. While the non-biological mother is referred to in the same article as "the *mother* who did not give birth" (emphasis added), there is at least some suggestion in the text that the non-biological mother occupies a slightly lesser status. *Civil Code of Quebec*, art. 539.1.

59 Ibid., art. 538.3.

60 Ibid. art. 538.2.

61 *S.G. v. L.C.*, [2004], para. 34.

62 Ibid., para. 54.

63 Ibid., para. 50.

64 *L.O. v. S.J.* (2006), J.Q. No. 450.

65 *A v. B, C and X* 2007 R.D.F. 217.

66 Without the knowledge of the non-biological lesbian co-mother, the child was conceived through intercourse rather than insemination during her relationship with the biological mother.

67 *M.A.C. v. M.K.*, [2009] ONCJ 18.

68 The donor had already successfully applied for access. *K.(M.) v. C.(M.) and D.(C.)*, 2007 ONCJ 456.

69 Jenni Millbank, "The Limits of Functional Family: Lesbian Mother Litigation in the Era of the Eternal Biological Family," *Int'l J.L. Pol'y and Fam.* 22 (2008): 149.

70 Ibid., 160.

71 Ibid., 161.

72 Ibid., 162.

73 Ibid., 158.

74 There have been six judgments in the *P v. K & M* case: *K v. M* (2002), 22 FRNZ 360; *P v. K & M* (Family Court, Auckland, unreported, Doogue J., 8 August 2002); *P v. K*, [2003] 2 NZLR 787; *P v. K & M*, [2004] NZFLR 752; *P v. K*, [2004] 2 NZLR 421; *P v. K*, [2006] NZFLR 22.

75 *P v. K*, [2003], para. 26.

Chapter 2: On Whose Terms? On What Terms?

1 *Rosenberg v. Canada (Attorney-General)*, [1998] 38 O.R. (3d) 577.

2 *Re K* (1995), 15 R.F.L. (4th) 129 (Ont. Prov. Ct.); *Re A* (1999), 181 D.L.R. (4th) 300 (Alta. Q.B.).

3 EGALE stands for Equality for Gays and Lesbians Everywhere. EGALE describes itself as a "national organization" that "advances equality and justice for lesbian, gay, bisexual and trans-identified people, and their families, across Canada" (http://www.egale.ca/).

4 See, e.g., Canadians for Equal Marriage, Press Release, "After the Vote: CEM Speaks," 28 June 2005, http://www.equal-marriage.ca/resource.php?id=464.

5 See, e.g., Susan Boyd and Claire Young, "'From Same-Sex to No Sex'?: Trends towards Recognition of (Same-Sex) Relationships in Canada," *Seattle Journal for Social Justice* 1 (2003): 763-65; Susan Boyd, "From Outlaw to InLaw: Bringing Lesbian and Gay Relationships into the Family System," *Yearbook of New Zealand Jurisprudence* 3 (1999): 31; Judith Butler, "Is Kinship Always Already Heterosexual?" *differences: A Journal of Feminist Cultural Studies* 13 (2002): 14; Julie Shapiro, "A Lesbian-Centered Critique of Second-Parent Adoptions," *Berkeley Women's L.J.* 14 (1999): 17; Shane Phelan, *Sexual Strangers: Gays, Lesbians, and Dilemmas of Citizenship* (Philadelphia: Temple University Press, 2001); Didi Herman, "Are We Family? Lesbian Rights and Women's Liberation," *Osgoode Hall L.J.* 28 (1990): 789; Ruthann Robson, *Lesbian (Out)law: Survival under the Rule of Law* (Ithaca, NY: Firebrand Books, 1992).

6 *Canadian Charter of Rights and Freedoms,* Part I of the *Constitution Act, 1982,* being Schedule B to the *Canada Act 1982* (U.K.), 1982, c. 11, s. 15.

7 *Law v. Canada (Minister of Employment and Immigration),* [1999] 1 S.C.R. 497, para. 6. The decision in *Law* confirmed that applicants bringing a claim under section 15 must identify a person, group, or groups with whom he or she wishes to be compared for the purpose of the discrimination inquiry.

8 Boyd and Young, "'From Same-Sex,'" 764.

9 Miriam Smith, *Lesbian and Gay Rights in Canada: Social Movements and Equality-Seeking, 1971-1995* (Toronto: University of Toronto Press, 1999), 85.

10 Shelley Gavigan, "Equal Families, Equal Parents, Equal Marriage: The Case of the Missing Patriarch," in *Diminishing Returns: Inequality and the Canadian Charter of Rights and Freedoms,* ed. Sheila McIntyre and Sandra Rodgers (Markham, ON: LexisNexis Butterworths, 2006), 317 at 320.

11 Some of the few exceptions are Katherine Arnup and Susan Boyd, "Familial Disputes? Sperm Donors, Lesbian Mothers, and Legal Parenthood," in *Legal Inversions,* ed. Didi Herman and Carl Stychin (Philadelphia: Temple University Press, 1995), 77; Fiona Kelly, "Nuclear Norms or Fluid Families? Incorporating Lesbian and Gay Parents and Their Children into Canadian Family Law," *Can. J. Fam. L.* 21 (2004): 133; Shapiro, "Lesbian-Centered Critique."

12 Nancy Polikoff, "The Deliberate Construction of Families without Fathers: Is It an Option for Lesbian and Heterosexual Mothers?" *Santa Clara L. Rev.* 36 (1996): 375; Nancy Polikoff, "This Child Does Have Two Mothers: Redefining Parenthood to Meet the Needs of Children in Lesbian-Mother and Other Nontraditional Families," *Geo. L.J.* 78 (1990): 459.

13 Miriam Smith, *Lesbian and Gay Rights in Canada: Social Movements and Equality Seeking, 1971-1995* (Toronto: University of Toronto Press, 1999), 70.

14 Ibid., 74-75.

15 Ibid., 69-70.

16 Ibid., 76.

17 Ibid., 85.

18 Smith describes "rights talk" as a "specific type of political discourse that ... privileges the law and the courts as the mechanism for the resolution and processing of political problems such as conflicts of interest and values between groups or conflicts between groups and the state. Rights talk assumes that the technical standards of constitutional law, enforced by courts, can resolve political problems and conflicts." Smith, *Lesbian and Gay Rights*, 74-75.

19 *Andrews v. Ontario (Minister of Health)* (1988), 64 O.R. (2d) 258 (H.C.J.).

20 *Human Rights Code*, R.S.O. 1990, c. H-19.

21 *Andrews*, para. 19.

22 Brenda Cossman, "Family Inside/Out," *U.T.L.J.* 44 (1994): 5-6.

23 For an analysis of these decisions, see Claire Young, "Spousal Status, Pension Benefits and Tax: *Rosenberg v. Canada (Attorney-General)*," *C.L.E.L.J.* 6 (1998): 435.

24 It is interesting to note that the amendments redefined "spouse," which had previously included married persons *and* those in opposite-sex common-law relationships, so that the word referred to married persons only. A new definition of common-law partner was added to the act. That definition included individuals who lived in a conjugal relationship with a person of the opposite or same sex for a period of at least twelve months. Despite the multiple categories of relationship, the tax rules applied in exactly the same manner to married persons, unmarried opposite-sex couples, and same-sex couples.

25 *Family Law Act*, R.S.O. 1990, c. F.3, s. 1(1); *M v. H*, [1996] 132 D.L.R. (4th) 538 (Ont. Ct. (Gen. Div.)).

26 Ibid., 615-16.

27 Boyd and Young, "'From Same-Sex," 763.

28 *Modernization of Benefits and Obligations Act*, S.C. 2000, c. 12.

29 *Civil Marriage Act*, S.C. 2005, c. 33.

30 Kathleen Lahey, *Are We "Persons" Yet? Law and Sexuality in Canada* (Toronto: University of Toronto Press, 1999).

31 Factum of Applicant couples, *Halpern v. Ontario in the Ontario Division* Court (28 August 2001), para 2 (on file with author), http://www.egale.ca/extra%5CON-ApplicantsFactum.doc [henceforth *Halpern* factum].

32 Gavigan, "Equal Families," 332.

33 *Halpern* factum, para 1.

34 Factum of the Intervenor, Interfaith Coalition on Marriage and Family, *Reference re Same-Sex Marriage*, [2004] S.C.J. No. 76, para. 1.

35 Affidavit of Lloyd Thornhill, *EGALE Inc. v. Attorney-General of Canada* (15 December 2001), EGALE Canada, http://www.egale.ca/, Issues, Equal Marriage, B.C. Marriage Case.

36 *Halpern* factum, para. 6.

37 The emphasis the litigants place on consumption – from property ownership to cars, refrigerators, and washing machines – helps make the litigants' relationships and lifestyle palatable to courts and politicians who increasingly understand family relationships through a privatized lens. By alluding to the middle-class, consumerist nature of their lives, the litigants place themselves squarely within what has been referred to as the "gayeoisie." Amy Gluckman and Betsy Reed, eds., *Homo Economics: Capitalism, Community, and Lesbian and Gay Life* (New York: Routledge, 1997).

38 Similar statements were made during the House of Commons Standing Committee on Justice and Human Rights hearings on same-sex unions in 2003. See, e.g., Canada, House of Commons Standing Committee on Justice and Human Rights, *Committee Minutes,* 37th Parl. 2nd sess., Meeting No. 29 (1 April 2003), 50 (Martha Dow) [henceforth Dow, *Committee Minutes*]; Canada, House of Commons Standing Committee on Justice and Human Rights, *Committee Minutes,* 37th Parl. 2nd sess., Meeting No. 29 (1 April 2003), 76 (Dawn Barbeau).

39 Boyd and Young, "'From Same-Sex,'" 773.

40 While the decision in *Andrews v. Ontario* rejected the "similarly situated" test and opened the door for section 15 to be interpreted through the lens of substantive equality, more recent Supreme Court decisions suggest that Canadian equality jurisprudence is retreating from a substantive equality framework. The trend began with the decision in *Law v. Canada* and has continued more recently in decisions such as *Gosselin v. Quebec (Attorney General),* [2002] 4 S.C.R. 429; *Walsh v. Nova Scotia (Attorney General),* [2002] 4 S.C.R. 325; and *Trociuk v. British Columbia (Attorney General),* [2003] 1 S.C.R. 835. It is thus not particularly surprising that the marriage case litigants presented their cases as claims to formal equality.

41 *Halpern* factum, para. 23.

42 Ibid., para. 27.

43 Ibid., para. 89.

44 Ibid., para. 4.

45 Gavigan, "Equal Families," 335.

46 Claire Young and Susan Boyd, "Losing the Feminist Voice? Debates on the Legal Recognition of Same Sex Partnerships in Canada," *Fem. Legal Stud.* 14 (2006): 213.

47 See, e.g., Tracey Tyler and Tracy Huffman, "Gay Couple Married after Ruling," *Toronto Star,* 11 June 2003, http://www.freerepublic.com/focus/f-news/926892/posts; Brian Morton and Nicholas Read, "Gay Marriage Makes B.C. History: Ceremony Minutes after Appeal Court Lifts Ban," *Vancouver Sun,* 9 July 2003.

48 Editorial, "Gays in the 'Hood," *Globe and Mail,* 31 January 2005.

49 For a critique of the role of race in the same-sex marriage debate, see Suzanne Lenon, "Marrying Citizens! Raced Subjects? Re-thinking the Terrain of Equal Marriage Discourse," *C.J.W.L.* 17 (2005): 405.

50   Robson, *Lesbian (Out)law*, 18.

51   Joan Nestle, *A Restricted Country* (Ithaca, NY: Firebrand Books, 1987), 123.

52   Butler, "Kinship," 28.

53   See, e.g., the following statement made by a lesbian woman before the House Committee: "I come to you as a traditional lesbian, who's been together for 19 years and has children. My partner is quitting work in a couple of weeks so she can stay home with our children. We need to be recognized with other couples who make choices." Dow, *Committee Minutes*. For an analysis of the submissions made to the committee, see Young and Boyd, "Losing."

54   Nancy Polikoff, *Beyond (Straight and Gay) Marriage: Valuing All Families under the Law* (Boston: Beacon Press, 2008).

55   Lenon, "Marrying Citizens!"; Boyd and Young, "'From Same-Sex,'" 771; Young and Boyd, "Losing," 218-19.

56   My use of the term "privatization project" refers to the movement of economic responsibility for the individual from the public or state domain to the private realm of the individual, family, or charity. The trend towards economic privatization is frequently linked to a neo-liberal political philosophy. For a feminist analysis of the impact of privatization in the family law context, see Brenda Cossman, "Family Feuds: Neo-Liberal and Neo-Conservative Visions of the Reprivatization Project," in *Privatization, Law, and the Challenge to Feminism*, ed. Brenda Cossman and Judy Fudge (Toronto: University of Toronto Press, 2002), 169.

57   Boyd and Young, "'From Same-Sex,'" 777.

58   In an Environics survey conducted almost a year after same-sex marriage was introduced at a federal level, 64 percent of the two thousand people surveyed supported the extension of marriage to include same-sex couples. Perhaps more telling, those who strongly agreed with equal marriage outnumbered those who strongly disagreed by 36 percent to 24 percent. Environics, *Canadians for Equal Marriage June 2006*, 14 May 2006, Media Room, http://erg.environics.net/.

59   Canada, House of Commons Standing Committee on Justice and Human Rights, *Committee Minutes*, 37th Parl. 2nd sess., Meeting No. 29 (1 April 2003), 61 (submission of West Coast LEAF).

60   See comments of Vic Toews (Canadian Alliance), Canada, *Committee Minutes*, Meeting No. 29 (submission of West Coast LEAF), (1 April 2003), 64.

61   Submission of Gary Kinsman, Canada, *Committee Minutes*, Meeting No. 35 (9 April 2003), 4, 5.

62   Butler, "Kinship," 18-19.

63   One of the few scholars to highlight the use of "best interests of the child" rhetoric in support of the right to equal marriage is Gavigan, "Equal Families," 332-39.

64   The one exception to this is *A.A. v. B.B.*, in which three parents (two mothers and a father) sought legal recognition. *A.A. v. B.B.*, [2007] O.J. No. 2. (C.A.).

65 *Re K*, para. 9.

66 Ibid.

67 Ibid., para. 37.

68 Ibid.

69 Ibid., para. 24.

70 *M.D.R. v. Ontario (Deputy Registrar General)*, [2006] O.J. 2268 (S.C.J.).

71 *A.A. v. B.B.* At the time *M.D.R.* was decided, the Court of Appeal decision in *A.A. v. B.B.*, which found that a child *could* have three legal parents, had not yet been handed down.

72 *Thomas S. v. Robin Y.*, 599 N.Y.S. 2d 377 (Fam. Ct. 1993). At the Family Court level, the mothers were successful.

73 The question of whether the donor should be considered to be inside or outside of the lesbian family caused a great deal of controversy within the lesbian and gay community itself. See, e.g., "Letters," *Lesbian/Gay Law Notes* 33.1 (1993): 1-4.

74 *Thomas S.* The New York Supreme Court overturned the Family Court decision and found in favour of Thomas S.

75 *S.G. v. L.C.*, [2004] Q.J. No. 6915 (S.C.); *L.O. v. S.J.*, [2006] J.Q. No. 450 (S.C.).

76 *Civil Code of Quebec*, S.Q. 1991, c. 64, arts. 538-42.

77 The mothers in *S.G. v. L.C.* were ultimately unsuccessful in their assertion, in large part because of the initial ambivalence that the non-biological mother had shown towards the idea of becoming a parent. While she subsequently supported the plan and became an active parent, the court treated her initial ambivalence as proof of the fact that the intention to parent was actually shared by the biological mother and the donor. However, the decision was based entirely on the uncontested affidavit of the donor. Its precedential impact is thus limited. In contrast, the court in *L.O. v. S.J.* found in favour of the two mothers. The court held that the intention to parent was clearly that of the two women and the donor was simply a third-party gamete provider. This conclusion was strongly supported by the limited role the donor had played in the child's life and the fact that the women already had two children conceived using the sperm of a different donor.

78 *M.A.C. v. M.K.*, [2009] ONCJ 18.

79 Prior to the decision in *A.A. v. B.B.*, a child could have two legal mothers but only if the donor was willing to relinquish his parental rights.

80 Shapiro, "Lesbian-Centered Critique," 31.

81 Similar scenarios might arise in situations where a child is parented by three or four individuals, some of whom have no legal recognition as parents.

82 Kelly, "Nuclear Norms."

83 For a discussion of the resurgence of the significance of biological fatherhood in Canadian family law, see Hester Lessard, "Mothers, Fathers and Naming: Reflections on the Law Equality Framework and *Trociuk v. British Columbia (Attorney General)*," *C.J.W.L.* 16 (2004): 165; Susan Boyd, "Gendering Legal Parenthood:

Bio-Genetic Ties, Intentionality and Responsibility," *Windsor Y.B. Access Just.* 25 (2007): 63.

84 For neo-conservative arguments, see, e.g., David Blankenhorn, *Fatherless America: Confronting Our Most Urgent Social Problem* (New York: Basic Books, 1995). For a discussion of the influence of neo-liberal rhetoric on child support law, see Cossman, "Family Feuds," 190-201.

85 Biological fathers have even been successful in gaining access to their children in situations where they have been violent towards the child's mother and may have engaged in abuse of the child. See, e.g., Linda Neilson, *Spousal Abuse, Children and the Legal System: Final Report for the Canadian Bar Association, Law for the Futures Fund* (Fredericton, NB: Muriel McQueen Fergusson Centre for Family Violence Research, UNB, 2001); Melanie Rosnes, "The Invisibility of Male Violence in Canadian Child Custody and Access Decision-Making," *Can. J. Fam. L.* 24 (1997): 31; Linda Neilson, "Partner Abuse, Children and Statutory Change: Cautionary Comments on Women's Access to Justice," *Windsor Y.B. Access Just.* 18 (2000): 115.

86 For example, in her review of reported Canadian custody and access cases from 1990 to 1993, Bourque found that "paternal access is viewed by judges as paramount in the 'best interests of the child' test, eclipsing virtually all other factors. A child's supposed 'need' for or 'right' to a father, irrespective of the quality or quantity of his parenting, has superseded virtually all other considerations." Dawn Bourque, "'Reconstructing' the Patriarchal Nuclear Family: Recent Developments in Child Custody and Access in Canada," *C.J.L.S.* 10 (1995): 6.

87 Shapiro, "Lesbian-Centered Critique," 21.

88 Ibid.

89 Ibid.

90 Jeffrey Weeks, Brian Heaphy, and Catherine Donovan, *Same Sex Intimacies: Families of Choice and Other Life Experiments* (London: Routledge, 2001).

Chapter 3: Defining Queer Kinship

1 Corinne P. Hayden, "Gender, Genetics and Generation: Reformulating Biology in Lesbian Kinship," *Cultural Anthropology* 10 (1995): 42. Hayden's position draws from Marilyn Strathern's argument that reproductive technologies also do not produce wholly new forms of kinship but rather make "new ideas out of old ideas." Marilyn Strathern, *Reproducing the Future: Essays on Anthropology, Kinship, and the New Reproductive Technologies* (New York: Routledge, 1992), 15.

2 Strathern, ibid.

3 Kath Weston, *Families We Choose: Lesbians, Gays, Kinship* (New York: Columbia University Press, 1991).

4 See, e.g., the literature of conservative Canadian organizations such as Focus on the Family, the Institute of Marriage and Family Canada, REAL Women of Canada, the National House of Prayer, and the Institute for Canadian Values. For a

discussion of the significant and growing role of these organizations in Canadian politics, see Marci McDonald, "Stephen Harper and the Theo-Cons," *The Walrus*, October 2006, 44. For a discussion of the "crisis of the family" literature, see Judith Stacey, *In the Name of the Family: Rethinking Family Values in the Post-Modern Age* (Boston: Beacon Press, 1996).

5 Weston, *Families We Choose*.

6 This lack of recognition was particularly acute in the United States, where Kath Weston conducted her research.

7 Though one Canadian province gives legal recognition (for some purposes) to non-conjugal, non-biological, long-term caregiving relationships, this legislation was not the product of any lobbying from the gay and lesbian community. *Adult Interdependent Relationships Act*, S.A. 2002, c. A-4.5.

8 Many of the mothers actually used this term without any prompting on my part. The expansive definition of "family" that many of the mothers adopted distinguishes them from the mothers in several other recent studies on lesbian parenthood. This may be because other studies have tended to focus on two-mother nuclear families. For example, American sociologist Maureen Sullivan *required* that the mothers in her study parent within a nuclear model, largely because she was interested in the relationship between gender and labour distribution within same-sex families with children. While Sullivan's mothers could still have defined "family" broadly, the construction of their own families arguably makes it less likely. In contrast, because my sampling strategy involved seeking as diverse an array of family configurations as possible, my study participants were more likely to voice a cross-section of opinions with regard to family definitions. Maureen Sullivan, *The Family of Woman: Lesbian Mothers, Their Children, and the Undoing of Gender* (Berkley: University of California Press, 2004), 234.

9 Neither of the men were the child's sperm donor.

10 See, e.g., Margaret Somerville, *The Ethical Imagination: Journeys of the Human Spirit* (Toronto: House of Anansi Press, 2006).

11 Tracey's resistance to having children is reminiscent of that expressed by lesbian feminists in the 1980s, who argued that lesbian motherhood would result in lesbians being absorbed into the mainstream.

12 Bountiful is a polygamous Mormon community in southeastern British Columbia near the town of Creston.

13 The recent decision of *A.A. v. B.B.* suggests that, in certain circumstances, this may no longer be the case (at least in Ontario). *A.A. v. B.B.*, [2007] O.J. No. 2 (C.A.).

14 Similar views were expressed by the lesbian mothers in Dunne's UK study. Dunne found that most of the mothers she interviewed chose gay donors, and all of the donors who were involved as co-parents were gay. While several reasons for choosing gay donors were cited, one of the most common was a view that gay men were "less likely to renege on agreements" because of their connection to the gay

community and its particular lifestyle. Gillian Dunne, "Opting into Motherhood: Lesbians Blurring the Boundaries and Transforming the Meaning of Parenthood and Kinship," *Gender and Society* 14 (2000): 16-17.

15 Stacey, *In the Name of the Family,* 142.

16 For a discussion of EGALE's approach to lesbian and gay advocacy, see Chapter 2, above.

17 This definition obviously does not limit the status of parent to two individuals.

18 Jeanette Edwards, "Explicit Connections: Ethnographic Enquiry in North-West England," in *Technologies of Procreation: Kinship in the Age of Assisted Conception,* Jeanette Edwards et al. (Manchester: Manchester University Press, 1993), 45.

19 This issue is discussed at pages 91-92, below.

20 The notion of "tying in" the non-biological mother comes from Maureen Sullivan's study of lesbian mothers in San Francisco. The mechanisms that some of the mothers used to "tie in" the non-biological mother were giving the child the non-biological mother's surname, securing a second-parent adoption, putting both mothers' names on the birth certificate, and providing for the total and equal involvement of non-biological mothers from the very beginning. Sullivan, *Family of Woman,* 59-61.

21 Ibid., 59.

22 In their study of stepfamilies in the United Kingdom, Edwards, Gillies, and McCarthy found that legal policies that emphasize biological ties often overlook the significant relationships children develop with step-parents. Rosalind Edwards, Val Gillies, and Jane Ribbens McCarthy, "Biological Parents and Social Families: Legal Discourses and Everyday Understandings of the Position of Step-parents," *Int'l J.L. Pol'y and Fam.* 13 (1999): 80.

23 Sullivan, *Family of Woman,* 67.

24 Stay-at-home parents, however, were extremely rare. Most families, particularly those living in Vancouver, simply could not afford to have a parent out of the workforce for any length of time.

25 These were not the only mothers in the sample who had separated from their child's other mother. However, they were the only cases in which either of the separated mothers suggested that there was some difference between biological and non-biological motherhood.

26 In one of these families, contact between the child and her non-biological mother was sporadic in the years immediately after separation, but they now have a mutually agreed-upon 50/50 parenting arrangement in place.

27 In fact, several of the separated non-biological mothers I spoke to had joint physical custody arrangements with their former partners.

28 In the remaining case, the non-biological mother showed little interest in being part of the child's life. Interestingly, the non-biological mother was the biological

mother of the couple's first child and *was* committed to maintaining a relationship between this child and the child's non-biological mother.

29 In fact, Simone had a biological tie with the children as the gestational mother, while Laurie had a genetic tie to them through her contribution of the eggs.

30 Identity release or "open" donors were not widely available in Canada when most of my study participants conceived. None of the mothers living in Alberta were able to access this option within their province, while the mothers in British Columbia had limited access (i.e., the group of donors who had agreed to identity release was very small). One couple used a US sperm bank for the express reason of being able to access a larger number of identity release donors.

31 David Blankenhorn, *Fatherless America: Confronting Our Most Urgent Social Problem* (New York: Basic Books, 1995); Maggie Gallagher, "Fatherless Boys Grow Up into Dangerous Men," *Wall Street Journal*, 1 December 1998; Jean Beth Elshtain, "Family Matters: The Plight of America's Children," *The Christian Century*, July 1993, 14.

32 See, e.g., Dawn Bourque's review of reported Canadian custody and access cases from 1990 to 1993 (please refer to note 86 in Chapter 2). Research also suggests that the presence of factors that diminish the benefits of access between biological fathers and their children, such as spousal abuse, has little effect on this pro-access position. Dawn Bourque, "'Reconstructing' the Patriarchal Nuclear Family: Recent Developments in Child Custody and Access in Canada," *C.J.L.S.* 10 (1995): 1; Linda Neilson, "Partner Abuse, Children and Statutory Change: Cautionary Comments on Women's Access to Justice," *Windsor Y.B. Access Just.* 18 (2000): 115.

33 See, e.g., *Re Patrick (An Application Concerning Contract)*, [2002] F.L.C. 93-096, 88, 891; *Thomas S. v. Robin Y.*, 599 N.Y.S. 2d 377 (Fam. Ct. 1993). For a discussion of these cases, see Fiona Kelly, "Nuclear Norms or Fluid Families? Incorporating Lesbian and Gay Parents and Their Children into Canadian Family Law," *Can J. Fam. L.* 21 (2004): 133; Katherine Arnup and Susan Boyd, "Familial Disputes? Sperm Donors, Lesbian Mothers, and Legal Parenthood," in *Legal Inversions: Lesbians, Gay Men, and the Politics of Law*, ed. Didi Herman and Carl Stychin (Philadelphia: Temple University Press, 1995), 77.

34 Most of the legal cases the mothers referred to, they had learned about through the press. The mothers often came across news stories about these disputes, most of which were located in the United States, when researching lesbian motherhood in books or on the Internet.

35 Sullivan, *Family of Woman*, 53.

36 Ibid., 49-50.

37 Ibid., 50.

38 Ibid.

39 In both of these families, however, no legal arrangements had been made, either between the mothers and donor or between the mothers themselves, leaving the donor's ability to claim custody unrestricted.

40 A significant number of study participants who parented within a nuclear model noted that this model had not actually been their first choice. They had wanted to parent with an involved known donor but had been unable to find a man who met their needs and was willing to take on the role.

41 See discussion at pages 55-56, above.

42 Strathern, *Reproducing the Future*, 15.

Chapter 4: Engaging with Reform

1 Nancy Polikoff, "This Child Does Have Two Mothers: Redefining Parenthood to Meet the Needs of Children in Lesbian-Mother and Other Nontraditional Families," *Geo. L.J.* 78 (1990): 459; Fred Bernstein, "This Child Does Have Two Mothers ... and a Sperm Donor with Visitation," *N.Y.U. Rev. L. and Soc. Change* 22 (1996): 1; Paula Ettelbrick, "Who Is a Parent? The Need to Develop a Lesbian Conscious Family Law," *N.Y.L. Sch. J. Hum. Rts.* 10 (1993): 513.

2 *Springer v. Graham-Newlin*, No. 642,975-5 (Cal. Super., Alameda Cty., 17 October 1988); *In the Matter of Alison D.*, 77 N.Y.2d 651(1991); *Jhordan C. v. Mary K.*, 224 Cal. Rptr. 530 (Ct. App. 1986); *In re R.C.*, 775 P. 2d 27 (Colo. 1989); *Thomas S. v. Robin Y.* 618 N.Y.S. 2d 356 (App. Div. 1994).

3 Polikoff, "This Child."

4 Ibid., 573.

5 All of Polikoff's reform proposals were also designed to apply to single (heterosexual) women, who she felt should also be in a position to parent autonomously from men. See, e.g., Nancy Polikoff, "The Deliberate Construction of Families without Fathers: Is It an Option for Lesbian and Heterosexual Mothers?" *Santa Clara L. Rev.* 36 (1996): 375.

6 Nancy Polikoff, "Breaking the Link between Biology and Parental Rights in Planned Lesbian Families: When Semen Donors Are Not Fathers," *Georgetown J. Gender and L.* 2 (2000): 57.

7 Bernstein, "This Child."

8 Ibid., 52.

9 Ibid.

10 Ibid.

11 Martha Albertson Fineman, *The Neutered Mother, the Sexual Family and Other Twentieth Century Tragedies* (New York: Routledge, 1995).

12 Ibid., 228.

13 Fineman does note, however, that the mother/child dyad is simply a metaphor and that "mothering" can be carried out by a person of either sex. Ibid., 234.

14 Ibid., 231.

15 Ibid., 229.

16 Alison Harvison Young, "Reconceiving the Family: Challenging the Paradigm of the Exclusive Family," *American Journal of Gender and Law* 6 (1998): 505.

17 Ibid., 518.

18 Marjorie Maguire Schulz, "Reproductive Technology and Intent-Based Parenthood: An Opportunity for Gender Neutrality," *Wis. L. Rev.* (1990): 349; Janet Dolgin, *Defining the Family: Law, Technology, and Reproduction in an Uneasy Age* (New York: New York University Press, 1997), 207-12.

19 Jenni Millbank, "The Limits of Functional Family: Lesbian Mother Litigation in the Era of the Eternal Biological Family," *Int'l J.L. Pol'y and Fam.* 22 (2008): 149.

20 Ibid., 150.

21 Ibid., 163-64.

22 Ibid., 164.

23 Ibid., 165-66.

24 Ibid., 168.

25 Please refer to note 19 in Chapter 1.

26 A successful challenge to Alberta's *Family Law Act* means that the parentage presumptions applicable in instances of assisted reproduction that applied only to the male partner of the birth mother now extend to the female partner of a birth mother. The legislation itself has not yet been amended. *Fraess v. Alberta (Minister of Justice and Attorney General)*, [2005] A.J. No. 1665 (Q.B.).

27 *Civil Code of Quebec*, arts. 538-42.

28 Ibid., art. 538.

29 Ibid., art. 538.3.

30 Ibid., art. 538.2.

31 It should be noted, however, that in a reported decision dealing with these provisions, the court found that the parental project was between the birth mother and the donor. This was despite the fact that the birth mother and non-biological mother had entered into a civil union prior to the birth of the child and had parented the child together from birth. The decision was an interim one and relied largely on the uncontested affidavit of the donor. However, it does suggest that the courts may be reluctant to apply the "parental project" provision in a manner that protects the lesbian family. *S.G. v. L.C.*, [2004] Q.J. No. 6915.

32 White Paper on *Family Relations Act* Reform: Proposals for a new Family Law Act, Ministry of Attorney-General, Justice Services Branch, Civil Policy and Legislation Branch, July 2010, http://www.ag.gov.bc.ca/legislation/pdf/Family-Law-White-Paper.pdf.

33 *Assisted Reproductive Treatment Act* 2008 (Vic).

34 Ibid., s. 147. Section 147 inserts a new Part III into the *Status of Children Act* 1974 (Vic). The *Uniform Parentage Act (UPA)* in the United States, revised most recently in 2002, includes a similar provision, though it applies only to married couples. While it clarifies the legal status of donors, the *UPA* does not apply to same-sex couples. The *UPA* has been adopted, though not verbatim, by a handful of states. *Uniform Parentage Act* (1973), Article 7.

35 Ibid.

36 Ibid., ss. 7-8.

37 See, e.g., *Artificial Conception Act* 1985 (WA), s. 6A; *Parentage Act* 2004 (ACT), s. 11. Unlike the Victorian legislation, the presumptions in the WA and ACT acts are rebuttable.

38 *Care of Children Act* 2004 (NZ), s. 41(2). Section 41 only applies to donor relationships and cannot be used by a third party who has not donated genetic material.

39 Ibid., s. 41(3).

40 Ibid., s. 41 4).

41 New Zealand Law Commission (NZLC), *New Issues in Legal Parenthood, Report 88* (Wellington: NZLC, 2005), paras. 6.58-6.73; Victorian Law Reform Committee (VLRC), *Assisted Reproductive Technology and Adoption: Position Paper Two – Parentage* (Melbourne: VLRC, 2005). Similar recommendations were made by the NSW Gay and Lesbian Rights Lobby in 1999. See Jenni Millbank, *And Then ... the Brides Changed Nappies: Lesbian Mothers, Gay Fathers and the Legal Recognition of Our Relationships with the Children We Raise, A Community Law Reform Project, Final Report* (Darlinghurst: Gay and Lesbian Rights Lobby [NSW], 2003).

42 VLRC, *Assisted Reproductive Technology,* para 4.32.

43 In order for parties to achieve recognition under Australian federal law, it was proposed that opting in be completed via adoption. Australian federal law recognizes relationships created through adoption, while state recognition of donor parental status would only be recognized if subsequent amendments were made to federal law. Given the conservative nature of Australia's federal government, there is little chance of such amendments being introduced.

44 VLRC, *Assisted Reproductive Technology,* para 4.35. Similar statements were made by the NZLC, *New Issues,* paras. 6.67-6.73. The NZLC also noted that what was being proposed was no different than children having multiple parental figures in their lives as a result of step-parenting, open adoption, or customary practices in Maori, Pacific Island, and other cultures where extended families exist.

45 *Family Law Act* 1975 (Cth), s. 65C. Similar provisions are available in a number of provincial family law statutes in Canada.

46 VLRC, *Assisted Reproductive Technology,* para. 4.26.

47 Ibid., para. 4.29.

48 NZLC, *New Issues,* Recommendation 10.

Chapter 5: (Re)forming Law's Family

1 The remaining five families felt that parenting should be an "all or nothing" category and that those who did not fulfill the role of a parent should not be entitled to any legal recognition.

2 A donor may still be able to apply for access as a non-parent under provincial family law legislation in some provinces. See, e.g., section 21 of Ontario's *Children's Law Reform Act*: "A parent of a child *or any other person* may apply to a court for an order respecting custody of or access to the child or determining any aspect of the incidents of custody of the child" (emphasis added). *Children's Law Reform Act*, R.S.O. 1990, c. C.12, s. 21.

3 The birth mother's ability to "opt out" of parenting would be limited to putting her child up for adoption.

4 This approach was recently rejected by the Alberta Court of Appeal in *Doe v. Alberta*, 2007 ABCA 50. The question for the court in *Doe* was whether a written agreement between a co-habiting couple, in which it was stated that the male party to the relationship (who was not the biological father of the child) had neither parental rights nor obligations to support the child, could be effective in law. Jane Doe decided she wanted to have a child but John Doe did not want to be a father. Neither party wanted to end their relationship with the other. Jane conceived via artificial insemination and together they agreed that any rights or obligations with respect to the child would be governed through an express written agreement. The agreement would stipulate that John Doe was not the father of the child and had neither parental rights nor any obligation to support the child. The Court of Appeal held that John Doe's subjective intent not to assume a parental role would inevitably yield to the needs of the child. In particular, his "settled intention" to remain in a close, albeit unmarried, relationship with the child's mother would inevitably "thrust John Doe, from a practical and realistic point of view, into the role of parent to this child" (paras. 21-22). Jane and John Doe sought leave to appeal to the Supreme Court of Canada, but the application was refused.

5 Jenni Millbank, "The Limits of Functional Family: Lesbian Mother Litigation in the Era of the Eternal Biological Family," *Int'l J.L. Pol'y and Fam.* 22 (2008): 149.

6 *Civil Code of Quebec*, S.Q. 1991, c. 64, art. 538. The focus on *mutual* consent in the Quebec provision and in my proposal is key, as it ensures that the intention of the biological mother is not prioritized over that of the non-biological mother.

7 Ibid.

8 A similar provision, applicable to heterosexual couples only, already exists in a number of provinces. See, e.g., *Family Law Act*, S.A. 2003, c. F-4.5, s. 13(3).

9 The one-year limit was recommended by the Victorian Law Reform Commission in its report on legal parentage. While an additional individual may become involved after the first year of the child's life and there may be some desire to have

his/her role legally recognized, the VLRC felt that in the interest of certainty and finality, both for the primary parents and the child, a one-year window was appropriate. Victorian Law Reform Committee, *Assisted Reproductive Technology and Adoption: Position Paper Two – Parentage* (Melbourne: VLRC, 2005), para. 4.33.

Chapter 6: Some Concluding Thoughts on Law Reform and Progressive Social Change

1 Michel Foucault, *Power/Knowledge: Selected Interviews and Other Writings, 1972-1977,* ed. Colin Gordon (Brighton: Harvester Press, 1980); Carol Smart, *Feminism and the Power of Law* (London: Routledge, 1989).
2 Ngaire Naffine, *Law and the Sexes: Explorations in Feminist Jurisprudence* (Sydney: Allen and Unwin, 1990), 36.
3 Roger Cotterrell, *The Sociology of Law: An Introduction* (London: Butterworths, 1984), 121-22.
4 Shelley Gavigan, "Law, Gender and Ideology," in *Legal Theory Meets Legal Practice,* ed. Anne Bayefsky (Edmonton: Academic Printers and Publishing, 1988), 293.
5 Ibid., 293-94.

Bibliography

Books and Articles

Anderson, Kermyt. "How Well Does Paternity Confidence Match Actual Paternity? Evidence from Worldwide Non-Paternity Rates." *Current Anthropology* 48 (2006): 511.

Arnup, Katherine, ed. *Lesbian Parenting: Living with Pride and Prejudice.* Charlotte-town, PE: Gynergy Books, 1995.

–. "'Mothers Just Like Others': Lesbians, Divorce and Child Custody in Canada." *C.J.W.L.* 3 (1989): 18.

–. "'We Are Family': Lesbian Mothers in Canada." *Resources for Feminist Research* 20 (1991): 101.

–, and Susan Boyd. "Familial Disputes? Sperm Donors, Lesbian Mothers, and Legal Parenthood." In *Legal Inversions*, edited by Didi Herman and Carl Stychin, 77. Philadelphia: Temple University Press, 1995.

Bernstein, Fred. "This Child Does Have Two Mothers ... and a Sperm Donor with Visitation." *N.Y.U. Rev. L. and Soc. Change* 22 (1996): 1.

Blankenhorn, David. *Fatherless America: Confronting Our Most Urgent Social Problem.* New York: Basic Books, 1995.

Bourque, Dawn. "'Reconstructing' the Patriarchal Nuclear Family: Recent Developments in Child Custody and Access in Canada." *C.J.L.S.* 10 (1995): 1.

Boyd, Susan. "From Outlaw to InLaw: Bringing Lesbian and Gay Relationships into the Family System." *Yearbook of New Zealand Jurisprudence* 3 (1999): 31.

–. "Gendering Legal Parenthood: Bio-Genetic Ties, Intentionality and Responsibility." *Windsor Y.B. Access to Justice* 25 (2007): 63.

–. "Is There an Ideology of Motherhood in (Post)Modern Child Custody Law?" *Social and Legal Studies* 5 (1996): 495.

–. "Lesbian (and Gay) Custody Claims: What Difference Does Difference Make?" *Can. J. Fam. L.* 15 (1998): 131.

–, and Claire Young. "Feminism, Fathers' Rights, and Family Catastrophes: Parliamentary Discourses on Post-Separation Parenting, 1966-2003." In *Reaction and Resistance: Feminism, Law and Social Change,* edited by Dorothy Chunn, Susan Boyd, and Hester Lessard, 198. Vancouver: UBC Press, 2007.

–, and Claire Young. "'From Same-Sex to No Sex'?: Trends towards Recognition of (Same-Sex) Relationships in Canada." *Seattle Journal for Social Justice* 1 (2003): 757.

Brewaeys, A., P. Devroey, F. M. Helmerhorst, E. V. Van Hall, and I. Ponjaert. "Lesbian Mothers Who Conceived after Donor Insemination – A Follow-Up Study." *Human Reproduction* 10 (1995): 2731.

British Columbia. Ministry of Attorney General Justice Services Branch. "Chapter 10: Defining Legal Parentage." In *Family Relations Act Review* (Discussion Paper). Victoria, BC: Civil and Family Law Policy Office, 2007.

Burgess, Robert. *In the Field: An Introduction to Field Research.* London: Allen and Unwin, 1984.

Butler, Judith. "Is Kinship Always Already Heterosexual?" *differences: A Journal of Feminist Cultural Studies* 13 (2002): 14.

Canada. House of Commons Standing Committee on Justice and Human Rights. *Committee Minutes,* 37th Parl. 2nd sess., 2003.

Coleman, Malina. "Gestation, Intent and the Seed: Defining Motherhood in the Era of Assisted Human Reproduction." *Cardozo L. Rev.* 17 (1996): 497.

Cossman, Brenda. "Family Feuds: Neo-Liberal and Neo-Conservative Visions of the Reprivatization Project." In *Privatization, Law and the Challenge to Feminism,* edited by Brenda Cossman and Judy Fudge, 169. Toronto: University of Toronto Press, 2002.

–. "Family Inside/Out." *U.T.L.J.* 44 (1994): 1.

Cotterrell, Roger. *The Sociology of Law: An Introduction.* London: Butterworths, 1984.

Dolgin, Janet. *Defining the Family: Law, Technology, and Reproduction in an Uneasy Age.* New York: New York University Press, 1997.

Dunne, Gillian. *Lesbian Lifestyles: Women's Work and the Politics of Sexuality.* London: MacMillan, 1997.

–. "Opting into Motherhood: Lesbians Blurring the Boundaries and Transforming the Meaning of Parenthood and Kinship." *Gender and Society* 14 (2000): 11.

Edwards, Jeanette. "Explicit Connections: Ethnographic Enquiry in North-West England." In *Technologies of Procreation: Kinship in the Age of Assisted Conception,* by Jeanette Edwards, Sarah Franklin, Eric Hirsch, Frances Price, and Marilyn Strathern, 42. Manchester: Manchester University Press, 1993.

Edwards, Rosalind, Val Gillies, and Jane Ribbens McCarthy. "Biological Parents and Social Families: Legal Discourses and Everyday Understandings of the Position of Step-parents." *Int'l J.L. Pol'y and Fam.* 13 (1999): 78.

Elias, Marilyn. "Gay Teens Coming Out Earlier to Peers and Family." *USA Today*, 7 February 2007, http://www.usatoday.com/news/nation/.

Elshtain, Jean Beth. "Family Matters: The Plight of America's Children." *The Christian Century*, July 1993, 14.

Environics. *Canadians for Equal Marriage June 2006*, 14 May 2006, Media Room, http://erg.environics.net/.

Ettelbrick, Paula. "Who Is a Parent? The Need to Develop a Lesbian Conscious Family Law." *N.Y.L. Sch. J. Hum. Rts.* 10 (1993): 513.

Fineman, Martha Albertson. *The Neutered Mother, the Sexual Family and Other Twentieth Century Tragedies.* New York: Routledge, 1995.

Foucault, Michel. *Power/Knowledge: Selected Interviews and Other Writings, 1972-1977.* Edited by Colin Gordon. Brighton: Harvester Press, 1980.

Gallagher, Maggie. "Fatherless Boys Grow Up into Dangerous Men." *Wall Street Journal*, 1 December 1998.

Gavigan, Shelley. "Equal Families, Equal Parents, Equal Marriage: The Case of the Missing Patriarch." In *Diminishing Returns: Inequality and the Canadian Charter of Rights and Freedoms*, edited by Sheila McIntyre and Sandra Rodgers, 320. Markham, ON: LexisNexis Butterworths, 2006.

–. "Law, Gender and Ideology." In *Legal Theory Meets Legal Practice*, edited by Anne Bayefsky. Edmonton, AB: Academic Printers and Publishing, 1988.

Gluckman, Amy, and Betsy Reed, eds. *Homo Economics: Capitalism, Community, and Lesbian and Gay Life.* New York: Routledge, 1997.

Harvison Young, Alison. "Reconceiving the Family: Challenging the Paradigm of the Exclusive Family." *American Journal of Gender and Law* 6 (1998): 505.

Hayden, Corinne P. "Gender, Genetics and Generation: Reformulating Biology in Lesbian Kinship." *Cultural Anthropology* 10 (1995): 41.

Herman, Didi. "Are We Family? Lesbian Rights and Women's Liberation." *Osgoode Hall L.J.* 28 (1990): 789.

Jaffe, Peter, David Wolfe, and Susan Wilson. *Children of Battered Women.* Newbury Park, CA: Sage, 1999.

Kelly, Fiona. "An Alternative Conception: The Legality of Home Insemination under Canada's *Assisted Human Reproduction Act.*" *Can. J. Fam. L.* 26 (2010): 149.

–. "Nuclear Norms or Fluid Families? Incorporating Lesbian and Gay Parents and Their Children into Canadian Family Law." *Can. J. Fam. L.* 21 (2004): 133.

Kerr, Grace, and Peter Jaffe. "Legal and Clinical Issues in Child Custody Disputes Involving Domestic Violence." *C.F.L.Q.* 17 (1999): 1.

Lahey, Kathleen. *Are We "Persons" Yet? Law and Sexuality in Canada*. Toronto: University of Toronto Press, 1999.

Lee, Raymond. *Doing Research on Sensitive Topics*. London: Sage, 1993.

Lenon, Suzanne. "Marrying Citizens! Raced Subjects? Re-thinking the Terrain of Equal Marriage Discourse." *C.J.W.L.* 17 (2005): 405.

Lessard, Hester. "Mothers, Fathers and Naming: Reflections on the Law Equality Framework and *Trociuk v. British Columbia (Attorney General)*." *C.J.W.L.* 16 (2004): 165.

"Letters." *Lesbian/Gay Law Notes* 33.1 (1993): 1-4.

Lewin, Ellen. *Lesbian Mothers: Accounts of Gender in American Culture*. Ithaca: Cornell University Press, 1993.

Maguire Schulz, Marjorie. "Reproductive Technology and Intent-Based Parenthood: An Opportunity for Gender Neutrality." *Wis. L. Rev.* (1990): 297.

McDonald, Marci. "Stephen Harper and the Theo-Cons." *The Walrus*, October 2006, 44.

McNair, Ruth, Deb Dempsey, and Sarah Wise. "Lesbian Parenting: Issues, Strengths and Challenges." *Family Matters* 63 (2002): 40.

Millbank, Jenni. *And Then ... the Brides Changed Nappies: Lesbian Mothers, Gay Fathers and the Legal Recognition of Our Relationships with the Children We Raise, A Community Law Reform Project, Final Report*. Darlinghurst: Gay and Lesbian Rights Lobby (NSW), 2003.

–. "Lesbians, Child Custody, and the Long Lingering Gaze of the Law." In *Challenging the Public/Private Divide: Feminism, Law, and Public Policy*, edited by Susan Boyd. Toronto: University of Toronto Press, 1997.

–. "The Limits of Functional Family: Lesbian Mother Litigation in the Era of the Eternal Biological Family." *Int'l J.L. Pol'y and Fam.* 22 (2008): 149.

–. *Meet the Parents: A Review of the Research on Lesbian and Gay Families*. Sydney: Gay and Lesbian Rights Lobby (NSW), 2002.

Mykitiuk, Roxanne. "Beyond Conception: Legal Determinations of Filiation in the Context of Assisted Reproductive Technologies." *Osgoode Hall L.J.* 39 (2001): 771.

Naffine, Ngaire. *Law and the Sexes: Explorations in Feminist Jurisprudence*. Sydney: Allen and Unwin, 1990.

Neilson, Linda. "Partner Abuse, Children and Statutory Change: Cautionary Comments on Women's Access to Justice." *Windsor Y.B. Access Just.* 18 (2000): 115.

–. *Spousal Abuse, Children and the Legal System: Final Report for the Canadian Bar Association, Law for the Futures Fund*. Fredericton, NB: Muriel McQueen Fergusson Centre for Family Violence Research (UNB), 2001.

Nelson, Fiona. *Lesbian Motherhood: An Exploration of Canadian Lesbian Families.* Toronto: University of Toronto Press, 1996.

Nestle, Joan. *A Restricted Country.* Ithaca, NY: Firebrand Books, 1987.

New Zealand Law Commission. *New Issues in Legal Parenthood, Report 88.* Wellington: NZ Law Commission, 2005.

Pagelow, M. "Effects of Domestic Violence on Children and Their Consequences for Custody and Visitation Agreements." *Mediation Quarterly* 7 (1994): 347.

Phelan, Shane. *Sexual Strangers: Gays, Lesbians, and Dilemmas of Citizenship.* Philadelphia: Temple University Press, 2001.

Plummer, Kenneth. *Documents of Life.* London: Allen and Unwin, 1981.

Polikoff, Nancy. *Beyond (Straight and Gay) Marriage: Valuing All Families under the Law.* Boston: Beacon Press, 2008.

–. "Breaking the Link between Biology and Parental Rights in Planned Lesbian Families: When Semen Donors Are Not Fathers." *Georgetown J. Gender and L.* 2 (2000): 57.

–. "The Deliberate Construction of Families without Fathers: Is It an Option for Lesbian and Heterosexual Mothers?" *Santa Clara L. Rev.* 36 (1996): 375.

–. "This Child Does Have Two Mothers: Redefining Parenthood to Meet the Needs of Children in Lesbian-Mother and Other Nontraditional Families." *Geo. L.J.* 78 (1990): 459.

Reimann, Renate. "Does Biology Matter? Lesbian Couples' Transition to Parenthood and Their Division of Labour." *Qualitative Sociology* 20 (1997): 153.

Rhoades, Helen, Reg Graycar, and Margaret Harrison. *The Family Law Reform Act 1995: The First Three Years.* Sydney: University of Sydney and the Family Court of Australia, 2000.

Robson, Ruthann. *Lesbian (Out)law: Survival under the Rule of Law.* Ithaca, NY: Firebrand Books, 1992.

Rosnes, Melanie. "The Invisibility of Male Violence in Canadian Child Custody and Access Decision-Making." *Can. J. Fam. L.* 14 (1997): 31.

Sevenhuijsen, Selma. "The Gendered Juridification of Parenthood." *Soc. and Leg. Stud.* 1 (1992): 71.

Shapiro, Julie. "A Lesbian-Centered Critique of Second-Parent Adoptions." *Berkeley Women's L.J.* 14 (1999): 17.

Smart, Carol. *Feminism and the Power of Law.* London: Routledge, 1989.

Smith, Miriam. *Lesbian and Gay Rights in Canada: Social Movements and Equality Seeking, 1971-1995.* Toronto: University of Toronto Press, 1999.

Somerville, Margaret. *The Ethical Imagination: Journeys of the Human Spirit.* Toronto: House of Anansi Press, 2006.

Stacey, Judith. *In the Name of the Family: Rethinking Family Values in the Post-Modern Age.* Boston: Beacon Press, 1996.

–, and Timothy Biblarz. "(How) Does the Sexual Orientation of Parents Matter?" *American Sociological Review* 66 (2001): 159.

Statistics Canada. *Family Portrait: Continuity and Change in Canadian Families and Households in 2006, 2006 Census* (Catalogue no. 97-553-XWE2006001). Ottawa: Statistics Canada, 2007.

–. *Income of Individuals, Families and Households: Highlight Tables, 2001 Census* (Catalogue no. 97F0024XIE2001014). Ottawa: Statistics Canada, 2003. http://www12.statcan.ca/english/census01/.

–. *Profile of Canadian Families and Households: Diversification Continues* (2001 Census Analysis Series, Catalogue no. 96F0030XIE2001003). Ottawa: Statistics Canada, 2002.

Strathern, Marilyn. *Reproducing the Future: Essays on Anthropology, Kinship, and the New Reproductive Technologies.* New York: Routledge, 1992.

Sudermann, Marlies, and Peter Jaffe. *A Handbook for Health and Social Service Providers and Educators on Children Exposed to Woman Abuse/Family Violence.* Ottawa: Health Canada, National Clearinghouse on Family Violence, 2000.

Sullivan, Maureen. *The Family of Woman: Lesbian Mothers, Their Children, and the Undoing of Gender.* Berkeley: University of California Press, 2004.

Victorian Law Reform Committee. *Assisted Reproductive Technology and Adoption: Position Paper Two – Parentage.* Melbourne: VLRC, 2005.

Weeks, Jeffrey, Brian Heaphy, and Catherine Donovan. *Same Sex Intimacies: Families of Choice and Other Life Experiments.* London: Routledge, 2001.

Weston, Kath. *Families We Choose: Lesbians, Gays, Kinship.* New York: Columbia University Press, 1991.

Wildman, Sarah. "Coming Out Early." *The Advocate,* 10 October 2000.

Young, Claire. "Spousal Status, Pension Benefits and Tax: *Rosenberg v. Canada (Attorney-General)*." *C.L.E.L.J.* 6 (1998): 435.

–, and Susan Boyd. "Losing the Feminist Voice? Debates on the Legal Recognition of Same Sex Partnerships in Canada." *Fem. Legal Stud.* 14 (2006): 213.

Cases and Court Documents

A v. B, C and X, 2007 R.D.F. 217.

A.A. v. B.B., [2007] O.J. No. 2. (C.A.).

A.A. v. New Brunswick (Department of Family and Community Services), [2004] N.B.H.R.B.I.D. No. 4.

Affidavit of Lloyd Thornhill, *EGALE Inc. v. Attorney-General of Canada* (15 December 2001). EGALE Canada, http://www.egale.ca/: Issues, Equal Marriage, B.C. Marriage Case.

Alliance for Marriage and Family v. A.A., 2007 SCC 40.

Andrews v. Ontario (Minister of Health) (1988), 64 O.R. (2d) 258 (H.C.J.).

Doe v. Alberta, 2007 ABCA 50.

Factum of Applicant couples, *Halpern v. Ontario in the Ontario Division* Court (28 August 2001) (on file with author). http://www.egale.ca/extra%5CON-ApplicantsFactum.doc.

Factum of the Intervenor, Interfaith Coalition on Marriage and Family, *Reference re Same-Sex Marriage*, [2004] S.C.J. No. 76.

Fraess v. Alberta (Minister of Justice and Attorney General), [2005] A.J. No. 1665 (Q.B.).

Gill v. Murray, 2001 BCHRT 34.

Gosselin v. Quebec (Attorney General), [2002] 4 S.C.R. 429.

In re R.C., 775 P. 2d 27 (Colo. 1989).

In the Matter of Alison D., 77 N.Y.2d 651 (1991).

Jhordan C. v. Mary K., 224 Cal. Rptr. 530 (Ct. App. 1986).

Johnson-Steeves v. Lee (1997), 29 R.F.L. (4th) 126 (Alta. Q.B.).

Johnson-Steeves v. Lee (1997), 33 R.F.L. (4th) 278 (Alta. C.A.).

K v. M (2002), 22 FRNZ 360.

K.G.T. v. P.D., [2005] B.C.J. No. 2935 (SC).

K.(M.) v. C.(M.) and D.(C.), 2007 ONCJ 456.

L.O. v. S.J. (2006), J.Q. No. 450 (S.C.).

Law v. Canada (Minister of Employment and Immigration), [1999] 1 S.C.R. 497.

M v. H, [1996] 132 D.L.R. (4th) 538 (Ont. Ct. (Gen. Div.)).

M.A.C. v. M.K., [2009] ONCJ 18.

M.D.R. v. Ontario (Deputy Registrar General), [2006] O.J. No. 2268 (S.C.J.).

P v. K & M (Family Court, Auckland, unreported, Doogue J., 8 August 2002).

P v. K & M, [2004] NZFLR 752.

P v. K, [2003] 2 NZLR 787.

P v. K, [2004] 2 NZLR 421.

P v. K, [2006] NZFLR 22.

P.C. v. S.L., 2005 SKQB 502.

Re A (1999), 181 D.L.R. (4th) 300 (Alta. Q.B.).

Re K (1995), 15 R.F.L. (4th) 129 (Ont. Prov. Ct.).

Re Nova Scotia (Birth Registration No. 1999-02-00420) (2001), 194 N.S.R. (2d) 362 (S.C.).

Re Patrick (An Application Concerning Contract), [2002] F.L.C. 93-096.

Rosenberg v. Canada (Attorney-General), [1998] 38 O.R. (3d) 577.

S.G. v. L.C., [2004] Q.J. No. 6915 (S.C.).

S.G. c. L.C., [2005] J.Q. No 7407.

Springer v. Graham-Newlin, No. 642,975-5 (Cal. Super., Alameda Cty., 17 October 1988).

T. (D.W.) v. British Columbia (Attorney-General) (2001), 90 B.C.L.R. (3d) 1.

Thomas S. v. Robin Y. 618 N.Y.S. 2d 356 (App. Div. 1994).

Trociuk v. British Columbia (Attorney-General), [2003] 1 S.C.R. 835.

Walsh v. Nova Scotia (Attorney General), [2002] 4 S.C.R. 325.

Legislation

Adoption Act, S.M. 1997, c. 47.

Adoption Act, R.S.B.C. 1996, c. 5.

Adoption Act, S.N.L. 1999, c. A-2.1.

Adoption Act, S.S. 1998, c. A-5.2.

Adoption Act, S.N.W.T. 1998, c. 9.

Adult Interdependent Relationships Act, S.A. 2002, c. A-4.5.

Artificial Conception Act 1985 (WA).

Assisted Reproductive Treatment Act 2008 (Vic).

Canadian Charter of Rights and Freedoms, Part I of the *Constitution Act, 1982*, being Schedule B to the *Canada Act 1982* (U.K.), 1982, c. 11.

Care of Children Act 2004 (NZ).

Child and Family Services Act, S.N.S. 1990, c. 5.

Child Status Act, R.S.P.E.I. 1988, c. C-6.

Child, Youth and Family Enhancement Act, R.S.A. 2000, c. C-12.

Children's Act, R.S.Y. 2002, c. 31.

Children's Act, R.S.Y.T. 1986, c. 31.

Children's Law Act, R.S.N.L. 1990, c. C-13.

Children's Law Act, S.N.W.T. 1997, c. 14.

Children's Law Act, S.S. 2002, c. C-8.1.

Children's Law Reform Act, R.S.O. 1990, c. 12.

Civil Code of Quebec, S.Q. 1991, c. 64.

Civil Marriage Act, S.C. 2005, c. 33.

Custody Jurisdiction and Enforcement Act, R.S.P.E.I. 1988, c. C-33.

Divorce Act, R.S.C. 1985, c. 3.

Family Law Act 1975 (Cth).

Family Law Act, R.S.O. 1990, c. F.3.

Family Law Act, S.A. 2003, c. F-4.5.

Family Maintenance Act, R.S.M. 1997, c. F20.

Family Relations Act, R.S.B.C. 1996, c. 128.

Family Services Act, S.N.B. 1980, c. F-2.2.

Human Rights Code, R.S.O. 1990, c. H-19.

Maintenance and Custody Act, R.S.N.S. 1989, c. 160.

Modernization of Benefits and Obligations Act, S.C. 2000, c. 12.

Parentage Act 2004 (ACT).

Uniform Parentage Act (1973), Article 7.

Vital Statistics Act, R.S.M. 1987, c. V60.

Vital Statistics Act, R.S.B.C. 1996, c. 479.

Index

LAW AND SOCIETY

Amanda Glasbeek
Feminized Justice: The Toronto Women's Court, 1913-34 (2009)

Kimberley Brooks (ed.)
Justice Bertha Wilson: One Woman's Difference (2009)

Wayne V. McIntosh and Cynthia L. Cates
Multi-Party Litigation: The Strategic Context (2009)

Renisa Mawani
*Colonial Proximities: Crossracial Encounters and Juridical Truths
in British Columbia, 1871-1921* (2009)

James B. Kelly and Christopher P. Manfredi (eds.)
*Contested Constitutionalism: Reflections on the Canadian Charter
of Rights and Freedoms* (2009)

Catherine E. Bell and Robert K. Paterson (eds.)
Protection of First Nations Cultural Heritage: Laws, Policy, and Reform (2008)

Hamar Foster, Benjamin L. Berger, and A.R. Buck (eds.)
*The Grand Experiment: Law and Legal Culture in British Settler
Societies* (2008)

Richard J. Moon (ed.)
Law and Religious Pluralism in Canada (2008)

Catherine E. Bell and Val Napoleon (eds.)
*First Nations Cultural Heritage and Law: Case Studies, Voices,
and Perspectives* (2008)

Douglas C. Harris
*Landing Native Fisheries: Indian Reserves and Fishing Rights in
British Columbia, 1849-1925* (2008)

Peggy J. Blair
Lament for a First Nation: The Williams Treaties in Southern Ontario (2008)

Lori G. Beaman
Defining Harm: Religious Freedom and the Limits of the Law (2007)

Stephen Tierney (ed.)
Multiculturalism and the Canadian Constitution (2007)

Julie Macfarlane
The New Lawyer: How Settlement Is Transforming the Practice of Law (2007)

Kimberley White
Negotiating Responsibility: Law, Murder, and States of Mind (2007)

Dawn Moore
Criminal Artefacts: Governing Drugs and Users (2007)

Hamar Foster, Heather Raven, and Jeremy Webber (eds.)
Let Right Be Done: Aboriginal Title, the Calder *Case, and the Future of Indigenous Rights* (2007)

Dorothy E. Chunn, Susan B. Boyd, and Hester Lessard (eds.)
Reaction and Resistance: Feminism, Law, and Social Change (2007)

Margot Young, Susan B. Boyd, Gwen Brodsky, and Shelagh Day (eds.)
Poverty: Rights, Social Citizenship, and Legal Activism (2007)

Rosanna L. Langer
Defining Rights and Wrongs: Bureaucracy, Human Rights, and Public Accountability (2007)

C.L. Ostberg and Matthew E. Wetstein
Attitudinal Decision Making in the Supreme Court of Canada (2007)

Chris Clarkson
Domestic Reforms: Political Visions and Family Regulation in British Columbia, 1862-1940 (2007)

Jean McKenzie Leiper
Bar Codes: Women in the Legal Profession (2006)

Gerald Baier
Courts and Federalism: Judicial Doctrine in the United States, Australia, and Canada (2006)

Avigail Eisenberg (ed.)
Diversity and Equality: The Changing Framework of Freedom in Canada (2006)

Randy K. Lippert
Sanctuary, Sovereignty, Sacrifice: Canadian Sanctuary Incidents, Power, and Law (2005)

James B. Kelly
Governing with the Charter: Legislative and Judicial Activism and Framers' Intent (2005)

Dianne Pothier and Richard Devlin (eds.)
Critical Disability Theory: Essays in Philosophy, Politics, Policy, and Law (2005)

Susan G. Drummond
Mapping Marriage Law in Spanish Gitano Communities (2005)

Louis A. Knafla and Jonathan Swainger (eds.)
Laws and Societies in the Canadian Prairie West, 1670-1940 (2005)

Ikechi Mgbeoji
Global Biopiracy: Patents, Plants, and Indigenous Knowledge (2005)

Florian Sauvageau, David Schneiderman, and David Taras, with Ruth Klinkhammer and Pierre Trudel
The Last Word: Media Coverage of the Supreme Court of Canada (2005)

Gerald Kernerman
Multicultural Nationalism: Civilizing Difference, Constituting Community (2005)

Pamela A. Jordan
Defending Rights in Russia: Lawyers, the State, and Legal Reform in the Post-Soviet Era (2005)

Anna Pratt
Securing Borders: Detention and Deportation in Canada (2005)

Kirsten Johnson Kramar
Unwilling Mothers, Unwanted Babies: Infanticide in Canada (2005)

W.A. Bogart
Good Government? Good Citizens? Courts, Politics, and Markets in a Changing Canada (2005)

Catherine Dauvergne
Humanitarianism, Identity, and Nation: Migration Laws in Canada and Australia (2005)

Michael Lee Ross
First Nations Sacred Sites in Canada's Courts (2005)

Andrew Woolford
Between Justice and Certainty: Treaty Making in British Columbia (2005)

John McLaren, Andrew Buck, and Nancy Wright (eds.)
Despotic Dominion: Property Rights in British Settler Societies (2004)

Georges Campeau
From UI to EI: Waging War on the Welfare State (2004).

Alvin J. Esau
The Courts and the Colonies: The Litigation of Hutterite Church Disputes (2004)

Christopher N. Kendall
Gay Male Pornography: An Issue of Sex Discrimination (2004)

Roy B. Flemming
Tournament of Appeals: Granting Judicial Review in Canada (2004)

Constance Backhouse and Nancy L. Backhouse
The Heiress vs the Establishment: Mrs. Campbell's Campaign for Legal Justice (2004)

Christopher P. Manfredi
Feminist Activism in the Supreme Court: Legal Mobilization and the Women's Legal Education and Action Fund (2004)

Annalise Acorn
Compulsory Compassion: A Critique of Restorative Justice (2004)

Jonathan Swainger and Constance Backhouse (eds.)
People and Place: Historical Influences on Legal Culture (2003)

Jim Phillips and Rosemary Gartner
Murdering Holiness: The Trials of Franz Creffield and George Mitchell (2003)

David R. Boyd
Unnatural Law: Rethinking Canadian Environmental Law and Policy (2003)

Ikechi Mgbeoji
Collective Insecurity: The Liberian Crisis, Unilateralism, and Global Order (2003)

Rebecca Johnson
Taxing Choices: The Intersection of Class, Gender, Parenthood, and the Law (2002)

John McLaren, Robert Menzies, and Dorothy E. Chunn (eds.)
Regulating Lives: Historical Essays on the State, Society, the Individual, and the Law (2002)

Joan Brockman
Gender in the Legal Profession: Fitting or Breaking the Mould (2001)